PRAISE

MW01257457

"Red Thread models the authentic sharing it encourages. It is a celebration of community and self-expression, with the tools, scripts and encouragement you need to move from dream to reality in creating your very own Red Tent space and growing into the fullness of yourself."
    -Lucy H. Pearce, author *Moon Time, Burning Woman, She of the Sea.*

"Reading Red Thread left me wholly fulfilled. This book is bold, thought-provoking, and eloquent. The sincerity expressed by Aj is not only authentic but delightful as well. Red Thread directs us inward, to a place we knew existed but were too afraid to go. The journey takes us on a spiritual path leading us through the muck and darkness to restoration and revelation. If you are looking for a read that is riveting and profound, this is it."
    -Marla Bautista Author, Philanthropist & Speaker
www.thebautistaprojectinc.org

Whether verbal or written, Aj's words are like being enveloped in a hug from your favorite human. This book is a poetic blend of levity, play, and poignant truths. It is both an invitation and an instruction manual to create a sanctuary to come home too, externally and within.
    -Jessica Smarro, LCSW Certified Life Coach and host of the podcast, Unblocked with Jessica Smarro
jessicasmarro.com

"Full of warmth and sparkle, Aj Smit expertly weaves personal stories with Red Tent wisdom, women's cultural predicaments with the path towards their resolution, broad vision with practical advice, while wrapping it all in a healthy dose of humor! You will find inspiration here, along with step by step guidance to create a Red Tent with passionate down to earth wisdom."

-DeAnna L'am, author of *Becoming Peers - Mentoring Girls Into Womanhood*, and A *Diva's Guide to getting Your Period* *www.deannalam.com*

"Reading *Red Thread* feels like a warm hug; it is a heartwarming, beautifully crafted book. An important read for anyone who is curious to engage more deeply with their own nature, and the perfect guide for anyone wishing to hold space for others to do the same."

-Alexandra Pope and Sjanie Hugo Wurlitzer, authors of *Wild Power*, and co-creators of Red School *www.RedSchool.net*

This book will nourish your very soul. I giggled and cried while I joined the women inside these pages as we processed, celebrated and reflected on our stories and the relationship we have with ourselves. I cannot recommend it enough. This book is tender, loving and so fierce, the way it advocates for women to embrace their experiences and step into sacred space to process is so alluring. It gives me all of the magical allure of my favorite novels while also reminding me that this is real life."

-Mary-Grace the Messy Healer www.TheMessyHealer.com

Reading *Red Thread* feels like getting a hug from both the wisest and funnest woman you know…oh wait, that's Aj for you! There's two things that sets this book apart from other personal development books out there. First, as a narrator, Aj never feels like she's talking to you from a pedestal. You can almost picture her sitting next to you as you laugh, cry, and grow together in a Red Tent. Secondly, the Red Tents for each section are a total game changer because they give you the tools to not only embrace yourself but to also share that gift with others. In simplest terms, this book is a gift to everyone who takes the time and dedication to not only read, but do the growth work inside. Be prepared to go on a beautiful journey!

-Ashleigh Magee, Health Coach for Military Women
www.ashleighmagee.com

As you will discover in this book, Red Tent Groups are an affirming space for women to be their authentic selves, and we surely need that affirmation at any age. It is at once fun and wise; motivating and challenging. It's an easy read in the sense that it's very straightforward, understandable and engaging and yet it contains a lot to think about and process so take your time and savor the ideas. Reading this book will be a great aid in discovering how to build a group that is an authentic expression of your gathered women's respective journey.

-Rev. M. Sylvia Vásquez

"Wise beyond her years and yet somehow overflowing with the fierce joy of youth, Aj is the guide I never knew I needed. This book could easily be called "How To Rock Womanhood 101" and it's a MUST READ for those who identify as a woman and those who love us. Can we all just pinkie promise to give this to the tweens in our life so they don't wander around in a body they don't understand like most of us did?"

   -Angela J Herrington MA, LSCC Faith Deconstruction Coach *AngelaJHerrington.com*

"Aj's book is an invitation to deepen one's relationship with themself. She provides tools and insights to help you connect more deeply with yourself and others. A must-read for all women and femme folk."

   -Anna Olson, coach and mentor *www.annaolson.com www.Instagram.com/coachannaolson*

"You know that person who walks into a room and immediately the energy shifts in the best possible way? You can tell right away that this person has a deeply rooted sense of self and it is magnetic. Aj is such a person and this book will help you become one too. Reading this book is like spending time with a wise, sparkly best friend who lovingly shares from her own pain and wisdom as you explore your own wild soul. It is both a practical guide to fully embody the beautiful, unique, and whole person you already are, and is an invitation to spread this energy to the people around you. I can't say enough good things about Aj and about this book!"

   -Kathleen Bertrand Board Member for SheLoves Society, Owner and Designer of Purple Thread Labels *www.PurpleThreadLabels.com*

Should be read by every woman and every mermaid. The self-examination questions alone are worth asking, even if they do not lead to a Red Tent. However, if you've been wondering about Red Tent—what it is or how to do one—this is the book for you. If you have been feeling like there must be more to life—this is the book for you. Theology, psychology, and good common sense are woven throughout. I highly recommend it.

-The Reverend Dr. Karen D. Brandon, Chaplain (Retired), United States Army

Red Thread is a warm hug from a best friend. It's also a safe space opening the channel for vulnerability, human emotion, and belonging. Smit has weaved a thread of love in and through a book that every woman needs to read and then buy for her best friend. As a clinician, I know the vital need for human connection. Through this book, Smit creates a blueprint for creating and fostering the community many of us have been longing for."

-Jessica Manfre, LMSW www.Jessicamanfre.com

Red Thread is an answered prayer for women who've felt like they are on the outside looking in or going through this life alone. With each page, Aj made me feel like I was at a weekend retreat full of beautiful women spirit guides placed there to support, educate, and honor what it truly is to be a whole woman. This book is for women of all ages. I have 3 young daughters and I am so grateful to have this as a resource to help them navigate the uncertainty and shame I felt in school and throughout adulthood. This book is a call to action for all women at any age or stage to be intentional, fearlessly share yourself with the world and receive others with open arms. *Red Thread* is the adventure in womanhood we all actually wanted but never knew was possible."

-Richelle Futch LICSW Author of *Her Ruck* *www.richellefutch.com*

"*Red thread* is a gorgeous and powerful read. Aj's wisdom, curiosity and joy radiate from every page. This book is a must read if you are wanting to connect with your body's deep knowing about authenticity and belonging. Learning how to create sacred space within Red Tents has taught me new ways to connect deeply with other women."Reclaiming the Skin You Are In" and "Dancing into Embodiment" spoke straight to my desire to unravel my unhealthy relationship with my body. Aj's insight and teaching about embodiment is beyond valuable. *Red Thread* breathes love and hope into all our weary souls. I know I will return to read it again and again"

    -Shaley Hoogendoorn

    www.instagram.com/messybeautywithshaley

"Are you a women that is longing for a place to belong... a place where not only do you understand "YOU", but all those around you meet you where you are and strive to understand "YOU" without questions or unrealistic expectations? Having a place like this is hard to imagine when you have never experienced such a space. Well in this book the search can cease. Aj, with a warm heart and tender care introduces us to a Red Tent experience. With every element of explanation and introduction of The Red Tent each component becomes more desirable. This book awakens the possibilities of exploring who you are without having to explain every step you make. With every page my desire to not only encounter a Red Tent grew, but I desired to create a space for others to experience such freedom. If you are ready to be free in your thoughts, be free in your actions, and embrace every element of "YOU" while gaining community this book is for you. Run and grab a copy for you and a friend."

    -Kennita Williams, Life Coach

    www.kennitawilliams.com

RED THREAD

WEAVING AN EMBODIED LIFE OF JOY

AJ SMIT

Sing your Soul Song
In Joy, Glitter & Grace,
AJ Smit

RISE, AN IMPRINT OF CLEAR FORK PUBLISHING

A portion of the proceeds from this book will go to The Bautista Project Inc. The Bautista Project provides basic living essentials, educational resources, support groups, and other necessary resources to assist homeless community members with reintegration.
www.thebautistaprojectinc.org

Rise - An Imprint of Clear Fork Publishing

P.O. Box 870 102 S. Swenson

Stamford, Texas 79553 (915) 209-0003

www.clearforkpublishing.com

Printed in the United States of America

Softcover ISBN - 978-1-950169-62-7

Dedicated to all of the women who came before me, especially Grandma Grace. May the communities and friendships cultivated from this book grow like the gardens and the people you loved.

CONTENTS

FOREWORD

I am Ida Gertruida, daughter of Ida Gertruida
Redelinghuys, granddaughter of Ida Gertruida Visser, great
granddaughter of Ida Gertruida Visser. That is the red
thread that runs in my veins, tying me to generations of
women before me who have carried the same name on
another continent. We have been pilgrims, farmers, teachers
and immigrants.

Years ago, when I read Anita Diamant's book *The Red
Tent*, I sensed it was more than an ancient story of ancient
times. It felt like reviving a memory, reminding me of
something that is as essential now: the gathering of women.
At the time, I was gathering with a group of women on
couches in my living room every second Thursday evening
—our own Red Tent spaces, ironically also around a red
couch. That led to an online community of women, a
continued heartbeat of gathering in authenticity, with Love,
seeing each other with dignity.

Gathering in circles has the power to heal us, connect us,
strengthen us and inspire us. It is like taking one deep
breath—together—collecting strength for the beautiful work

we each need to do in the world. It reminds us we are loved exactly as we are.

When I show up in Red Tent spaces, I am an immigrant woman, far from the land of my birth and the language of my heart. When I dare to show up as my whole and authentic self, I get woven into the fabric of the global sisterhood of Love that connects us from East to West, South to North. It is so beautiful and powerful and that invitation is here for every one of us.

I've had the privilege of walking with Aj in an online community for several years and I have seen her embody her authentic joy, while bringing much wisdom to the spaces she finds herself in. She's an old soul in a young body with such an effervescent spirit. Here's what I know: You *want* to be in Aj's circle. You *want* Aj to hold space for you.

From Aj, I also learned this beautiful phrase: "I have spoken." It is to know when we have said all there is to say for that time and that moment. It reminds me how much our words matter.

In *Red Thread: Weaving an Embodied Life of Joy*, Aj has invited us into a Sacred Circle together—our own Red Tent space—right here in the shape of a book. She has much to teach us and I am so grateful for the beautiful spaces that will ring out from here.

May your soul be sparked, with joy, and may you find exactly what you need here.

I have spoken,

Idelette McVicker (she/her)

Founder of SheLovesmagazine.com and DangerousWomen.org

Written on the unceded territories of the Kwantlen, Semiahmoo and Sto:lo peoples, also known as Surrey, BC in Canada.

WELCOME IN, LOVELY

*I*magine walking into a room where your whole self is welcomed and wanted.

Imagine a place with comfy places to sit with soft blankets, delicious hot tea and cocoa on the stove, and people with kind eyes and warm hugs to greet you.

Imagine a place where you can put down the mask you feel you have to wear every day, and you can say what's actually on your mind. Where you can share your vulnerability, in a sober space, without being afraid it's going to be weaponized against you.

Can you imagine what it would be like to share a problem and have someone respond with "I hear you. What do you need?" instead of trying to fix you?

If you can't imagine this yet, I understand.

Sometimes it's hard to imagine something we haven't seen or been a part of yet, but places like this exist. One of them I've found is called a Red Tent, and being a part of one has changed my life.

Many women don't have a place or a Red Tent where they can safely share and relax without the pressure to perform, to be on with the societal expectations of the right answers. After leading multiple Red Tents for the last five years, Tent has become a place to learn tools of language, vulnerability, and boundaries to create better relationships for myself and others.

This book is itself a Red Tent to explore who you are and what it means to live an embodied life. As you read you will also be invited to create Red Tent spaces for yourself, your family, or your community.

What is a Red Tent evening? Settle in, and I'll bring you along to experience a Red Tent evening in my home.

We hear laughter from the kitchen as a few fellow Tent Keepers start the Tea and share about their week and the shows they are watching. Another woman grabs the corner of the blanket we're holding and helps us drape the red fabric over the couch to create the ambiance for the women coming shortly. We walk around turning on the battery-operated candles as quiet, peaceful music flows from the speaker.

The first knock of many is heard at the door as women start arriving in my home. They are greeted with, "Would you like a thumbs-up, hive-five, or a hug?" We asked this before the pandemic, but after, it's become even more welcome to have the choice.

As the clock strikes seven, we settle in and around my oversized red couch and some sprawl on the floor with tea and snacks in hand. Last-minute purse digging is heard as women turn their phones on silent, retrieve a pen, and crackling paper signals opening journals. I lead us in shaking out the worries of the day and deep breathing to help us settle into our bodies. The music still streams in the background as eyes close around the circle, and I share our opening blessing:

*"We are gathered here in our Red Tent as women, as
daughters, as mothers, as workers and dreamers.
We come here to speak our hearts desires, our
mind's thoughts, and share the song of our souls.
We see with our eyes, hear with our ears, and
will hum along in our hearts. Let this space be
open, sacred, and grounded for us here tonight.
Let us hold hands and travel deeper together to
learn to love ourselves, each other, and the
world."*

After the blessing, we set the tone by sharing our
guidelines for Tent and how we keep it a sacred space.

I ask the women to:

- Please do not advise unless requested.
- Speak what you mean, and ask for what you
  need.
- Only speak of your own story while also keeping
  the stories heard tonight confidential.
- When you finish, say, "I have spoken."

Saying "I have spoken" signals that it can be someone
else's turn and gives you the dignity of claiming the words
you have shared. There's no, 'Here's what I did when that
happened to me," or here's my sister's dog sitter's solution to
that same problem. No. We are here to hold space and
listen.

Before we introduce ourselves, we sing our "Call Down
a Blessing" song.[1] As we sing it over each woman, she
speaks what she would like for a blessing for that evening,
maybe friendship, laughter, kindness, or peace. As the song
is sung, she places her token into the communal bowl and
passes the bowl to the next woman. The bowl accumulates
trinkets, keys, rings, and jewelry until it comes back into my
hands. It is placed in the center of the circle, representing

every woman in the room. At the end of the evening, each woman will retrieve their given piece.

Our theme guides our gathering, and tonight it's Curiosity.

Each woman shares her name, intention, and what the theme means to her. The stories start already as you hear the memories they call to mind. They share their first instinct about curiosity, whether feeling adrift, inspired, or relate to curiosity like an ex-lover who keeps drawing them back in. Just this question alone may bring tears to their eyes just thinking about it, *which is perfectly normal.* There's a Tent saying we have: "It's not Tent until someone cries."

After introductions, another Tent Keeper shares a poem, and we hear responses from those who want to share, and then we move into our first activity. Our activities bring us together to learn as a community of women. Being silly and doing an activity as a group can help break down barriers we have quicker than a glass of wine.

Sharing our ideas, knowing we can disagree, while fully recognizing the humanity of each other, and still accept one another cultivates trust when vulnerability is a rare gift. Red Tent evenings are sacred precisely because they are full of curiosity, tears, emotions, and laughter all at the same time.

As we write down our thoughts from our activity, a knowing sets in around the room. It's time to hear a story and not just any story, a womanhood story. This story one woman shares could be about anything, ranging from first periods, a miscarriage, a first kiss, birth control, or how the meaning of womanhood has changed for them through the years.

These musings of the soul have involved tears, laughter, silence, shouting, and even show-and-tell items.

Stories are sacred.

Tales are usually locked up tight in fear of being shamed. Accusations are slung every day of 'It was your fault,' 'You should have known,' and the onslaught of advice after finally

reclaiming your body after an assault can lead to women
secreting away their stories in fear.

But.

Not.

Here.

There's a space in Tent for the pain and the joy; it's not
an either-or situation. In our Tent, it's more often a yes/and.
We listen with open hearts, open hands, silent lips—and
healing happens.

In our Tent, we have a tradition of giving the person
sharing her womanhood story a necklace, a single red stone
in the shape of a crescent moon, marking those who said yes
and stepped into the wilderness of vulnerability, sharing her
story with the community we all adore.

It is after this moment we have our 'Soul Care Time.'
Twenty minutes to do whatever your heart needs. Maybe
you are craving a nap, a stretch, trading a mini massage, or
indulging in snacks! Curious women often dive into the Red
Library.

Our Red Library houses books about womanhood and
growth—everything from *Eat, Pray, Love*, to *Burning Woman*,
to *Jesus Feminist*. Books challenge us to grow, so ours are
loaned out between Tents. Pages become marked up over
time with notes in margins, collecting the wisdom not only of
the author but of the women who have read the same novel.

We reconvene for a second activity, a guided visual
meditation to breathe and connect to our hearts, followed by
journaling and honest, reflective sharing.

Tent women believe we are more alike than we are
different, all of us connected to each other going back to the
beginning, through our mothers, grandmothers, and
ancestors. To weave the evening to a close, and mark this
connection of us being here, at this moment, surrounded by
these remarkable women, we do a Red Thread ceremony.

Red Thread is laden with connective imagery across the
world, bringing people together despite all odds from

Ariadne's thread in the labyrinth, the thread of lovers in China, the thread of fate in Japan, and even in Jewish mystical traditions. Red Thread becomes a marker of how we've all been drawn into the space of the Red Tent and reminds us we can pull on our thread to get help when we need it too, because we are all connected.

We wrap the red thread around our wrists, as one by one, each woman recites her matriarchal spiritual lineage: the names of the women and those who have brought her to this moment. Those who have born her mind, body, or soul, any children she has, and whoever she would like to claim in the end, whether God, Spirit, Eve, possibilities, or even the women around her.

I start at a near whisper and end my lineage with my head held high in Gratitude. "I am Aj, daughter of Linda, daughter of Julie, daughter of Bertha, daughter of Grace, Annie, Holly, and the wild women before me, daughter of daughters, daughter of God, moon, fire and flame."

After everyone has wrapped their red thread, we can literally feel our connection as the red thread ties us all together in a giant circle. Still threaded together, we sing our *We are the Flow* song.[2] In our Tent and many other Tents through the years, hundreds of women have sung this song together, and it always gives me chills.

There's always a pause in the air after this song. An exquisite liminal space where you can simply be, where the whole of you is welcome to the table, where your story is valuable and a part of BUT NOT ALL of who you are.

After singing, with the song still echoing in our minds, we cut our bracelets and say our favorite part and takeaway of the evening. As the scissors make their way back into my hands, I share an invitation to explore the theme in the upcoming month, and we close our Red Tent circle.

Some women have to leave after Tent closes, finding just enough time in their day to rest for the time we are in the space, and others snuggle in with a book or ask someone to braid their hair and catch up about life. Others move to the kitchen table to debrief about a moment they had when they cried in Tent together. The buzz of energy rises as we all feel grounded, loved, and safe.

After the last woman leaves and the red fabric is folded back up into the suitcases, my living room looks like a regular room. Except for the few pens on the counter, extra plates in the sink, and chocolate cake someone left you wouldn't know there were just 20 women in here feeding one another mind, body, and soul, and yet, you can feel it in the air. Like many other Red Tent women that evening, I'll fall asleep still smiling about our night.

Welcome to the Red Tent.

YOUR GUIDE

You may be wondering who I am; I'm Aj, a colorful joy-filled Red Tent Keeper, henna artist, and professional mermaid entertainer — *which is like hiring a clown for a party, but with the added bonus that your children won't come away scarred for life.* I'm also an Air Force spouse who has been traveling the world with my husband Jer and two pups for the last ten years, walking alongside others to weave joy, curiosity, creativity, and wonder into their lives, whether they're six or sixty.

Through my work in the last ten years, I've learned we often stifle our creativity and imagination out of fear of being too much or not enough. As women, we spend an excessive amount of time beating around the bush, *no pun intended*, worrying about appearing polite and pleasant, which means we rarely call it as it is.

Leading workshops about our bodies, Red Tents, and retreats for women has allowed women to ask everything from "*How do you ask for what you need?*" to "*How do you say no?*"

The silent questions women held were bursting at the seams, and I saw the real questions underneath the questions:

> *"Am I normal?"*
> *"Am I enough?"*
> *"Am I worthy of love and goodness?"*

Maybe you've wondered some of these questions.

I know I have.

When I was 27, I was struggling with serious life questions, frustrated with birth control, my cycle, and weighing if I was going to have children or not. I felt alone and crazy. I had friends but didn't think I could talk to anyone about my REAL questions. Red Tents entered my life during this period of wrestling, nestled into two paragraphs of a book about understanding your menstrual cycle called *Moon Time* by Lucy Pearce.

As I read the part about Red Tents, my soul yelled, "*I NEED THIS!*" I looked up the closest Red Tent. It was two and a half hours away and in German.

I speak enough German to buy my groceries but not to talk about my soul's innermost feelings[3]. As I brought my new menstrual cycle learnings and the wild hair idea to start our own Red Tent to friends, they shared their own heartbreaking stories of their wombs, hearts, and bodies. They all had stories different yet frustratingly similar to mine, and here we were, suffering in silence.

Together, but alone.

We needed a Red Tent.

Elissa, a Tent Keeper, shares,

"I remember sitting at my first Red Tent Retreat, and how many of us were sharing stories that were rooted in trauma. So many of us experienced pain and shame that we've suppressed. I realized I'm not alone. It's never been just me. You think you're the only one that something is broken within you. Red Tent is awkward and intimate, and vulnerable. It gets to the core of who you are and allows another person to reach inside you and say, 'It's okay.'"

Red Thread is your own personal Red Tent to hear stories from other women, myself, and to explore your stories. Each chapter highlights a new way to look at the world, yourself, and how you are uniquely wired through a different theme. *Red Thread* is also a guide to cultivating a Red Tent if you choose for yourself, your close friends, or your community.

None of us have to be alone with our stories ever again.

For some of you, this is the first book you've read about Red Tents and sacred spaces and are wondering if this might be too 'woo.' Some of you may, like me, have a stack of themed books on how to cultivate yourself and friendships on your bookshelf and this is just one of many! Some of you might be the "All-of-my-friends-are-guys" type and picked this up because the idea of living embodied sounds nice. Others, yet, might have picked up the book because the cover is pretty (I agree) and feel a tug somewhere inside that you needed this book.

No matter what brought you to this moment, where you

are from, or what you believe, you are ALL welcome here. All women: Cis, Trans, Intersex, and femme folk have a seat at this table. Even if you don't identify as a woman, I promise you; there will be goodness in this book for you as well.

Red Thread gives you the tools to show up in the world bolder, kinder, and armed with new knowledge to see yourself and your life in a way you didn't before. When we have new concepts and language, we can show up fully embodied in the world, ready for whatever may come our way.

The subtitle for this book is *Weaving an Embodied Life of Joy*. Embodiment doesn't merely mean you are bold enough to wear that red lipstick (although I am a massive fan of red lipstick), ask for the pay raise you deserve or even speak the truth on your heart. It means you recognize the unique soul you have, and you are present, mind, body, and soul in the here and now.

Because of the way I see the world, I talk about God, faith, possibilities, and glitter throughout this book.[4] As I do so, I want to offer you an inclusive invitation to explore the word *God* from *The Artist's Way* by Julia Cameron.

She believes we are all creative beings, and when we can imagine there is a force greater than ourselves rooting for our flourishing, it can remove some energetic blocks we create in our lives—beliefs about how you can't set boundaries, how it's selfish to have soul care time, that you aren't creative, and one of the most harmful I believe: that your Inner Voice isn't worthy of being trusted. She encourages in her book the below, and I'd like to encourage the same here,

"When the word *God* is used in these pages, you may substitute the thought *good orderly direction* or *flow*. What we are talking about is a creative energy. *God* is useful shorthand for many of us, but so is *Goddess, Mind, Universe,*

Source, and *Higher Power*...The point is not what you name it. The point is that you try using it."[5]

I concur with Julia that each person's interpretation of God is their own and encourage you to use words that resonate the most with you. My views about Spirit might be different than what you believe, and that is okay. Take what works and leave what doesn't. Trust the flow and that this book is in your hands for a reason.

I encourage you to sit with the questions within and at the end of each chapter. Journal about them, or talk them out with a friend. Grab your favorite pens to highlight and write all over this book! If anything in these chapters brings you a sense of discomfort, try asking yourself: what is discomfort inviting you to unveil and see? Often when a hint —or a heap—of defensiveness rises in us, it's our body's way of trying to tell us something.

So be gentle with yourself when reading. You might just be surprised what comes up for you when you believe you are worthy of goodness, tenderness, grace, and love.

As a white American who mainly serves women, I have done my best to be inclusive of various experiences and use "friend" or" lovely" when addressing you. Woven throughout this book are the perspectives of thirteen women who have led or been in Tents. Their experiences vary in beliefs, age, ethnicity, and neuro-diversity. I include these to expand the perspective written in this book and let you know you aren't alone if you feel different or aren't sure if there is a Red Tent or place you belong. The stories shared here are told as honestly as possible to the best of my and others' recollection. Some names and details have changed for confidentiality.

Our Thirteen Red Ladies who have contributed their stories, experiences, ideas, and love to this book:

1. Elissa:

Elissa is a 40-year-old Bi Ambivert that has always marked "other" in the race box. As a mixed-race person of color, and a Libra, Elissa has always been keenly aware of the dualities of her life and understands the struggle to find balance in all things. She is drawn equally to the sun and the moon, the mountains and the ocean, the garden, and the kitchen, nights together with friends, and early mornings alone. Elissa is a mother, mil-spouse, writer, Red Tent Keeper, Meditation Creator, and self-proclaimed nerd who enjoys bringing more diversity into the different facets of her life and art mediums.

2. Michaela:

Michaela is enthusiastic about being 40, an eternal student, and a forest witch in training. Most of her ancestors came from Celtic countries. She makes good snickerdoodles. Her love language is gifts of interesting dead insects and bones from the forest. She spends a lot of time talking about mental health and the power of language.

3. Leah:

Leah is 52 years young, a mother of two amazing young adults, a Nana of two precious grandchildren, a military wife, and a dog mom. She is caucasian with a mix of Scot-Irish and Norweigan ancestry who grew up in the hills of Kentucky. She loves to dance, craft, be in nature and learn new things that challenge her to grow or see new perspectives. Life has led her to be a vet tech, sign language interpreter, police officer, Reiki provider, and many things between.

4. Obbie:

Obbie was born and raised in the South Bronx and is Puerto Rican. She is loud, opinionated, and a whole lot of sass. She loves reading, K-Dramas, drawing, and video games. Obbie is a military wife and Mom who was lucky enough to be introduced to Red Tent and made some of the best friends she could ever wish for, with some of the most amazing women she's ever met.

5. Ayesha:

Ayesha is an ambitious 28-year-old multiracial dreamer with a passion for animals and conservation education. She lives with her soldier that lured her from the sea and their two feline furbabies. She enjoys mermaiding, practicing aerial arts, and aspires to live life fully and authentically.

6. Taylor:

Taylor is an Autistic camping enthusiast from North Dakota and a 27-year-old American with Norwegian and Irish Heritage and traditions. She is a graduate of Independence Inc's Community Leadership Academy and DeAnna L'am's Red Tent Academy. She absolutely maintains a spreadsheet with all of her closest friends' different personality test results. She's a Chaotic Good Slytherin INTJ.

7. DeLandrea:

DeLandrea is a 30 something who was born and mostly raised in Oklahoma. However, she claims Oklahoma and Texas as her homes. She is mom to a 12-year-old man-child and three dogs. She's a five-year military spouse and unapologetically black. She is pursuing her degree in psychology, emphasis in gender and minority studies, and wants to work with teens and adolescents, especially minorities, to be the voice and sounding board she was missing growing up. She is a diehard Potterhead [Gryffinclaw] and Disnerd for life. She enjoys laughing, making people laugh, and a nice Chianti with fava beans.

8. Jill:

Jillian is a 33-year-old white pansexual military spouse, mom of humans and fur people, writer, and daughter of the Universe. Jillian was diagnosed with ADHD/ASD in adulthood and is now pursuing a degree in Psychology, intending to become a behavioral therapist, hoping that she can help others overcome the obstacles that come with being neurodivergent. She lives by an old Klingon motto: "Own the day."

9. Bruna:

Bruna is a ten-year Navy veteran and mother of twins. She loves God, the ocean, surfing and is married 23 years to a retired Navy guy. Bruna is an American of Mexican descent and a first-generation American citizen, and the first person to graduate from college in her family. She currently provides concierge services to health plan members ages 65 and older.

10: Lindsay:

Lindsay Briley, nearing 30 years old, is a true dreamer, Cancer and Enneagram 7 and a white American of Irish descent, and lived in Texas her whole life except for one summer in Australia that rocked her world. She's obsessed with her husband and five-year-old daughter. Lindsay teaches second graders and loves ALL things Disney and intentionally incorporates it into every day. She's loud, whimsical, and a welcoming lighthouse for others.

11. Tara:

Tara M. Clapper (she/her) is a disabled cis white writer, pagan, live-action role-playing game designer, healthcare advocate, and digital marketer. She loves dogs, immersive experiences, exploring Irish American culture, and tarot readings.

12. Mary-Grace:

Mary-Grace is a creative leadership coach who, after a transformational experience in California, founded The Messy Healer in 2019. She lives in Michigan with her husband, cat, and two dogs. She is 25 years young and is of French, Irish, and Mi'kmaq lineage. She nourishes her heart with long walks, a good book, a steaming kettle of tea, and the reminder that the nature of all truth is simply love.

13. Brooke:

Brooke is a caucasian redhead from Texas, born and raised, where she lives with her husband, daughter, three dogs, and a cat she's had since high school. At the age of 31, she's come full circle from the witchy-esque teenager, where she loves herbalism, nature, and animals. She let others dictate what an adult was supposed to look like and went on a ten-year journey that led her back to her animals and plants.

SO...WHAT EXACTLY IS A RED TENT?

Red Tent is a newer term for a place where women gather and share stories in sacred space, passing down wisdom they've learned. Throughout history, communities of women have come together during their bleeding times or other times of celebration, whether through coming of age ceremonies, weddings, births, and crossing into menopause.

Whether in places like a Red Tent or a Menstruation Hut, the idea of a separate time during menstruation has shown up through time in both healing and harmful ways. Some renditions have been safe places for women to seek wisdom while menstruating, like in the Lakota tradition of Moon Lodges.[6] In other societies, women can be separated from the rest of their communities while menstruating, and this can lead to highly negative consequences like missing school, malnourishment, and even death.[7]

Over time with the hustle and bustle of our lives in Western society, the importance of intentional gathering of women faded into a dull ember. When the book *Red Tent* was published in 1997, it ignited women across the globe on a larger scale to come together in sacred spaces to honor and share our lived experiences.

Anita Diamont's book *The Red Tent* and the Lifetime series based on her book is a fictional retelling of the story of Dinah in the Bible, who is Jacob and Leah's daughter. Diamont explores Dinah's experience of growing up with a Red Tent, a place women go when bleeding as they were considered 'unclean,' and thus not 'fit to be around men.' The Red Tent in her novel is a place for women to share stories about womanhood, joy, loss, birth, the sacred, and the secular. Exhausted women are refreshed by sharing tea, massage, art, and songs in a private space. Seeing this in the book inspired women worldwide to ask, "Where are OUR Red Tents?"

Since *The Red Tent* being published the Red Tent movement has gained traction in the last 20 years. Since then, leaders such as DeAnna L'am, Alissa Starkweather, Dr. Isadora Leidenfrost, the Red Tent Directory, and women worldwide have stepped up to lead under the Red Tent banner. All of them helping those who feel the tug of the red thread to join the movement and create Red Tents.

Authors of *Red Tents* and leaders of the Red Tent Directory Mary Ann Clements and Aisha Hannibal share,

"We think of Red Tents as community-held spaces where women can come to connect with each other in ways that aren't necessarily common or familiar to us. And we think of the practice of doing this, of meeting each other monthly to share, and rest, as something that allows us to connect to one another in a different kind of way from what we might be used to. Connecting by intentionally listening and deliberately seeking not to 'fix' or critique. Doing this we think can be a liberatory practice that helps support change in our lives and in our world."[8]

For our usage here, Red Tents are open faith,[9] sober sacred places where you learn tools of embodiment, and you don't have to perform—a place where all women are welcome. There is no proof of blood or wombs needed here.[10]

Although inspired by menstrual gathering traditions, Red Tent is not about your cycle; it's about your soul.[11]

A Red Tent is a place where you can leave your shame at the door.

When there was no Tent accessible to me, I asked my friends in a not-as-subtle-as-I-thought way, "Would you like to be in a Red Tent with me and talk about our innermost feelings and cycles of our lives?"

Reactions varied from, "That sounds amazing! Of course!" to, "No, thank you, it sounds like a weird vagina cult with red robes." To be fair, we sit in a circle and talk about our wombs on occasion, although not as often as people may expect. We also sing songs together during our evening, and while wearing red is encouraged because it's Red Tent, and matching is fun, there is no actual dress code, except for being comfy.

With the 'this-is-not-a-cult' disclaimer out in the open, if anyone would like to give me a red robe with pockets, I'm here for it.

Our first Tent's theme was based on the old proverb, "When sleeping women wake, mountains move." This theme has been a rallying cry of what Tent is and what happens when women join ever since. There are hundreds of Red Tents around the world, and each one is different.

I mentioned earlier this book is also a Red Tent for *you*. At the end of each themed chapter is a Red Tent Script you can use by yourself as a mini personal retreat or utilize to lead a Red Tent with your friends. These Tents are tools to help you dive into the thirteen different themes through activities, questions, and guided visual meditations. Doing the Tents is not required either. There are no grades, or extra credit points here, just opportunities to explore.

HOW TO USE YOUR RED TENT SCRIPTS AND MEDITATIONS

Red Thread is composed of 13 chapters, one for each new moon of the year. Did you know the average moon cycle is 28 days? So is the average woman's hormonal cycle. Throughout history, a women's cycle has often been linked to the new moon, and Red Tents are generally on or near a New moon. You can read all the chapters straight through and host a Red Tent once a month to create a new tradition in your life or do the Tents as you read each corresponding chapter. There's no right or wrong way.

You could have a tent tomorrow with no plan other than self-care and a few question starters.

But if you want intimate conversation starters, circle ideas, and a game plan you can follow either alone or in a group—which has been tested and tried—refined over and over again?

Then I've got you, babe.

I don't want one thousand Aj tents or women who see the world just like I do. I want one thousand Red Tents unique and marvelous as her Tent Keepers will be.

You have three options for using the Red Tent Scripts at the end of the chapters:

1. You can use it by yourself as a mini-retreat
2. You can use it with a friend or a daughter as an activity, where it's more relaxed, and you go through it together.
3. You can use it to lead a Red Tent with others, whether with a few friends or a more substantial gathering.

If you choose option two or three, whether in-person or online, I would suggest reading through the Tent beforehand, so you understand the rhythm of the Tent. You can even have a more private Tent with a few friends in addition to leading a larger public Tent.

The scripts in this book are more like guidelines than actual rules to help you get your feet under you. To use them word for word or as a jumping-off point. They are a way to inspire you to envision your own Red Tent, which may be pretty similar or different from mine. Take this idea and run with it. The torch is in your hands now.

THINGS TO KEEP IN MIND

Don't rush. It is easy to sprint through the parts where you do grounded breathing or meditation, but the way the Tents are written allows you to breathe throughout. Take your time. If you find yourself overwhelmed or your mind swirling, it is okay to pause re-center yourself. You can say a prayer or say, "Hold on; I need a few seconds." Take a deep breath, imagine your breath coming from your toes, and release it slowly, and remember you don't have to do this flawlessly. Red Tent is about showing up, just as you are, for yourself and those around you.

Set the stage. When preparing a space for a Red Tent, keep in mind different people's body needs. Some may want chairs or something soft to sit in, whereas others may be comfortable on the ground. Having various pillows or blankets for warmth can allow your women to choose what feels best for them to settle into the room.

How do you want your space to look? Your Tent may be a living room, a backyard, or a room at your church or community center. Even if you are by yourself, decorations can make the space feel cozy and sacred. I buy red curtains and blankets on sale at goodwill, and after washing, pin them on the walls using push pins on Red Tent night. I use other red sheets to cover tables, and we pull pillows and blankets from beds for extra comfort, which can extend the sense of safety.

Depending on your setup, it could take you 10 minutes to an hour to set up. I like to hang up curtains, make soup, and bring out many blankets, so I usually give myself an hour to go slow and get in the zone as I prep. Sometimes other women come to help set up as well and hang out beforehand. Clean-up usually is quicker as you can ask the women to help you fold blankets or put things in bins.

. . .

What to bring: Having your women bring a journal and pen is helpful as there is often at least one journaling portion in Red Tent. I tell my women to bring their token,[12] donation, water bottle, journal, pens and wear comfy clothes. After everyone has finished the Red Thread Ceremony at the end of the Tent, each woman will take her item out of the bowl.

Bring red yarn and scissors for your Red Thread Ceremony at the end of the Tent. Bringing spare paper and coloring goodies is helpful in case anyone doesn't have a journal. You will also need a bowl for tokens, which could be a pretty abalone shell or a kitchen soup bowl. If you are virtual, encourage each woman to bring a pen and a journal, but you will need nothing except your script.

You may have heard of a talking stick, but because we use battery-operated tea lights to decorate the space, we pick one of those tea lights to pass around as we speak, and then it's one less thing for you to think about having to pack. Outside of these, what you bring personally to Tent is up to you. Essential oil roll-ons have been a nice touch I have found for helping women pick their scents for the night.

If we are in person, I invite my women 30 minutes before Tent starts. Pre-Tent time allows them time to relax, eat food, and catch up before we start. Relaxing before will enable women to meet each other, catch up, and settle in, which helps everyone find their groove for Tent quicker. If virtually, I usually open the Zoom room 15 minutes ahead of time with music playing allowing women to sort out technical difficulties before we begin.

Time Boundaries: This is more important than you realize. Women are often trying to fit more into their day than is humanly possible, and for them to come to Tent means they have prioritized Tent above other needs. Following through on time boundaries means you need to start and end on time for the active Red Tent portion, for whatever timeline your Tent agrees on.

I've put timestamps in front of each activity to help you gauge how long things may take. My online Tents are usually one and a half hours, and our in-person Tents are generally two and a half. Depending on the number of women in your group (Three women vs. thirteen), you may have to adjust activities or sharing accordingly, where the circle is a one-minute answer instead of two to three. I've also put in modification ideas throughout Tents with pairing up vs. whole circle sharing.

Time management is a skill you learn with time. Depending on your group, you can take out the Womanhood story, the Call Down a Blessing song, or the Quote and Response question if you need a shorter evening. Maybe your Red Tent consists of just the intro questions and one activity, and the rest of the time is relaxing and sharing. Use the script however feels best to you. You DO NOT need to include every item in the script into your Tent.

Manipulating the Soul Care Time is also a possibility. For example, we were a bit past the timestamps at one Tent, so instead of twenty minutes of Soul Care Time, we had ten minutes. Don't ever cut this out entirely because you need a mental break. Ten minutes is the minimum you should have for your break, so women can grab a snack, use the bathroom, and chat. Five minutes will have everyone mainly stand up and sit back down.

A Red Tent is a place for everyone to share their lived experience without having to prove it. Having vulnerability in a space like this can feel daunting, and not everyone is always ready for it. Allow people to pass when it's their time in the circle or only share as much as they feel comfortable.

It's also crucial that a Red Tent is a sober space precisely because of the topics of conversations. To be fully present mentally and own the words you say, you need to be in a clear state of mind. It can be easier to be vulnerable when we drink or do drugs, but we slowly teach our bodies how to be courageously present in a safe space when we show up without mood-altering substances. It's amazing what people share when high or drunk. It's even more astonishing when they share their stories sober.

Italicized words in the scripts are for you to think about as a leader. These thoughts will help you create an engaging and thoughtful atmosphere for your women. The words for you to speak will be after a section labeled **Leader**. The two songs can be listened to in the downloadable resources for the book, as well as examples of some of the activities and a womanhood story print out.[13]

If you want to do it online, you 100% can! The average Tent in the book is 2.5 hours long. Here's an outline of what I do instead with a Tent to make it a 1.5 hour Virtual Red Tent:

1.Opener (shakeout, grounded breathing, call in, the first question) I leave out the Call Down a blessing song.

2. 1st Activity, questions, and 2nd activity. You can skip the Womanhood Story and Soul Care Time because it's a short evening.

3. Closing. If you would like to sing the final song, you may do so, but everyone but you will have to be on mute because of the way zoom works. If you feel uncomfortable singing, you can also just have people say their Matriarchal Spiritual lineage, whether that is "Descendent of those who ____" or "Daughter of ____" along with their favorite part and takeaway.

If you want to have a Tent for everyone, not just women and femme folk, or do it with a sibling or partner, that is fabulous! You are invited to switch the language throughout the Tent scripts to be gender-neutral. Included in the introduction questions in each script are Pronoun check-ins as well.

During the Red Thread Ceremony, it is helpful to be

aware of women's different relationships with their lineage. Some only know their mom's name, whereas others can go back five generations. Adoptions, slavery, immigration, record keeping, and trauma all impact the names women want to or feel comfortable sharing. We've used 'descendent or daughter of those who _____' as an option for those who would instead claim a community of people.

It's essential to make sure your women know there is no right or wrong way to do this in how they want to claim themselves. We've even had one lady say I am Kristen, daughter of myself. If someone is uncomfortable with the lineage idea, they can just share their favorite part of the evening or wrap without saying anything.

In addition, because Tent is open-faith, you can have a wide variety of people and belief systems in the room. Holding the space for all experiences can be perspective changing in and of itself. Open faith means all perspectives are welcome as long as no one is being shamed or demeaned for their beliefs. The world may define us outside of Tent, but inside of it, we can express ourselves.

If you want your Tent to be open and inclusive when inviting people, you can say so when you post it online, and say "At this Tent, we believe all women are women: Cis, Trans, Intersex, and Femme folk are welcome in this space." The Red Tent Directory also has deeper resources around creating inclusive Red Tents.

MEDITATIONS WITHIN THE RED TENTS

Let me start with the acknowledgment that there are hundreds of ways to meditate. You can meditate in a particular position by watching your thoughts, going on a journey, or sitting in silence for five minutes or two hours. Some people meditate on a scripture, a word, or verbally chant to help them meditate.

Simply put, "Meditation is a practice where an individual

uses a technique – such as mindfulness or focusing the mind on a particular object, thought, or activity – to train attention and awareness, and achieve a mentally clear and emotionally calm and stable state."[14]

Any person, in any faith, can meditate. It comes down to finding the way that works best for you. There is no one right or wrong way to meditate.

I'm a very visual person, so most of the meditations in our Red Tent—and in this book— are guided visual meditations to tune in to how we feel and ground ourselves in the present moment. The first time I ever did a visual guided meditation was with Amber Kuileimailani Bonnici through her Woman Unleashed Retreat, and I was surprised with how focused I was, and what came up for me, and I've never looked back. When we do our meditations, sometimes we meet an archetype. Archetypes are a way for us to meet our subconscious in a more accessible way. They remove the blocks we have in place that keep us from listening to our core desires. Our archetypes are facets of ourselves that want to be seen and heard.

Just because your subconscious is a part of you, it doesn't mean meditations are always fun. Sometimes we have to face reality while meditating. For example, a Maiden archetype in the cycles meditation might be scared instead of free and flowing because you feel like you aren't allowed to let your guard down in your day-to-day life. Your perceptions of archetypes influence the experience you have with them.

Another example could be an Inner Sanctuary in need of repair and tending. Each person is different, but across the board, whatever you need to see will be there, even if you just see colors or don't see anything. I've had people fall asleep during meditations, and sometimes, a nap is just what the body needs at that moment.

Think of guided meditations as a two-way street for your conscious and subconscious to connect and see the next steps. For one woman, the realization in her meditation turned into putting her writing out into the world. For others, it has looked like setting boundaries or leaving a toxic situation.

In my experience, sometimes what seems like a small step to others feels like a giant leap for ourselves. When we can see the fear and the story we have about what our next step would mean for us, we can set boundaries and pursue our curiosity and longings. Along the way, we just might discover there is more space for us in the world than we realized initially. Meditations, where you can connect with your Inner Voice and remove the mental clutter and the clanging of the outside world, can help you feel grounded, calm, and clear on your next steps.

 Leah shares,
"You think about meditations like 'Oh, it's Woo-Woo.' But honestly, if you think about it, prayers, and talking to Jesus is meditation. It all could be meditation, walking in the woods, just looking at the trees is a meditation. I think doing the meditations we do in Tent helps because it helped me get in touch more so with my Inner Voice and brought more self-awareness to that Inner Voice. It helped me to relax, accept and promote more compassion and kindness for those parts of myself I am sometimes afraid to embrace."

If you aren't sure how to tap into your authentic Inner Voice, meditations may be a good place to start. The Cycles and the Wild Soul Self meditation can help walk you back to yourself. The Curiosity meditation will help you navigate your life path. Your Sanctuary meditation will be a place you can find rest. The Body Meditation will remind you to tend your body in this journey with kindness, and the Values meditation will remind you of the value you have and how you are allowed to protect and nurture your space and life.

If you are reading them outloud, pace yourself as you read the meditations, let the music guide you on speed, and remember there's no need to rush. You are allowed to go slow, both during meditations and in life. If you'd rather not read, I've also recorded the meditations for you to play in the downloadable resources. If you need music, my personal favorites are *Ocean* and *Any Other Name* by Thomas Newman. Your experience may be different each time you listen to a meditation and that's okay. It's all a part of the journey, and meditations are just one more tool you can use along the way.

If you feel the tug of the Red Thread to try out the Tents and meditations, I encourage you to, even if that means your Tent is just you. You will be making ripples that will be felt for years to come. I'm reminded of a Marianne Williamson quote I love: "...And as we let our own light shine, we unconsciously give other people permission to do the same. As we are liberated from our own fear, our presence automatically liberates others."[15]

I believe…
Everyone is worthy to be walked alongside.
That sacred space is accessible for everyone who claims it.
I believe life can be imbued with more vibrancy, possibilities and joy.
I believe living a grounded life of embodied joy is kind and necessary for our world.
You are welcome and wanted here.
You, lovely one, are full of creative potential, joy, and wonder.
May this book tend the flames of your soul in a nourishing and liberating way.
Welcome to your Red Tent.
-Aj

BODY IS A TEMPLE

CW: Bulimia/Eating Disorder/Body Dysmorphia

I don't know about you, but the struggle between feeling too much and not enough has followed me for most of my life. The whiplash between the two can be exhausting. My struggle to feel like I could be my whole self is ironic because I come from a big extended family with a variety of unapologetic eccentric people within it.

My Ferry family—yes, my maiden name is Ferry—has huge reunions. My grandpa has twelve siblings, and every two years, we all gather in a different state for fun, food, songs, and drinking. We'd have an impromptu band thrown together, and our talent show was always a blast. We claimed we were Irish but recently found out not really: mostly Bohemian (a part of the Czech Republic)—with a sprinkle of Scottish and a dash of German. Honestly, I think my grandparents just said, "We're Irish," and no one ever had reason to disbelieve or correct them.[1].

These reunions are an absolute blast. One of my second cousins, Sarah, is a ball of energy. She's always excited to meet everyone and passionately expresses her emotions and ideas. When I was 12, she was in high school, and I remember her effortlessly chatting by the side of the pool in her colorful swimsuit and pixie haircut, and I thought she was the coolest.

I also had Aunts who wore over-the-top colors, laughed loudly, lived creative lives, and even moved far from home to explore lives outside of Iowa, and I was in awe of their bravery to live lives aligned to who they were.

I heard the adults talk through the years about how some family members were over the top and a little zany. I wanted to be just like them when I grew up, but I was nervous about also receiving the label of "too much."

I thought, "They can get away with it, they're older and cooler. Regular people can't dress like that! Who do I think I am?"

My Aunt Holly, to me, is the epitome of an embodied woman. Maybe you have a cool aunt or woman you know — or perhaps you are the cool Aunt now — the one who wears bold lipstick, a lucky pair of boots that have been through the wringer, or a hand-painted jacket. When they walk into a room, you feel stronger and more centered just by them being there.

My Aunt Holly is a savvy single mom and business owner, and one day in my Grandma's kitchen, I brought up the nerves to ask, "How are you able to wear bold lipstick and fashion in the world? Aren't you afraid of being too much?" I told her when I was older, after 50, I'd wear the red lipstick and clothes I wanted of capes and fantastic boots, but I needed to wait till it was the proper time to 'take up space.' In my mind, I had to wait to wear what I wanted.

Aunt Holly put down her coffee and said, "Sweetie, you don't have to wait. You can wear what you want and be who you want to be now. Why would you wear anything other than what brings you joy?"

I was shocked, not having planned for receiving permission to live fully the way I wanted at that moment. Could I dress like a super cool 50-year-old aunt *now*? Layers of clothes, fun makeup, and stride into a room like I belong and *not apologize* for standing there? A whisper of insecurity brought my elation back down to earth as I thought, "Aj, you don't deserve to take up the amount of space you dream of." And with that thought, I wrapped my old blankets of shame and self-doubt back around me, but not for long.

I used my extra energy in our drama program at church and school, which eventually led me to join pageants. I loved it. I wasn't the best, but I won two local pageants and Miss Congeniality when I competed for Miss Iowa in the Miss America circuit.[2]

I made sure everything I did was in line with the perfect pageant girl's image. *This image wasn't hard for me; I grew up in Iowa as a white, blond-haired, blue-eyed Christian girl. The stereotype was the spitting image of my life.* As I entered college, I became curious about who I wanted to be and how I wanted to look without feeling the need to reflect others' ideas of who I should be;

The more we seek to be other people's vision of us, the more we forget what makes us feel radiant in our skin.

During my Freshman year of college, I started exploring more of what ignited my inner fire. As a theatre major, I heard about a small Burlesque show looking for belly dancers and signed right up, which launched me into a five-year whirlwind of performing and choreographing with *Sissy's Sircus*.[3] We sang and danced in a way that made me feel powerful and bold, and we grew as a supportive community.

I could play with crazy makeup, and it introduced me to a world of people whose rainbow of being was quite different from my own and what I was usually around. I met many beautiful humans who felt stunning but didn't fit the 'Barbie' mold I thought I needed to be. These people paved the way for me to start making my own more colorful choices.

I married Jer in the middle of college, and my sparkly exuberance for life was well balanced with his grounded Iowa farmer temperament. After getting married, a photo on Pinterest stuck me with inspiration in it was a lady with purple hair, red lipstick, and tattoos. I decided I needed *color* and promptly got a pixie cut and dyed my hair pink. *Who was this rebel woman?!*[4]

If you've ever made a drastic hair change, you know how wild this can feel. It feels like anything is possible. I was feeling equal parts, limitless and inconspicuous. As I looked in the mirror that night, I saw a truer reflection of myself. Have you ever looked in the mirror and felt recognition deep in your bones like, *"Hey! That's me!"*? Like many people, my style was whatever was on racks, but this was the first time I was surprised at how doing something different made me feel intrinsically aligned. I did eventually go back to being blonde for a time, but I wanted something to say "I'm going to choose from here on out."

Sometimes we don't look like ourselves; we look like the version society wants us to be. And then there are moments where you look how you feel inside. I've had purple hair for the last four years and recently felt the nudge to go blue, and it's been a blast. Changing the way we show up in the world allows us to see ourselves in new ways; when we do the same old, we usually *feel* the same old.

MERMAID DREAMS

Every birthday I can remember, I wished, "I know I'm a human with these legs, but If I could have a tail and be a mermaid, that would be the coolest. I don't even need to breathe underwater, just the tail. I know it's impossible, but it'd sure as heck be the best thing ever."

On my 23rd birthday, I came across an article about a lady who was a professional mermaid. I was astounded and almost fell out of my chair, "WHAT!? You can be a mermaid, and people will pay you for it? Why didn't anyone tell me this earlier?" Glee flooded my body as I realized my impossible dreams were about to become my new reality.

A few months after discovering being a mermaid was possible, the Air Force gave us orders[5] to move to Hawaii. It felt like the stars had aligned for me to launch my mermaid business. I found a tail maker (someone who makes tails) and designed my tail with galaxy colors and sparkles. Certainly not how I expected my transformation to happen, but I was stoked nonetheless. I had an actual mermaid tail! I wholeheartedly embraced the over-the-top muchness of mermaid life. Endless permission to be eccentric, and it gets written off because I perform as a mermaid? Yes. Please.

Younger me could not imagine the real magic I would feel in being a real mermaid. When I put my tail on and swam underwater for the first time, I felt a peaceful gloriousness. Everything in the world faded away, and all I could hear was the thrum of my heartbeat and the sound of the water around me. It was as if I was swimming in an ocean of stars.

I performed as Mermaid Harmony by singing songs, playing games, and swimming in the ocean with kids. When you are a mermaid or in any public-facing profession, some people think you are perfect and have it all together. On occasion, I receive messages from people letting me know I'm their idol. My first thought is, *"WAIT, what? Pump the breaks; I don't want to be anyone's idol!"*

Way too much pressure.

I feel fierce about this because I put being the perfect mermaid above my health under that same pressure. Instead of using mermaiding as a tool to better my life, I used it as a measuring stick for how I wasn't enough.

My first tail was good, but then I found a pre-made tail with sparkles and beautiful colors. It was fairly smaller than my measurements, but I thought I could make it work if I lost some weight.

The tail had some stretch, so I reasoned getting my figure down to a size four would be doable by summer when the tail would arrive; after all, I had been a size four before. Unfortunately, the last time I was a size four was due to a milk and egg allergy, which caused me to throw up half my meals. Milk and eggs are in quite a few things, so at the time, I was acquainted with the toilet more often than not. Understanding my allergies brought me back to a healthier and current weight as a size eight.

I worked hard to tailor my diet and workout through the early spring, but the realization that summer was just around the corner meant panic quickly set in. None of my efforts were paying off; I hadn't lost any weight.

I can almost remember the moment I had the thought, *"You were sick once before. You can make yourself sick again. It's nothing you haven't already been through, and this time you can control it."*

Bulimia, an eating disorder I thought I would never wrestle with, entered my life with those words.

I convinced myself it was a decent bargain if I could fit into the tail in the end.

Back then, I saw skinny mermaids worldwide, getting gigs, swimming in tanks, and traveling as models. In my mind, I equated the slim mermaid look with getting better gigs, even though I was slender, and people adored my own blossoming company.

Nowadays, the mermaid world numbers in the thousands and is diverse in color, gender, and size. The evidence that you can be yourself and go after your dream is everywhere now. But back then, there were maybe 100 of us in the world, and the most popular and highest-paid were white, blonde, and supermodel thin.

The fear of not being enough, alongside the whispers of control from Bulimia, constricted me so tight I ignored my better sense. Dr. Hillary McBride, an embodiment therapist shares, "Fitting in, being a part of something, is so important to us that we can get so easily trapped in a game of denying ourselves what we know and believe for the sake of belonging."[6]

I hid my eating disorder from everyone, including my husband, from early spring into summer. I deluded myself into thinking no one would notice because I didn't even realize how bad it had gotten.

It just so happened that my best friend Kelsey's wedding was the same summer my mermaid dream tail would be arriving. I was excited for her yet mentally tied up in the whirlwind of trying to lose weight. I had bought a new fitness program and started a new clean eating regime on top of forcing myself to lose half my meals. There was progress; however, I wasn't getting the results I wanted—I was still a size eight.

I was miserable and used alcohol to cope with the frustration I had at myself for not losing enough weight. The evening of the bachelorette party, we all ended up at a friend's house after attending a comedy show. After having some snacks and drinking with everyone, I went to the bathroom to get rid of it all. When I came back out, Laura and Kelsey realized something was wrong but could not quite put their fingers on it.

I breezily placed the blame of my puffy eyes on allergies and a long day. Laura, who is all of five feet with the bluest eyes you've ever seen, always sees straight through any nonsense any of us say.

She was the first to see through my cracking veneer and asked me if I had been throwing up. My mind raced as my body froze and my hands shook. I had been found out. I stuttered out a lie, but the tears that were streaming down my face told a different story.

The four of us crawled into bed as I explained why I was struggling. Kelsey placed her hand on my stomach, with tears running down her face, and cried, "I feel like I can put my hand through you. You feel broken". Her words shattered me.

As I admitted everything I had put myself through for the last four months, my friends wrapped themselves around me, and the Bulimia marginally loosened its grip on my soul. I would spend the next three months relapsing and rewriting my thoughts to keep myself from falling back into the habit.

I was lucky enough to get out of my Eating Disorder trance with the support of my friends and Jer after I told him, but I know that not everyone is so fortunate. I still have days where the thoughts weasel their way into my head, and I'd be lying if I said I haven't had a few days where I have relapsed here and there over the years. I've rewired my brain to remember, "I keep what I eat, and my food feeds my body and soul." I say body and soul because I don't make deals with food anymore, and ice cream and margaritas are not something I will feel guilty for having ever again.

Some who struggle like I did need more help or in-house hospitalization. If you need assistance, reach out to me, and I'm happy to point you in the right direction, or call/text the National Eating Disorders Association's helpline at 800-931-2237. Just because it might not be as bad as someone else's story doesn't mean you aren't worthy of help and encouragement in finding freedom from the confines of an eating disorder. I'm grateful I had someone see me, but I wish *I would have seen me* before it got to the point it did.

All that to say: after seven months of wrestling with an eating disorder, stress, and worry, the time finally came to try on the tail...and it fit.

Like.

A.

Glove.

Do you know what size I was when I tried it on?
An eight.

Don't sacrifice who you are for a dream that won't fit you.
Your dreams will take you just as you are.

RECLAIMING THE SKIN YOU ARE IN

One of the ways I show my story is through tattoos and
henna. After struggling with an eating disorder, I decorate
my body with reminders to hold the stories I don't want to
forget.

 Nadia Bolz-Weber, a Pastrix in Colorado, shares
how our bodies keep track of memories.
"Everything that happens to us happens to
our bodies, every act of love, every insult, every
moment of pleasure, every interaction with other
humans. Every hateful thing we have said or
which has been said to us has happened to our
bodies. Every kindness, every sorrow. Every
ounce of laughter. We carry all of it with us
within our skin. We are walking embodiments of
our entire story."[7]

Tattoos personally help me celebrate the idea of showing
my story on the outside. If your body is an archive of
memories, tales, and lessons you can decorate, how would
you love to adorn yourself? Adorning could be clothes,
henna, jewelry, a hairstyle, or the way you move. Magazines
may tell us, 'this is the way you need to be,' but what if you
started looking at yourself less like a dress-up doll and more

like the Library of Alexandria? A place treasured and filled with knowledge. A haven of goodness.

How would that change the way you perceive yourself?

When I shared the Library of Alexandria reference to Tara, who struggles with a chronic illness, she laughed,
"Yes, my body is like the Library of Alexandria in that it's burning down, and it's old. I approach it more from the mind because I'm really creative, so I keep my mind sharp and accentuate my eyes because I get compliments on those. It's like when the body has dysfunction, and it shows up in your nails or hair falling out, sometimes I have to do the shadow work and be like, what does this actually say about me? I don't think I'm quite there where some women find it powerful to embrace the hag's identity. I wonder if I do honestly hate my body or hate the fact that I live in a country that enables me to do very little with the options I have healthcare-wise. It generates healthy righteous anger when it comes down to the systemic issue, which helps me be a healthcare advocate and help other people. I can't bypass my health; I have to do the work."
There's a push in society to love your body, but maybe your relationship status with your body is "It's complicated." That's okay. I think it's even more crucial to give yourself grace as you navigate these questions in these cases. Explore if kindness can enter into your relationship with your body even if you've 'blocked your body's number' because you feel betrayed and hurt by it. Even complicated relationships with our bodies can help us do inner work and see what is calling us.
If you are struggling with permitting yourself to show up in the way you want, having women around you who are honest about their struggles and explorations can help take

weight off your shoulders. We can think we are the only
ones who think and feel one way until we're in a community
and realize others harbor the same desires.

> Michaela, one of our tent women, came to a
> place of decorating her body after being around
> others in Red Tent who had embraced their
> bodies:
> "I thought I had to wait till my body was a
> certain size and shape before I could decorate it
> the way I wanted to. Because of the Tent and
> the kind of environment it fosters of gathering
> women to support and edify each other, it
> naturally attracts women who want to lift other
> women. Being with women in other places in
> their journey than I was, I realized my body is
> good enough. I can treat my body the way I
> want to treat it right now. I don't have to wait
> for my body to earn the decorations and clothes
> and things I want for it. One day after a Tent, I
> told my husband, "I want a tattoo." I have three
> tattoos now, and I have plans for more. It is
> because of the Red Tent that I finally feel like I
> am allowed to decorate my body in the way I
> wanted to."

Maybe you don't want tattoos. What is it you have always
wanted to do that is within your purview, but you haven't
felt like it's possible? Maybe it's a hiking trip, making art, or
a nose ring. Other times doing the things that resonate in
our souls helps us feel embodied. When you accomplish
something you haven't been able to do before or move in a
way you love, it can feel like everything is aligned and will
create ripples you might not expect.
    Another way to tap into feeling good is the way we

dress. Hilary Rushford Collyer is a stylist and entrepreneur who runs her company Dean Street Society. In her class Style & Styleability, she shares how magazines love to tell us 'you are chic or preppy,' but she tells us we each have a unique signature that is our own, and we are allowed to uncover and claim it, regardless of others' approval. For me, my vibe is magical everyday wear. I wear clothes that make me feel adorned and gorgeous and like I could go dance in the woods with them.[8]

Decorating your body as a temple is not just how you wear clothes or what color you paint your nails, but it's about how you want to feel when you're by yourself, out in the world, or in your soul. Dressing for joy may not be an immediate shift for everyone, but it's something to keep in mind when making your daily choices. When you're getting dressed, pause, and ask yourself, "what would bring me joy to wear today?"

The way we present ourselves to the world physically is just as much about how we feel energetically as how we feel in our bodies. For those with body dysmorphia, this can feel like a trick question. While navigating body worth and self-value, it can be helpful to bring others along the journey to help you see yourself in a new light.

" Cat Anderson, a teacher and the fabulous developmental editor for this book, shares, "I've struggled with body dysmorphia since I was a sophomore in high school. All I saw in the mirror were flaws and a person who weighed twice as much as I actually did. My college needed a figure model for the painting classes on campus. It paid well, and I figured 'if they don't care what size I am, and it's not about being sexy (they paint gnarly old men most of the time), then I suppose I can do it. If I hate it, I don't have to come back.' What I didn't realize was that it was something I needed.

Seeing how others saw me--seeing the many different paintings of me, all different but similar--helped me heal. Instead of what I saw in the mirror, flaws and rolls and weight, I saw a girl. And she was actually kind of pretty. She had curves and soft shoulders, and she looked like a painting you'd see in a museum from the renaissance. I realized after modeling a few times that the girl they were painting was me — what I really looked like — and that my brain was wrong. It helped me start to see myself closer to how others see me and closer to how I actually look."

If you struggle with seeing goodness in your body and soul, how could others help you uncover the truth, and speak kindness to you? In what ways could you cultivate tenderness towards yourself with the help of those around you?

" Author Jen Hatmaker asks, "What would have to happen for us to honor our bodies? What is the opposite approach from this toxic cycle of comparison, impossible standards, shame, and self-harm? What might it look like if a

generation of women started celebrating their
outsides on their insides?"[9]

What might it look like indeed...

DANCING INTO EMBODIMENT

Have you ever read a book placed in another realm or world
and wished, "Oh, I wish I could spend even a day there!"?
How would you feel if you found out you could be a
character in your favorite fictional world (or one similar to
it) for a weekend? Ecstatic? Thrilled? Elated? Me too,
which is why when I first heard about the College of
Wizardry (CoW) online from a friend who posted it, I said
sign me up. Being able to go to wizard college in Poland and
be a student at a place like Hogwarts for a weekend!?[10] Yes
Please![11] The CoW is a Live Action Role Play (LARP) for
adults who pretend to be wizarding college students for a
weekend.

After getting my character of Nyxie, a half fairy-half
nature witch, I knew I wanted to create a beautiful dancing
moment for all the players. For me, the times I feel most
aligned are when I'm in a sacred space that involves
dancing, so after seeing the druid scene in *Outlander*, where
women danced through the night with lanterns, I knew
someday I wanted to dance in the woods. At CoW, I told
everyone around me that we would dance in a clearing by
the castle at midnight; I wanted a moment of wonderment
and joy in the woods.

I planned that we would dance, and then a fairy queen
would come out and offer each of us blessings. We turned on
our lanterns, and fifteen of us danced and twirled in the
woods. Our skirts and jackets glimmering against the
lantern lights as we moved. Our fairy queen walked out
slowly after we danced, offering us a blessing as a group,
and then went around the circle whispering a blessing to

each dancer. She told us magic was within our bones and how dancing with joy creates sacred space. She reminded us that dancing and gathering could bring a community together. We were all crying, and as she left, we stood around the circle taking in the new moon sky sprinkled with bright stars, holding hands and feeling gratitude. As we gathered our things, I realized I had to do this again.

Even though we took part during a LARP as characters, it struck a genuine chord within each of us. I realized the sense of sacred dancing and ritual wasn't just for a weekend whirlwind but could be brought home and woven into my life.

I also realized we all have the opportunity to be the fairy queen for those around us, to create and give blessings others can accept and weave together space for people to feel like their whole selves are welcome and wanted.

Embodiment for me is when you feel present and aligned in mind, body, and soul. It's tangible in the simple way we do things, and sometimes we can get deeply rooted in how it feels by going all-in on an evening or event. Have you had a moment where you can recall, "*Yes, this was good.*" Maybe it was a night with friends by the fire, and you can still recall the warmth, or a board game night with your family filled with laughter.

 For Tara, larping helps her explore aspects of herself and feel embodied as well. "I feel most embodied when de-rolling (a debriefing discussion about what the LARP meant for you after the LARP ends) after an intense LARP experience. It's about me; I internalize a lot of the empowerment I play; the people I de-role with also went through the same LARP, so there is no shame or judgment in the de-rolling and debriefing process. It's like the creative flow state I experience when writing fiction, but much easier to access. The more I learn, the more I can access that state of being."

McBride says embodiment "is the experience of being a self in and through the body, not just paying attention to what the body looks like."[12]

Use this knowledge, and look for those moments when you feel embodied and present. When do you feel like yourself? When you dance, when you're trying something new or solving a problem? Maybe it's when you bake or when you cuddle with your kids.

Use these as clues along your journey. Taking steps towards celebrating your body might not be receiving a tattoo but could take form in the words you use, the boundaries you set, and changing the perspective you have of yourself.

When you feel good, it impacts the way you talk, your perspective, and your energy. When you feel exhausted or depleted because you deny yourself joy and goodness, it affects your mental and physical health.

Our bodies deserve kindness, whether that's a walk, getting out in nature or a hot bath. We can disconnect and distance ourselves from our bodies because of what society has told us they 'should' be. Bodies that don't cooperate with plans can feel like living in a state of betrayal. Broken healthcare or doctors who don't listen can widen the gap even more between you and your body. Fear of our bodies has been the pervasive story of the century, so trust me when I say you are not alone if you've ever felt like you couldn't trust your body.

How have you punished yourself for not having a body yourself or others approved of? How did you distance yourself or ignore your body? Self-body punishment can look like excessively working out, eating disorders, wearing uncomfortable clothes, or even ignoring warning signs something may be wrong. You've been in a relationship with your body since before you were born. Just like any relationship, there are ups and downs.

What would reconnecting and cultivating trust with your body look like for you? Can you befriend your body or become an acquaintance by doing a weekly check-in? Maybe you can rebuild your relationship with your body by tuning in to how your body would like to move, dress, or what they are craving. It doesn't have to be a complete overhaul of how you talk or treat yourself, but what is 1% more of kindness or gentleness?

As women, we have complicated stories with our bodies, but we can start writing a new tale. We take out our frustration on our bodies when they are just trying to be bodies. Sometimes our bodies don't cooperate the way we want them to, and illness, injuries, and age all impact our perspective of our body's capabilities. We do not exist apart from our bodies in this life, so instead of being angry at our one body we have, is it possible to give our bodies and ourselves some grace?

 Erin Brown, an author, advisor, and artist, says, "It's not like you can make all your junk magically go away overnight. But you can name it. You can notice it immediately when it arises, and you can address it. Your old stories don't have to be your forever story. It's up to you... What would happen if you let love rule your life? What would change if you stopped asking, 'Am I beautiful enough' and started asking, 'Am I living a beautiful life?'"

If you were to allow your whole self (mind/body/soul) to partake in living a beautiful life here on out where you feel true, whole, and free, what would that look like for you? Can you imagine it?

FURTHER DISCOVERY

What does embodiment mean to you?

When have you felt fully present? Whether it was an activity or a moment. Where nothing else existed except for what you were doing?

If you were to adorn and treat yourself like a 'Library of Alexandria,' what would that look like for you?

Book Recommendations:
As Is by Erin Brown
Mothers, Daughters, and Body Image by Hillary McBride
The Body Keeps the Score by Bessel van der Kolk

Body is a Temple Red Tent

Five minutes before the Tent Begins:

Leader: Lovelies, please put your phones on silent or off, grab your water, snacks, journal, and token and join me in the circle.

Opening:

Leader: Before we begin, I would like to state that this is a safe space. In order to make it so, there needs to be agreement around keeping what is said in circle, in the circle. I'm asking you all to agree to only speak of your own experiences, and only give advice when asked. We will be talking about deeply personal things in the Red Tent. A gentle reminder that we can disagree and still accept each other. Can I have a show of hands for everyone willing to keep this space confidential, for themselves and everyone here tonight?

Shakeout and Grounded Breathing:

Leader: Let us take a minute to stand up, shake out any worries, or frustration from your day. Twist your body, shake your booty, kick your legs, jump up and down. Audibly make sounds while relaxing your jaw. Stretch, or move in a way that feels supportive.

Please have a seat in this circle, and let's do some ground breathing. You can close your eyes, start to relax your shoulders. You can roll your neck from side to side, rest your hands on your stomach, knees, or the ground, whatever is most comfortable for you. Start breathing in from your belly. Take a deep breath. As you exhale, release anything that came before tonight that is on your mind.

Breathe in again, releasing anything to come in the future. Keep breathing, focusing on the sounds around you,

the breath of other women, and your heartbeat. As you release your breath, feel your body settling into this space. In this moment, here with us. You are safe. You are loved. We are glad you are here with us.

Call in:

Leader: We are gathered in our Red Tent, as women, as daughters, as mothers, as workers and dreamers. We come here to speak our heart's desires, our mind's thoughts, and share the song of our souls. We see with our eyes, hear with our ears, and will hum along in our hearts. May this space be open, sacred, and grounded for us here tonight. Let us hold hands as we travel deeper together, learning to better love ourselves, each other, and the world.

Gender Neutral Option:

We are gathered in our Red Tent Tent as humans, as explorers, as workers and dreamers. We come here to speak our heart's desires, our mind's thoughts, and share the song of our souls. We see with our eyes, hear with our ears, and will hum along in our hearts. May this space be open, sacred, and grounded for us here tonight. Let us hold hands as we travel deeper together, learning to better love ourselves, each other, and the world.

Song:

Leader: Close your eyes and think of what you want from this night and this week. It might be friendship, laughter, wisdom. We'll pass the bowl around one person at a time, and you'll say your blessing request, we'll sing the song with your word inside of it, and then after we sing over you, pass the bowl to the next woman. She'll share her

blessing word, and we'll sing a blessing over her until we reach the end of the circle.

Call down a blessing x3, Call down, ____before you, ____behind you, ____Within you, and around you*
  Repeat for each person in the group, end with three call downs.

15: 1st Circle:
  Leader: When speaking, please use the talking light, and when you finish, please say "I have spoken," so we know you have completed your thought. You can react with hand snaps, hand on your heart, and facial expressions. Please speak only of your own story, and don't give any advice unless asked.
  For our first circle, please share your name, pronouns, our intention for tonight, and what embodiment means to you?

25: Quote and Response *Depending on the size of the group, you can ask for a one word reaction, or a one minute response.*
  Leader: I'll share the poem below, and then we'll go around the circle, and you can share in a few words what resonated or didn't resonate with you.

My bones say,
    I need more magic.
    More sacred.
    More real
    More tangible rest.

My bones ache for strength for words,
    And to stretch tall,
    My bones scream for believing they won't break.
    My bones are ready and await.

My belly says, I'm full of snacks,
    But hungry for truth.
    For more.

To listen to my craving.
    To stop snacking and start feeding.

My heart says peace.
    You are okay.
    You are okay.
    You are okay.
    -Aj Smit

35: Activity 1: Body Scan Meditation
Located at the end of this script

50: Journal
Leader: Draw a blank figure on the paper. Starting at your feet and working your way up, draw in what you

experienced in your meditation. What are you grateful for, what did you notice? What colors show up for you?

1: 2nd Circle
    Leader: Share what came up for you in your meditation

1:15: Soul Care Time:
    Leader: Now is our soul care time. This is 20 minutes to stretch, nap, chat, get food, go to the restroom. We do ask that you don't use this time to be on your phone. I'll give us a five-minute heads up to Tent, and a one minute come to circle heads up.

1:35: Activity Two: Body Letter
    Leader: For this activity write a letter from your body to yourself. What would your body like you to know? What is she (your body) trying to tell you? I'll put on some music and give us a few minutes to write our letters.

1:40: Womanhood story:
    Leader: Womanhood stories are a core part of Red Tent, sharing our stories is a brave act. Sometimes they are joy filled, sad, frustrating, or a mix of all of it. The story may include periods, sex, birth, or any part of the woman and human experience. ___ has offered to share her story tonight. ____ the floor is yours.
    See the appendix of the book for reaching out to your women to see who would like to share before the tent day.

After her story:
    Leader: Thank you ___ for sharing your story. Is there

anything you need from us? Hug, encouragement, a listening ear during break?

If they say yes, do what you can to fulfill that need if possible.

1:50: Closer *Grab your red thread (yarn) and make sure scissors are within reach.*

Leader: Red thread represents our connection to the women around us and those who have come before us. You will take your red yarn and wrap it around your wrist. You can wrap as many times as you want, as you recite your matriarchal spiritual lineage. Your lineage are the women and people who have influenced and loved you.

They don't have to be biologically related, you can claim or not claim anyone you would like. You can say your name, mother of (any children), daughter of x, daughter of y, daughter of daughters, daughter of whatever resonates (Eve, Spirit, the moon, etc). You can also say descendent instead, or daughter of those who _____ instead of names.

When you have finished wrapping, pass the thread to the next person until it has gone all the way around the circle.

You can start the process and do your lineage and wrap and then pass it to the person on your right.

After the Red Thread has come back to you.

Leader: As we are connected, let us sing our song, we'll sing it three times, it goes flow, ebb, weavers, thread, weavers, thread, spiders, web. Sing it with me:

Song: We are the flow we are the ebb,
We are the weavers we are the thread,
We are the weavers we are the thread,
we are the spiders we are the web.
x3

. . .

Leader, pick up the scissors, and cut your thread, and as you explain the below, you can have the person to the left tie your thread.

Leader: When cutting the thread to tie bracelets, share your favorite moment and a takeaway. Have the lady to your left tie your yarn, twice in a square knot, and one slip knot, and this way, your thread will not come undone. After you have spoken, pass the scissors to the right, and the next person can go.

After the scissors make their way back to you, and everyone has tied their thread, you can hold hands if you'd like.

Invitation to curiosity

Leader: How can you notice this month how your body is enjoying moments? How can you be kinder to the body you are currently in? Thank you for being a part of tonight's Red Tent. You are all a treasure, and I'm glad you are here. Our Red Tent is now closed.

Body Scan Meditation

This is a meditation to recall how your body remembers some of your favorite memories. Tune in to how you would be most comfortable and happy in this moment. Whether it's curled up with a blanket, leaning back in your chair, or tucked into a comfy couch.

Imagine you're lying underneath the warm summer sun with a breeze in the afternoon. Your body is warm and relaxed. Let your breath rise to your face like the tide, your exhale leaving calm, sleepy muscles.

Let yourself be in this space, sinking deeper and letting your muscles relax, where nobody needs anything from you in this moment.

(pause)

Bring your awareness to your toes. What was the time that they helped you reach for something where you got on your tiptoes? To stretch? Maybe it was to reach your favorite cereal in the grocery aisle, or to put a kayak on top of a car.

(pause)

What things do your feet love to stand on? What do they love to dig into? What textures do they love? This might be a fluffy carpet, lush grass or the cool waters of a creek. Maybe it's the warm waves of the ocean. Bring to your memory what that feels like underneath your feet.

(pause)

Sense the strength of your legs. How strong they are, how they've held you up and helped you get back up time and time again. When was a time where you lifted someone's spirits? When you felt kind and loving.

(pause)

In your mind, ask yourself, What kind of things do your hips love to wear? How do they love to move? This might be a salsa twist or jamming to music in your kitchen while you cook or the way your hip shifts as you hold a child.

(pause)

Bring your thoughts to your stomach. What does your stomach love to eat? What feels delicious in your stomach? It might be your grandmother's lasagna recipe or the gelato you had when you traveled overseas. Remember the taste of it, and how your stomach fuels you.

(pause)

Raise your thoughts higher to your chest. When was the time where you met something face forward, head on. Where even if you were afraid you still stood your ground? How did that feel, knowing you weren't shrinking back?

(pause)

Tune into your heart. What does your heart have gratitude for? Your heart holds so many emotions. What would it like to tell you right now about your body and who you are?

(pause)

What do your arms enjoy holding? Who do they love wrapping in hugs? Can you recall the best hug you've ever gotten in your life? Who was it with? How did it make you feel?

(pause)

Our hands create so much. Imagine every type of art you've ever touched covering your hands, from paints to pottery, crayons and markers and pens and pencils. See your hands covered in the colors of creativity. What is your favorite thing you've ever made with your hands? It might be a piece of art or a poem or a coloring page you did with a young one. How did you feel when you made that piece? Let that joy and pride radiate up your arms into your heart center.

(pause)

Feel into the tips of your fingers. What is the softest thing you've ever touched in your life? Soft as the lightest feather? Maybe it's the way the wind feels when you go on a walk, or the perfect blanket. Or a newborn's tiny cheeks. Let your fingers remember that touch.

(pause)

Feel your back and the surety inside of it. What was the time when you stood in your truth and you stood tall? When was the last time you felt tall and sure and strong? Where you stood in your knowing? Let it radiate in your back and through your body.

(pause)

Can you sense your lips? What was the last thing that made you smile or laugh so big that it almost hurt? Can you pull it to mind? What did that feel like? What did they say? Let those emotions wash over you.

(pause)

What is your favorite smell? Maybe it's parchment and fresh grass or maybe it's brownies just out of the oven or the smell of a rainstorm coming. When was the last time you smelled this? What memories are associated with the smell?

(pause)

And your eyes, all the things they have seen, good and bad, beautiful and heart-wrenching. What is one of the most beautiful things you've ever seen in your life? It might be a sunset or a memory of a loved one. Bring it to mind now, recalling what it was like to be in that moment. How lucky you were to be in that moment to be able to witness that.

(pause)

What sound when you hear it makes you smile and close your eyes in cozy glee? It may be the sound of a lover whispering to you, or the sound of a thunderstorm when you're wrapped in bed, raindrops pitter-pattering on the windows outside. Let that sound you love wash over you.

(pause)

Tune in to your whole body, brimming over with memories and gratitude and joy. All of these rememberings remind you that you are made with purpose, created to experience each one of these sensations and to create so many more.

(pause)

Take a minute to soak in the gratitude, letting it course through your bones and your veins.

When you're ready, you can stretch, yawn, wiggle, and bring yourself back to the circle.

CYCLES

Grab some chocolate—we're going to need it.

First off, you need to know my uterus tried to kill me. Maybe not with as much enthusiasm as other uteruses have attempted to take out other people, but enough for me to get the hint. Between the pill that caused a blood clot and the IUD which sent me to the hospital twice —once in China because I thought my uterus was exploding (it wasn't) and once in America, I've had my share of womb centered battle. I was sent home both times and told I shouldn't make such a big deal out of it. This isn't even to mention the low-hormone Depo shot, which made me feel like a shell of myself.

I was so exasperated with my uterus I was going to take it all out.

My goal: get the tubes tied or get everything removed—I honestly didn't care. "Take the lot. It's a warehouse sale!"

So there I was legs in stirrups, asking my doctor about getting a hysterectomy at 27. While laughing at me, he disregarded my fears about birth control, even after the pill gave me a blood clot, and promised me this birth control would be better.

But would it be?[1] I left with a pamphlet about the Progesterone Shot, hysterectomies, and counseling. Because, of course, any woman who has questions about her uterus must need counseling. God forbid we be curious or want to make informed decisions.

Silenced by my doctor, I felt exasperated with the various forms of birth control wreaking havoc on my body and nervous I'd have to rely on condoms, hope, and the rhythm method not to get pregnant. Feeling scared and intimidated by my womb is when Red Tents entered my life, nestled into two paragraphs of a book called *Moon Time* by Lucy Pearce. I had picked up the book in hopes of understanding my cycle to figure out the aforementioned rhythm method.

I was at war with my own body. All I wanted was a clockwork period. Not that I knew what that meant, as I was on some form of birth control since I was seventeen, even though I wasn't having sex. I got on the pill because I thought that's what one did as a woman. I didn't realize my hormones created phases I was moving through each month. Instead, I let my emotions go through the wash cycle and drive my life.

You may have felt like you have been in a similar place or be in one now where you feel lonely, even if you know people. It can be hard to share your simmering fears and questions about your cycle and body out loud. Everyone has opinions on the 'right way to be': the perfect birth control, free bleeding, natural tampons, and even planned moon-bleeding.

I had never understood why your cycle was important. Yes, your ovaries take turns releasing an egg each month, yes, your uterus is doing an 'ex-lover spat cleanout' of your uterine wall, and yes, it can hurt like hell. However, the way Lucy wrote about bleeding and the impact of our hormones, regardless of your menstrual cycle, put it into a new light for me.

Within the four stages of your cycle, your hormones fluctuate. Your body craves different things, and we long for action or times of solace. A light switched on my brain as to why I felt crazy sometimes and not others.

I say this not because you need to know my entire story but because my story is similar to many others who use birth control to make our hormonal cycles easier or fix one thing or another. Sometimes they do, sometimes they don't. Sometimes birth control makes a bad situation even worse.

I wish someone had told me these things before I almost got a hysterectomy. I spent so many years yelling at my uterus, not pausing to ask any questions, *but she was only trying to send me messages!*

Every woman is different, and I highly encourage you to talk to a doctor who listens to you. What works for your sister, or your neighbor, could make you feel at odds with yourself. Hormones can be your best friend or your worst enemy. Perhaps a hysterectomy or bi-lateral salpingectomy (removal of your tubes) is the right choice for you. Maybe you had to have your ovaries removed, and you wished you didn't. Perhaps your PCOS or endometriosis forced your hand in making decisions. Knowledge and information are what lessens the overwhelm and the layers of shame. That's why talking about this is so important.

When we know our options, we can make smarter choices, and we can help those around us see more perspectives. I hope this chapter starts a journey to mend and create a better relationship with your cycle.

Growing up, talking about your cycle is like talking about Bigfoot: full of urban legends, interesting factoids, and close calls.

You hear horror stories of the cave and are told not to talk about 'down there.' In middle school, shushed whispers are shared on how you'll bleed for life and not die. This non-death bleeding sounds like a superpower, but it's also a time where you also curl up on a bed with a warm sock filled with rice. You find yourself watching sappy Hallmark movies and crying while eating brownies, wondering where your self-control went, which was exceptionally strong two weeks ago. We receive warnings about the blood but not about the actual hormones.

Sound familiar? *I see you smiling.*

We call it shark week, Aunt Flo, that time of the month, Mr. P, and the clinical sounding menstrual cycle, *which all of us can say, but can any of us spell?*

We learn to think of the women around us as our competition, so bring out the claws. Yet our periods are the mark of womanhood! Besides the hippie lady who came to your 4th-grade class to talk about pads and tampons, you don't get much else besides conflicting experiences. Perhaps a special dinner or hushed-up tampon shopping at the supermarket. Congratulations! You're a woman. Isn't that a grand celebration of a once-in-a-lifetime milestone?

Welcome to the war in your pelvic bowl.

What if it didn't have to be like that? What if there was a different way? Let's talk about all the things you wish people told you about cycling and how to utilize your monthly shifting hormones for the better, instead of believing the 'woman's curse' will always be hell.

All of your stories have a safe place here.

A note on the proper way to cycle:

Within the realm of women's wellness, people can put an amplifier on bleeding with the moon as extra magical. As cool as this is, you are enchanting and fabulous regardless of whether you bleed or not—and it doesn't matter what phase the moon is in if you do. Not all women bleed, and not all those who identify as women bleed.

Each body is unique, yet each has phases it flows

through, making your life more manageable when you acknowledge them. I've had many conversations with women asking if they were welcome in Tent because they had hysterectomies, were transwomen, on birth control, or were going through menopause. We have so much to learn from one another. The competitive stories run deep on how we shouldn't trust one another; let's not create more layers of distance between one another by one-upping or gatekeeping one another by using our periods and cycles.

Not bleeding makes you no less of a woman.

When people talk about their cycle, they are usually referencing the time when they bleed, thinking, "Blood comes and goes, and that is all there is to it."

There is so much more to your cycle.

There are four stages of your cycle: Waxing Moon, Full Moon, Waning Moon, and New Moon. We are using these labels in this book because your hormones vary whether you are on birth control, menopausal, or don't bleed. If you aren't bleeding, use your emotions or energy levels as benchmarks to discover how your body moves through each month. Each phase of our cycle plays out more extensively throughout the four stages of our life as well.

I'll break down each cycle phase below and include in-depth ways to move through your life with your hormonal cycle, along with a table to reference after. I'll also incorporate the corresponding archetypes to each phase and your energy levels. Archetypes are a way of using characterization to see yourself in a new light. We shift throughout the month, and by having the archetypes, we can identify how that may come across to others in a more personal way. Each phase has two options for you to use the Archetype that resonates with you the most. I encourage you to read *Moon Time* by Lucy Pearce for a more in-depth exploration of cycle archetypes.

WAXING MOON

In this phase, all the fresh, bright energy you have is ready to explode! Estrogen is starting to rise, and it is the perfect time to make plans. For some women, your new womb lining is growing. Your pituitary gland releases follicle-stimulating hormones (FSH) to help an egg prepare to release. It's Go Time! The archetypes here are Maiden and Virgin. One definition of Virgin is "a woman who belongs to herself." Think of this as a beautiful time to start fresh on goals and projects. Be careful not to overpack the end of your cycle, thinking you'll have the same energy then as you have now; you'll regret it.[2]

> In her book *Woman Code*, Alisa Vitti writes, "Fresh, vibrant, light foods make you feel more energized during this phase when all hormone levels are at their lowest...think: pressed salads, (kimchi and sauerkraut), plenty of veggies, lean proteins, sprouted beans and seeds, and dense energy-sustaining grains."[3]

This first stage of 5-8 days is a great time to reach out, love people, and be spontaneous. Others may lack the energy you have, so be gracious and generous. If people ask you for a big decision, tell them you need a month to think about it. Although you may feel you can take it on now, you'll want to think about it when you have quiet time and higher intuition.

You'll be able to commit or turn down an opportunity during your next Waxing Moon stage, knowing you didn't hop on it just because you could but because it's something you want to do. Often as women, if we feel we have enough energy, we will say yes. We may then feel guilty or coerced into said activity, which can cultivate resentment.

Not that any of us have ever said yes in those circumstances.[4]

FULL MOON:

During the Full Moon stage of your cycle, you may feel nurturing, sexy, or even on top of the world. Your Estrogen is at its peak, creating a high fertility window, and releases an egg. *Be careful if you don't want to get pregnant.*

To understand your high fertility window, you can check your cervical fluid, which at this time is a white discharge with a stretchy, almost egg white feel. You can also use ovulation strips. An egg's life is about 24 hours. Many women believe the egg releases on day 14, but everybody is different. Your egg could release on day ten or day seventeen. Your cycle length can vary depending on sleep, stress, food, alcohol, medication, and the like. Checking your cervical fluid will help you know whether you ovulate on day ten or day seventeen.

The Full Moon stage is also known as your Mother or Creatrix stage. In this 3-5 day window of your cycle, you can feel loving and want to have everyone over for dinner or write notes to your family on handmade paper. Let your creativity flow and see what is 'created,' whether it's a baby or a new idea. Cramps can occur as your ovaries take turns releasing an egg each cycle. You may feel untouchable or crave attention. Be aware, if you are crossed, nurturing Mommy Dearest can turn into a raging Momma Bear, so be sure to tend yourself in this and all stages, so you don't burn out from over-promising and feeling over-extended.

If you feel led to reach out or make amends, now is the perfect time to do it because you have the extra capacity to hold space for hard conversations. **Don't put it off**. It is alluring to front-load during this time, but be careful not to do too much, as you are about to switch over into your Waning Moon stage, where your energy can start to become more frantic.

A word of wisdom from Alexandra and Sjanie, the founders of Red School, which empowers women to harness their cyclical nature to the fullest potential, "Particularly watch out for superwoman around ovulation. She reckons you can do it all regardless and is blissfully unaware of what lies ahead."[5]

WANING MOON:

The 5-8 days of Waning Moon stage brings loud pronouncements of, "I want the truth and nothing but the truth!" In this cyclical shift of hormones, you may have fierce mood swings. You feel feisty, ready for a nap or a fight, all while frantically searching for an emergency chocolate bar, and that's just the first thirty minutes of your day before breakfast.

Progesterone rises like the tide, and Estrogen goes down like the *Titanic*,[6] paving the way for the archetypes of The Enchantress and Wild Woman. This is my favorite stage because I can put this energy towards my creative endeavors from my Full Moon stage.

You may, like me, have more energy at this stage, but if you do not begin to slow down, you will regret it soon. Your body is transitioning to prepare to bleed, so use the energy well—don't let it use you. Were you thinking of leaving your energy unregulated? In this 24/7, 365 world we live in, if you keep going at the pace you were earlier in the cycle, you will be crying into a box of brownies at three a.m. with a glass (or bottle) of wine, wondering why this happens every few months because YOU'VE BEEN SO GOOD AND ON TOP OF IT LATELY.

Seem familiar?

Not at all?

I thought so.
Words of wisdom for this phase, lovely:
Watch.
Your.
Words.

When you share truth or opinions during the Waning Moon stage, they can become bitter, bitey, and unnecessary if not well minded. It's important to ask yourself if the words you are saying are true, kind, or necessary. Some things need to be given to God, the journal or screamed into a fluffy pillow. Thoughts and impulses rising to the surface are your mind's way of letting you know about crossed boundaries or unresolved issues. They're critical red flags but should be addressed with care in this stage.

In *Wild Power,* they share, 'You're being shown exactly what needs your attention, what needs to change, and what isn't working. You get feedback on your overall health and stress levels, how well you're caring for yourself, your relationships, creative projects, spiritual life, and more. Your task is to stay present and receive the feedback with as much self-kindness as you can muster."'[7]

Don't shove your emotions into a knapsack the size of a makeup bag; grab your journal, and write them down. Freewriting is a great way to get ahead of resentment, burnout, and anger before they take over your life. When your gut tells you something is wrong, trust it. Trust yourself enough to tune in and make shifts when you think something is off.

Your creative juices may be flowing during this time! Get out your markers, and make something. Go ahead and put your energy towards something productive. Heavy workouts with weights help me channel my energy and frustration when they float to the surface during this time. A good exercise can help direct your frenetic energy while also making you feel accomplished.

Even small things count during this time, as you are

about to start bleeding. Being aware you are in this stage can give you grace when your emotions rise to remember that your feelings don't control you. Being mindful can help you take a step back and realize you aren't angry at your partner for X, or you are frustrated with yourself for forgetting a deadline and feeling dumb. The people around us want to be supportive. Ask for what you need, and don't guilt yourself for the asking; it helps others know what would help you the most.

NEW MOON

Your energy starts dropping during your New Moon stage. If you are bleeding, you see the blood, and your brain clicks into place. Oh yeah! My period—that's why I was off last week. Your Estrogen is low, and your uterine wall is shedding. All your body craves is a soft blanket, some sangria, and a good movie or book. Some may joke that your uterus is taking a knife to redecorate her walls. While this is theoretically true, it's essential to realize that this is your time to breathe and rest. She's doing a lot of work; can you imagine if she wasn't self-cleaning? (Yeah, you're welcome.)

Give yourself grace and salty chocolate. Take naps, and journal during these 3-7 days. Your New Moon time is also a time of deep connection, a great time to vision and dream for the month ahead. Ask yourself, "In my life right now, what do I like, what do I not like?" and "What truth am I avoiding right now?" These can be big questions—but you aren't acting on them yet—you are just brushing off the busyness of the month to do an accurate check-in with yourself.

The archetypes in this phase are The Sage and The Wise Woman because your intuition is through the roof. Your dreams may be more vivid, so don't panic if they are different than usual. I sleep with a journal next to my bed if anything pops up in my dreams I want to remember.

As women, we often say yes without knowing how many activities we are genuinely balancing and can overcommit ourselves for others' approval. If you have to make a big decision, bleed on it (or Moon Mull if you don't bleed). Lisa Lister wrote about "bleeding on it," and I thought it was such a weird but witty phrase because it reminds you that the awareness you get during this time is more evident. It's been a game-changer for my life, so I pass it off to you now.[8]

Feed your body well during this time. As much as you crave junk food, eat some vegetables and protein, and drink approximately a boatful of water. Half your body weight in ounces is a general rule of thumb.[9]

Exercise helps cramps and sluggishness —so do hot baths and showers, vitamin B, and sleep. If you rest now and use the time to reset, you'll have a fresh vision and be ready to go when you cycle back into your Waxing Moon stage. If you do not rest, you will go into your next phase frantic and exhausted. Overwhelm is often people's default —because we don't know any different. We keep going at full speed, and then our bodies break down every few months. *Oh, look at that lovely self-perpetuating cycle.*

Our bodies get us to rest, one way or another.

You cycle whether you choose to or not; it's your choice to work with it or rage against it.[10]

"Leah, a grandmother of two shares, "One of the things I realized is that just because at this stage in my life, and due to not having the flow, I still cycle, I still go through all these stages, they're still there. And they will always be there. I don't think I recognize them sometimes. As I learned the phases, I started to have favorite ones, like the Wild Woman and Crone helped me not feel so disconnected from myself. In this part of my life, I feel like I'm more definitely the Crone. I didn't think I would relate to Wild Woman, but the more I learned about her, I do because to me, it represents more of that natural instinct."

Here is a simple chart to reference on your own. You can also make a chart with your lived experience of your cycle.

Moon Phase: Waxing Moon
Menstrual Phase: Pre-Ovulation
Archetypes: Virgin and Maiden
Hormones: Estrogen rises, as Progesterone lowers.
Energy: Your energy rises along with your excitement for your ideas.
Tip to Remember: Engage your dreams with action.

Moon Phase: Full Moon
Menstrual Phase: Ovulation
Archetypes: Mother and Creatrix
Hormones: Estrogen is at its height.
Energy: High, outward nourishing energy is in abundance.
Tip to Remember: Cultivate and nurture growth in yourself and those around you.

Moon Phase: Waning Moon
Menstrual Phase: Pre-Menstrual

Archetypes: Enchantress and Wild Woman
Hormones: Your Progesterone rises, as Estrogen recedes.
Energy: Energy levels can fluctuate, and feel frenetic.
Tip to Remember: Harness and use your fluctuating energy. Use it well, or you may feel like a live wire.

Moon Phase: New Moon
Menstrual Phase: Menstruation
Archetypes: Sage and Wise Woman
Hormones: Progesterone is high, and your Estrogen is at its lowest.
Energy: You may feel low, inward directed energy.
Tip to Remember: Use this time for rest and visioning.

CYCLE CHARTING

Anytime I talk about cycle charting, people feel overwhelmed and aren't even sure where to start. There are apps you can use, and some are more user-friendly than others.[11] Keeping track in a google calendar or paper calendar allows you to see trends. You can mark when your ovulation days are, and it's easily noticeable. I kept track with an app no longer in service and lost all of the information I had entered. If you keep track with an app, also keep track in your calendar with a little P or stickers, just in case. When you go to the doctor, this is valuable information when you wonder if you are late or have more pain than usual.

A simple way to chart is to mark your first day of bleeding on your calendar. I usually write a letter P and then a number 1 on that day in my month layout. I write out numbers 2-25 (about my cycle length) on the following days. If I started bleeding on the 3rd, it has P1 in the corner. The

4th has a 2 in the corner, the 5th, a 3, and so on. This method helps me know when to expect my future period and the energy forecast of my cycle.

For example, let's say I'm in my Full Moon stage and feeling kind and nurturing. I realize we haven't done a big family dinner night in a while with our neighbors. My first impulse is to schedule the next dinner night two weeks out, so people have time to plan. Looking at the calendar, however, I'll realize two weeks from now, it is day 30/day 3 of my next cycle (if I do indeed start bleeding on day 27).

I don't know about you, but all I want to do when I am in my New Moon stage is take a hot bath, nap, and devour all the salted chocolate I can find; I can pass on the people.

> Lisa Lister writes, "... being able to see on my calendar when the monthly emotional maelstrom will probably be at its worst has been an absolute revelation. Turns out being able to differentiate between menstrual mood swings and impending mental breakdown is really, really useful. Who knew?"[12]

Charting is a tool you can do to be aware of your body's rhythms and moods, so you can prepare and not be surprised each month.

Even when things land on your calendar while you are in your New Moon stage, knowing when it is around the corner allows you to schedule in grace space.[13] If I'm serving with kids at church while in New Moon? Then we will grab a rotisserie chicken and have a leisurely lunch, just Jer and me. Are you feeling feisty in the Waning Moon phase? Have a girls' night in instead of a girls' night out. Scheduling with your cycle in mind allows you to have wiggle room in the schedule and the forethought to say "No."

Phases may feel like a giant expanse of time between

New Moon stages, so you may wonder why chart? Your cycle is changing throughout the month, and knowing what your hormones are doing gives you ownership of your emotions and body.

For those who ovulate, many believe that their ovulation is in the smack middle of their periods, but frequently it can be at the ⅓ mark, or 6/10th mark, not falling precisely in the middle. If you are uncomfortable using the Creighton method of checking your cervical fluid. I suggest buying ovulation strips from Amazon in bulk, allowing you to notice when you are most fertile. Some women even ovulate twice in a cycle.[14] Regardless of whether you are trying to get pregnant, ovulation strips and energy level tracking give you knowledge of what is happening in your body. Knowledge is power, and when you know what your body is doing, you are more aware when something is off, allowing you to speak up and advocate for yourself.

For those with Endometriosis, PCOS, PMDD< or sporadic cycling, charting is even more important for you to have a fuller picture of how your body is cycling through your hormones. Charting can also help doctors understand and believe you more if you have documentation. I wish this was not a true statement, but I have found it to be an accurate assessment through the years of listening to stories and my own experience. May period trackers will also track symptoms, mood, sleep, and water intake, so you don't have to have multiple charts spread across different apps.

ITEMS YOU CAN USE WHEN BLEEDING

On the days you are bleeding, buying pads and tampons can be a to-do item that slips your mind until the horror of realization dawns on you as you reach under the cabinet that you, my dear, are out of menstrual products. Don't know what to use for your period? In the last few years, there has been a resurgence of period awareness and various products. Everyone is different with what they use and love, so there is no room for period product shaming in this house.

Pads

Pads are the modern-day version of the old-school bits of cloth shoved into pants. Now our pads have sticky backs and are preshaped! Pads are treated as a secret object, much like the triangle with the Illuminati. You could have an arch-enemy in high school, but ask for a pad, and you are suddenly together in a secret society no one else knows about as you sneak a pad from one purse to another with a coat draped over your arm to disguise the transfer. (Subtlety is not a bleeding teen's strong suit). In 1888 Kotex came out with its first pad, and for the next century, companies created suspenders or belts with a tiny hammock to hold your pad in place. [15]

Although it's fun to smell like a field of lavender, make sure to get unscented pads, as scented ones can disturb your PH balance. You can wear pads on a plane, on a train, in a house, or near a mouse. You can even wear them anywhere from one to six hours. Word of warning, though, any longer, and your inner thighs will start getting red like a sober Irishman in Florida summer and as angry as one too. No one needs razor burn and diaper rash put together, so change out your pads when you are sweating and bleeding heavily to spare yourself the extra angst.

Reusable pads have been around since women started bleeding, but now they come with fancy things like snaps and pretty fabric! They last for years before wearing out, allowing less waste to go to the landfill and less risk of running out if you have plenty at the house. You MUST wash these with cold water before going into your washing machine, [16] which means if you faint at the sight of blood….these might not be the items for you. Many companies are making reusable pads utilizing various fabrics, including bamboo, and as much as I'm a fan of sparkles, I'd say keep the sequins and shiny fabrics for your capes, not your pads. Many companies who create these products also donate pads to those in need, creating a ripple effect of menstrual equality, of which I'm a massive fan.

Period Underwear

Period underwear and menstrual cups were GAME CHANGERS for me. Period underwear is similar to reusable pads, except the 'pad' part is woven into the underwear. Thinx makes silky pairs, letting you feel beautiful while absorbing up to three tampons worth of blood. Padkix makes you feel like a Viking warrior as they have reusable pads and underwear that will last you overnight by themselves. You can even wear period underwear for a full day, depending on your flow. Some use period underwear in addition to tampons or cups.

Tampons

Tampons are the garbage disposals of the period product world. They will absorb blood, water, moisture, happiness — they'll soak it all up. They are indiscriminate in doing their job. They also force you into doing blood divination. Do you know how heavy your bleeding will be five hours from now?

No? Better get it right!

If you grab the wrong tampon and grab a super on a light day, you'll regret that later when it comes time to pull out your tampon, and you feel like the Sahara has relocated to your nether regions. Use a light tampon on a heavy day, and you wonder why you dared underestimate yourself. It's risky business, either way you play your cards, and so most people wear a pad or liner with their tampon to hedge their bets.

Tampons can cause Toxic Shock Syndrome if left in too long.[17] Try not to leave your tampon in for longer than six hours. Tampons are like a Set-It-And-Forget-It kitchen cooker, but there's no timer, and it's easier to forget because you won't smell anything burning. Tampons are fantastic for going swimming when you can't wear a pad. However, remember tampons soak up everything, which means when swimming, your tampon will absorb both your blood and the water you were in, whether lake, ocean, or a chlorinated pool: so take out your tampon immediately afterward.

Finally, avoid scented tampons.[18] You want minimal chemicals inside your vagina walls, as they absorb quickly into your bloodstream. Your cervix is PH balanced and sensitive to changes, so any new bacteria or chemicals can throw everything off-kilter and make for an annoying vaginal yeast infection — which is totally as fun as it sounds. *Not.*

PS. Cardboard tampons can go to hell. Avoid them at all costs.

Menstrual Cup

A menstrual cup is an excellent option for those who bleed heavily but don't like the feel of cotton tampons. Besides being the awkward mental picture of shot glasses for vampires, menstrual cups are also great for those who are morbidly curious about how much blood loss they have each day. Many cups are lined with measurements so you can keep track: no calorie counting here, just ounce checking.

Whereas tampons have strings you can pull, cups need a bit more finesse. If you've ever wanted to work on a bomb squad, this is your time to shine each month. The reason being, if you slip and drop your cup... it's a bit of a mess. With a bit of practice inserting, cups should feel like nothing is there. Many companies have a variety of sizes. Some even promote the possibility of lessening cramps.

When in public, you can empty your cup into the toilet and insert it right back in without washing it, although washing your cup once a day is preferred. At the end of your cycle or about every five days, clean your cup with sex toy cleaner or boil your cup in hot water for ten minutes.[19]

Now that periods are becoming less taboo, you can find menstrual cups at affordable prices online and in stores.

Something to keep in mind is that all bodies have opinions. They just do. Sometimes it lines up with ours, and sometimes it doesn't. If a menstrual cup doesn't feel good, it doesn't feel good—no matter how people tell you it should feel. I was hardcore team cups until I had my tubes removed via surgery, and now if I try using a cup, she (my uterus) throws a total hissy fit—complete with body aches and cramps that make me want to just curl up with my fluffy blanket and never move again.

Our bodies and hormones change as we grow older. Maybe you used to love pads, and now you are living an only tampon life. It's okay to shift and go with what feels good to your body. Just like with birth control, if it's not a good fit, it's not a good fit, and you'll know with every fiber of your being. Everyone else has opinions on what your body and vagina should like, so let your body have her own opinion as well, *and then listen to her when she speaks*. You'll be on much better terms with your body if you pay attention, I promise.

All in all, our cycles impact our lives whether we acknowledge them or not. By bringing mindfulness to our hormonal cycle, we allow ourselves to get 'ahead of the wave' as it were and not feel so surprised when our New Moon phase begins. Each person's cycle is different, and each product has its place and time it's needed. If you are experiencing more pain than average, please talk to your OB/GYN.

QUESTIONS FOR DISCOVERY

What have you called your cycle through time?

Is there a stage you like more than the others or relate to more?

Are there any stages of your cycle that you don't like?

Journal out your relationship with your cycle. Does anything pop out at you?

BOOK RECOMMENDATIONS

Moon Time by Lucy Pearce
The Pill: Is it for you by Alexandra Pope and Jane Bennett
Wild Power: By Alexandra Pope and Sjanie Hugo Wurlitzer
I want to punch you in the face, but I love Jesus by Sherri Lynn

Cycles Red Tent

Five minutes before the Tent Begins:
Leader: Lovelies, please put your phones on silent or off, grab your water, snacks, journal, and token and join me in the circle.

Opening:
Leader: Before we begin, I would like to state that this is a safe space. In order to make it so, there needs to be agreement around keeping what is said in circle, in the circle. I'm asking you all to agree to only speak of your own experiences, and only give advice when asked. We will be talking about deeply personal things in the Red Tent. A gentle reminder that we can disagree and still accept each other. Can I have a show of hands for everyone willing to keep this space confidential, for themselves and everyone here tonight?

Shakeout and Grounded Breathing:
Leader: Let us take a minute to stand up, shake out any worries, or frustration from your day. Twist your body, shake your booty, kick your legs, jump up and down. Audibly make sounds while relaxing your jaw. Stretch, or move in a way that feels supportive.

Please have a seat in this circle, and let's do some ground breathing. You can close your eyes, start to relax your shoulders. You can roll your neck from side to side, rest your hands on your stomach, knees, or the ground, whatever is most comfortable for you. Start breathing in from your belly. Take a deep breath. As you exhale, release anything that came before tonight that is on your mind.

Breathe in again, releasing anything to come in the future. Keep breathing, focusing on the sounds around you,

the breath of other women, and your heartbeat. As you release your breath, feel your body settling into this space. In this moment, here with us. You are safe. You are loved. We are glad you are here with us.

Call in:

Leader: We are gathered in our Red Tent, as women, as daughters, as mothers, as workers and dreamers. We come here to speak our heart's desires, our mind's thoughts, and share the song of our souls. We see with our eyes, hear with our ears, and will hum along in our hearts. May this space be open, sacred, and grounded for us here tonight. Let us hold hands as we travel deeper together, learning to better love ourselves, each other, and the world.

Gender Neutral Option:

We are gathered in our Red Tent Tent as humans, as explorers, as workers and dreamers. We come here to speak our heart's desires, our mind's thoughts, and share the song of our souls. We see with our eyes, hear with our ears, and will hum along in our hearts. May this space be open, sacred, and grounded for us here tonight. Let us hold hands as we travel deeper together, learning to better love ourselves, each other, and the world.

Song:

Leader: Close your eyes and think of what you want from this night and this week. It might be friendship, laughter, wisdom. We'll pass the bowl around one person at a time, and you'll say your blessing request, we'll sing the song with your word inside of it, and then after we sing over you, pass the bowl to the next woman. She'll share her

blessing word, and we'll sing a blessing over her until we reach the end of the circle.

Call down a blessing x3, Call down, ____before you, ____behind you, ____Within you, and around you*
Repeat for each person in the group, end with three call downs.

15: 1st Circle:

Leader: When speaking, please use the talking light, and when you finish, please say "I have spoken," so we know you have completed your thought. You can react with hand snaps, hand on your heart, and facial expressions. Please speak only of your own story, and don't give any advice unless asked.

For our first circle, what is your name, your pronouns, what is your intention for tonight? How would you describe your relationship with your cycle?

25: Activity 1: Cycle charting the four phases[20]

Leader: We're going to do an activity to explore the four stages of our hormonal and energetic cycle. Whether you bleed or not your hormones shift through the month so you can use this guide to explore your energetic phases as well. Please grab your journals and a pen. I want you to draw a line down the middle and across as well. You are making a giant t. In the first section top right corner, I want you to write Waxing Moon, in the bottom right, write Full Moon, bottom left, Waning Moon, and top left, New Moon. Under each of those write 'archetype:' As we go through each phase, I'll let you know what each archetype is, and tips on maneuvering through that specific phase, so leave some room for notes. In each section: draw a circle close to the center, which we will fill with the correlating moon phases.

In your Waxing Moon box, your archetypes are Maiden and Queen. Which references being a woman unto yourself with bold ideas. Your circle will have a waxing moon inside it, which means the white crescent is on the right side of the moon

This is your Pre-ovulation time. Your new womb lining is growing during this 7-10 day stage. Estrogen is starting to rise, so make plans with your infectious energy! This Waxing Moon time is a great time to reach out and take action on projects. Others may lack the stamina you have, so be gracious and generous. Don't overpack the end of your cycle, thinking you'll have the same enthusiasm then as you do now. If people ask you for a big decision, tell them you need a month to think about it. Although you may feel you can take it on now, you'll want to mull it during your New Moon, or menstruation phase, when your intuition is higher. You'll be able to commit or turn it down, knowing that you didn't just hop on it because you could, but because it's something you want to do. Women often say yes on default, which can cultivate resentment if you are running on fumes.

Pause for a minute to let people write.

In your Full Moon box, your archetypes are Mother and Creatrix, which references being able to cultivate life both in your womb and in your world. Your circle will have a full moon inside it, so you don't need to add anything.

Your Estrogen is at its peak, so this is the ovulation stage of the cycle. One of your ovaries releases an egg, which can cause cramping. A white discharge may note these three to four days with a stretchy egg white feel. You may feel loving, sexy, and ready to go. If you need to step out in action, reach out to make amends, or stand tall, now is a perfect time. Don't put it off. However, just because you have more energy doesn't mean you need to pick up more commitments and activities. Doing too much can make you snap and angry. Being overwhelmed can be a sign you are about to switch over into your pre-menstrual stage, as your energy becomes more frantic. Keep balance during this time as much as any others.

Pause for a minute to let people write.

In your Waning Moon box, your archetypes are Wild Woman and Enchantress. Which references the significant frenetic energy you feel, and the hormone swings. Your circle will have a waning moon inside it, so your white crescent is on the left side of the moon. This is also the Premenstrual stage and lasts 7-10 days.

In this stage Progesterone rises, as Estrogen goes down. In this cyclical shift of hormones, you can feel fierce, fraught, ready for a fight, and a nap—all before breakfast. Your body is transitioning to go slower. In this 24/7 365 world we live in; if you keep going at the pace you were earlier in the cycle, you will be crying into a box of brownies at 3 am with a bottle of wine wondering why you aren't good enough. Don't let your Inner Critic win, be gentle with yourself and try to give yourself good food and sleep.

Anger and impulses rise to the surface, bringing your attention to crossed boundaries, or situations that you need to address. Trust yourself enough to tune in when you feel something is off. Watch your words as they can become bitter, bitey, and unnecessary. Awareness of this stage can give you the grace you need to respond, and not just react. Channel your energy by working on something creative or moving your body.

Pause for a minute to let people write.

In your New Moon box, your archetypes are Sage and Crone. These archetypes reference the wisdom you seek, the insight you may have, and your energy level for doing things. Your circle will be a New Moon, so fill it all in.

This is also the menstrual stage where you will bleed, and this phase lasts 3-7 days. Your Estrogen is low, and soft blankets call your name. Remember to have patience for yourself and others. It is a time to go slow—vision and dream for the month ahead. As much as you crave junk food, eat vegetables, get protein, and drink all of the water. Exercise helps cramps, as do hot baths, vitamin B, and sleep. If you do not rest, you will go into your Waxing Moon stage, frantic and exhausted. People's first choice (not always consciously) is often to keep going at full speed until they crash. Our bodies will get us to rest, one way or another.

40: 2nd Circle

Leader: What comes up for you around these four phases and archetypes? Thoughts? Feelings?

55: Womanhood story:

Leader: Womanhood stories are a core part of Red Tent, sharing our stories is a brave act. Sometimes they are joy filled, sad, frustrating, or a mix of all of it. The story may include periods, sex, birth, or any part of the woman and human experience. ___ has offered to share her story tonight. ____ the floor is yours.

See the appendix of the book for reaching out to your women to see who would like to share before the tent day.

After her story:

Leader: Thank you ___ for sharing your story. Is there anything you need from us? Hug, encouragement, a listening ear during break?

If they say yes, do what you can to fulfill that need if possible.

1:05 Soul Care Time:

Leader: Now is our soul care time. This is 20 minutes to stretch, nap, chat, get food, go to the restroom. We do ask that you don't use this time to be on your phone. I'll give us a five-minute heads up to tent, and a one minute come to circle heads up.

1:25: Activity 2: Cycles Meditation
Meditation is located at the end of this Red Tent script.

1:45: Journal
Leader: Grab your journal and pen to write down your meditation experience. You can answer these questions, or free write your experience.

Describe your path. How were your stairs crafted? What did your Door to the Feminine look like? Were there words around it? How did you open your door? What was in your Feminine Soul Scape? Did you see fields, mountains, or a river? How big was your fire? How did it make you feel? What were you wearing?

Go through each archetype individually:

Maiden/ Creatrix/ Wild Woman/ Wise Woman

What does she look like? What is she doing? What do you want to call her? Does she remind you of anyone? How did she make you feel? Did she say anything to you?

How did you feel when you watched your archetypes?

Give the women another minute or two to write any other thoughts

2:00: 3rd Circle
Share what you'd like from your meditation.

• • •

2:15: Closer *Grab your red thread (yarn) and make sure scissors are within reach.*

Leader: Red thread represents our connection to the women around us and those who have come before us. You will take your red yarn and wrap it around your wrist. You can wrap as many times as you want, as you recite your matriarchal spiritual lineage. Your lineage are the women who have influenced and loved you.

They don't have to be biologically related, you can claim or not claim anyone you would like. You can say your name, mother of (any children), daughter of x, daughter of y, daughter of daughters, daughter of whatever resonates (Eve, Spirit, the moon, etc). You can also say descendent instead.

When you have finished wrapping, pass the thread to the next person until it has gone all the way around the circle.

You can start the process and do your lineage and wrap and then pass it to the person on your right.

After the Red Thread has come back to you:

Leader: As we are connected, let us sing our song, we'll sing it three times, it goes flow, ebb, weavers, thread, weavers, thread, spiders, web. Sing it with me:

Song: We are the flow we are the ebb,
We are the weavers we are the thread,
We are the weavers we are the thread,
we are the spiders we are the web.
x3

• • •

Leader, pick up the scissors, and cut your thread, and as you explain the below, you can have the person to the left tie your thread.

Leader: When cutting the thread to tie bracelets, share your favorite moment and a takeaway. Have the lady to your left tie your yarn, twice in a square knot, and one slip knot, and this way, your thread will not come undone. After you have spoken, pass the scissors to the right, and the next person can go.

After the scissors make their way back to you, and everyone has tied their thread, you can hold hands if you'd like.

Invitation to curiosity

Leader: Keep track of your cycle. You can do this by writing in your calendar the four main phases of the moon, or writing the day of your cycle in your planner, or app how you feel. Notice if you see similarities or differences throughout the month.

Thank you for being a part of tonight's Red Tent. You are all a treasure, and I'm glad you are here. Our Red Tent is now closed.

Cycles Meditation

Leader: This meditation is for meeting your cycle archetypes. Archetypes are facets to see and view yourself through.

You may like one or more of your archetypes more than others. Strong feelings are welcome here; this is soul work of figuring out where you are, how you are stuck, and how to move through this world purposefully. Whatever comes up for you is normal, and okay. Give yourself permission to explore the visuals and ideas that come to the surface.

Find a place to rest and be comfortable — Check-in with your body on how she would like to sit, or lay. You can rest your hands on the ground, your stomach, heart, or sprawl out.

Let your body sink into the ground, or the chair, almost like you're melting into yourself. Any thoughts that come in, acknowledge them, and let them pass.

Breathe in from your belly, and audibly exhale. Letting go of any fears, or notions of what's to come.

(pause)

With each breath, let yourself sink deeper into your seat, and into the ground. You are safe and you are held. Sinking deeper and deeper.

Relaxing your muscles and letting it be.

(pause)

Envision a path before you.

Begin to walk down it.

What does this path look like? It could be gravel, dirt, or a small stream, or something else entirely.

(pause)

The way soon starts going downwards, almost like a winding staircase. Walk down them.

Maybe your hand glides down on the railing as you go down. What does it feel like? What are your steps made of? Stone? Wood? Is it a slide?

(pause)

Keep going down, pass your heart door. Keep walking, pass your soul door, and keep going down the stairs until you're almost at the end.

(pause)

Soon in front of you is another door. Your Door to the Feminine.

Take a moment to look at it. Touch it. Is it painted or stained? What is it made of?

See if there is anything written on it or above. There may or may not be.

It may not even look like a door.

Take a moment to explore the textures and design of your door.

(pause)

On the other side of this door is a place where you feel safe and free.

Take a breath, and know you understand how to open the door, regardless if there is a handle.

When you are ready, open the door and walk through.

What do you see?

Take a moment to explore the area around you. Is it a forest? A beach, mountains? A backyard garden, your favorite gathering place?

(pause)

Up ahead, you see a fire and some women around this fire.

If you would like, walk towards it.

What does this fire feel like to you?

(pause)

Can you warm yourself by the fire? Does it make you want to sit and sing, or burn things? What kind of fire is this?

This is your Feminine Flame. Like a phoenix, and like a cycle, it may be larger sometimes than others, and your flame or fire can go out — but there is always a way to light it again.

Check-in with your body and how you feel as you watch the firelight.

(pause)

You look at one of the women. She is your Wild Woman.

What does she look like?

What is she wearing?

What is she doing?

She is also known as the Enchantress or Crazy Woman. Does one of those feel more true to you, or would she like to be called something else?

(pause)

Does she remind you of anyone? How does she make you feel? Ask her if there is anything she would like to tell you. She may speak in words, images, or just a feeling you get in your body, or she may not say anything at all.

(pause)

Another lady catches your eye. This is your maiden.

What does she look like? What is she doing?

You can go closer and talk with her.

She is also known as Queen and Virgin.

Does she remind you of anyone?

How does she make you feel?

You can ask her if there is something she would like to tell you.

(pause)

A different lady leans over to tend to the flame.

She is your creatrix or mother archetype.

What does she look like? What is she wearing or doing?

How does she make you feel?

Does she have anything to say to you?

(pause)

You see the fourth woman near you as well. She is your Crone, also known as Sage, Wise Woman, or Witch.

What does she look like? What is she wearing?

What is she doing? How does she look at you?

How does she make you feel? Take a moment to get acquainted with her.

(pause)

With your four ladies around the fire, I'll give you a few minutes to chat, be, dance, tend to the flames, do with this time as you see fit.

(a two minute pause)

When you are ready, say your goodbyes.

(pause)

As you walk back to your door, take a moment to look at how you are dressed. Are you barefoot? What is your hair like here? Are you wearing any jewelry?

Before you open the door take a moment to look around in your Feminine Soul-Scape.

(pause)

This place is yours to explore, breathe, and get advice. Whatever you need.

Go through your door and start walking back up your stairs.

Up up, past your soul door.

Keep walking.

(pause)

Pass your heart door, keep walking, all the way to the top where light starts to shine through. Come up to fresh air on the path you started on, and start walking back to you, to the room or space you are in, and the way your body feels.

(pause)

Lay for a moment taking in the sounds, the smells, and how your breath fills your body. When you feel finished, stretch, wiggle, yawn and slowly open your eyes.

CURIOSITY

$\mathcal{A}$ few years ago, I came to a place of feeling like my curiosity was a curse because if I brought up questions, I was shot down and presumed a trouble maker or told I didn't trust enough. I thought God didn't want me anymore because I was being disruptive and asking too many questions. It was with this fear and worry—and me avoiding God for a month in fear of being struck by lightning, that I decided to pray and meditate to discern if I was indeed a lost soul.

Midway through the meditation, I heard Spirit whisper into my soul: "Your curiosity is a gift, not a burden."

As I wrote this statement in my journal, I sobbed. A gift? I felt like curiosity was my curse. I wasn't someone that just wanted to know the reason why. I wanted to know, "Why not?" "What if?" And" What would happen if?" In response to asking these questions, I was answered with, "Don't ask that question," from friends, "We just don't talk about it," from a pastor, and "That's a slippery slope," from a mentor.

I felt exasperated and cut off by those responses. I wasn't a three-year-old requesting ice cream before dinner. I wondered, "If God hates my curiosity, why is it planted deep in my soul?"

I've come to learn that curiosity is a gift we have for exploring our world, but we don't always treat it as such.

 Bruna recalls getting brushed off for her excitement and curiosity when she was younger as well, "You're not supposed to ask questions when you are curious. I asked my fabulous older cousin, 'What's that?' and they retorted, 'You shut up. It's none of your business. Get out of here; you don't know what you're talking about.' But all I wanted was to comment on how fantastic something was. So now, when my curiosity pipes up, I think, 'don't say anything you're dumb.' It's unfortunate, I know."

There's a quote you have probably heard before, "Curiosity killed the cat." This feels like a clear-cut statement, but the end of the phrase is, "but satisfaction brought it back." That's the part our society doesn't quote nearly as often, and we need to because it completely changes the meaning of the passage.

What if curiosity can be a guide towards satisfaction, awareness, and goodness?

I believe the God of our universe can handle our questions. Find people who are open to your questions and exploring. There is a whole wilderness full of folks, dancing, asking, questioning, and finding. When I found my question welcoming communities in the Evolving Faith conference, Red Tents, Dangerous Women online community, and my little 100-year-old Episcopalian Church in San Antonio, it felt like coming home.

I want you to find the same—a home where you are surrounded by people who are curious, seeking, and welcome your whole self, whether this is a Red Tent, online forum, AA, neighborhood gathering, gaming group, or a small church in your town.

Listening to your curiosity can show you where there are things yet to discover, whether about yourself or the world.

> Obbie shares, "If anyone feels their inner nudge or sees something that speaks to them, they should take a chance. Try it out, follow, analyze, adjust, and move in the ways that you need. Not what's decided for you or what you are allowed by religion, family, or friends. Explore, experience, and then decide. Don't decide first. When we take chances on things we are skeptical about, it might reward us tenfold. You won't find treasure unless you look."

Friend, know that questions, curiosity, and wondering are okay.

You are okay.

Don't let someone's pearl-clutching choke you out of Spirit's presence.

ASKING THE QUESTIONS

Curiosity is a gentle hand-raising of "I wonder." In those moments of seeking knowledge and understanding, would we shame and belittle a kindergartner who wondered why Z, 2, and S are similar but different? No? Then why do we shame ourselves for asking questions on a path we've never been on before, in a life we've never lived before?

Maybe these questions are small, like, "What if I wore red lipstick today?" or "What if I signed up for this training class?"

Curiosity can also bring daunting questions to the table, such as: "Why is our marriage falling apart?"

"What if I took this job across the country?"

"What if I'm not crazy?" and even, "Is this the real life? Is this just fantasy?"[1]

Each question can feel like a massive leap off a cliff. Asking a question about a previously held idea you hold can show you its impact on your life. An idea is a mental object you are holding onto, so as impossible as it may seem, you can indeed let go of the ones that are eating you up from the inside out.[2]

For example, the idea, "I'm bad and ruin everything," might come up a lot for you. When this plays out, it colors every situation, making you wait for the shoe to drop and ready to take the blame even when it might not be your fault.

Curiosity might ask, "What if it wasn't my fault?" which may reframe thoughts to say, "Sometimes things don't work out, but I'm doing the best I can." With this new, more accurate thought, you can give yourself more grace without taking on the world's weight if things go sideways.

We get so freaked out by asking the question that we don't even feel we can come close to tuning into our bodies, wisdom, and Spirit to see what the answer may be.

Friend, let me speak some truth to you.

Curiosity can be a revealer of truth. Structures and systems often rely on you consistently playing your role to keep everything at status quo. So what happens when the truth shows things could be different, better, or more holy?

Well...your curiosity just became an issue.

Tara is a content developer and works in the LARP and gaming community to make it more diverse and accessible through safety and consent guidelines and gets pushback quite often.

"I'm met in my community mostly with good responses, but sometimes I say, 'The design of this game isn't in a way that's accessible for people with wheelchairs and me. A solution could be to have the event on the first floor so everyone can participate, but I receive pushback asking 'if it's worth the hassle.' A big component is having other people to support me. I feel more comfortable because I know others also have the same objection."

When you ask questions that reveal places that need new solutions, it can be troublesome to bring up. It means walking into the unknown and hearing "who knows" and the "we'll see" response that comes with risks and trying new things. The world is usually more comfortable when the options seem like absolutes. When you think you only have to choose between black and white, grey becomes quite intimidating. Still, the innovative holistic solutions we need in our world right now are only going to be found by asking new questions and holding the tension of being in-between.

Relationships can also feel the in-between tension. Curiosity can be a door to understanding people who have different perspectives as well. If someone confides in you, and you aren't sure how to respond, try asking questions about their lived experience instead of slinging accusations and assumptions.

Questions to try on in curious conversations:
"What is the journey you went on to reach this understanding?"
"How did you know this was the right path for you?"
"What have you been reading lately?"
"What does this mean to you?"

These types of questions can feel vulnerable on your end and are a delicate way to tend to a fragile moment. These queries show you care about the person you are talking to because you want to find a common base with them.

Curiosity can form the common denominator we need in friendships, especially if we're coming at things from different angles.

CURIOSITY AS A SCOUT

In Disney's *Beauty and the Beast*, Belle's dad Maurice is on a trip out of town and has to go through the woods. He comes to a fork in the road: one way is a lovely dusk-filled forest, and the other feels eerie and dark. Between the ominous music in one direction and birds chirping in the other, it's a clear choice on which path is more desirable.

As a viewer, we know he should take the charming path, which is why I screamed at the screen when Maurice nonchalantly tries to cut time by gallivanting off into the deep, dark, scary woods. *He didn't even have a GPS.*

In movies, they make decisions with one great choice and one dangerous choice. When our lives come to a crossroads, it often seems like both paths look fine.

Friend,

Maybe you feel lost.

Or like you are drowning.

It's okay to say that out loud and admit you don't have directions.

Regardless of what came before this moment, you are at a fork in the road.

It's important to know where you are so you know how to move forward. Maybe you have gone off the beaten path, or you've been in dangerous territory.

Are there things that are dangerous to look into? Yes. *Hello, beehives and bear caves.*

Are there longings you have that are not life-giving? Yes.

Because underneath your curiosity, there may be some unresolved issues and heart wounds that need to be processed.

But the desire under the desire? It's pure.

It's to be loved.

It's to be seen.

It's to feel whole.

The lies we've believed about ourselves can place layers of misunderstanding on our most genuine desires, making them seem shallow, but we can reclaim what we are created for if we dig deep enough and let Spirit guide us.

What if curiosity is a scout instead of that mysterious dark stranger in the tavern with a questionable back story everyone wants us to avoid?[3]

If you are at a fork in the road, use your curiosity to 'scout out' the different paths in front of you and imagine what each direction could look like to help you make a more intentional choice.

> DeLandrea's husband is military, and they move every few years. When mold started growing in her military base housing, they had to decide with one possible year left at their station whether to buy a house and move, or continue to rent, and she used her curiosity to weigh her options.
>
> "I was getting sick all of the time, but I thought as soon as we buy a house, we'll get orders to move again to a new station. We had already been in Mississippi for five years. Another year went by, and my headaches were worse, and there were no orders on the horizon. We talked about it and went looking for houses to get an idea of what we'd like and fell in love with our current house on the first day. I'm a firm believer that everything happens for a reason, but when I loosened the reins a little bit and went with the unknown path, it was worth it. Scary, but worth it."

Friend, you'll only know the answers to your "What would it be like" questions if you ask them. If you refuse to let curiosity be your scout, you won't have any idea what could go right, wrong, or sideways. You might get blindsided by what's around the corner regardless of what choice you make, but at least with curiosity, you'll have a heads up of when to duck.

CURIOUS IMAGINATION

When we were kids, we imagined sticks were swords, boxes were boats, and a tablecloth wrapped around our legs was a mermaid tail. Our world was anything we wanted it to be. A changing society with reduced benefits, alongside the lectures of "This is just how it is, nothing will ever change," beat down many and quieted our imaginations because we didn't have the time or energy anymore.

Don't let the busyness of our world take away from the vast incredibleness that is your creativity, joy, and curiosity. Take baby steps towards what makes your heart wonder.

Curiosity is an allowance to experience life like a tourist, to ask questions and explore what ignites a spark inside you. Curiosity shifts our perspective and helps us see things in a new light. If you still feel reluctant to give curiosity a foot back into your life, it might be because it feels wrong or off-limits.

What no one tells you is that you are the one who gets to determine your possibilities.

So if you feel stuck, try writing yourself a permission slip that allows you to play with your curiosity.

 Here's an example from Ayesha:
Dear curiosity,

I give you permission to try new things. To explore so, you can identify and establish what boundaries you need while enjoying life without guilt. To smile genuinely, to feel and embrace each emotion as it flows through you. Stop apologizing without need, take up space meaningfully, get messy, make mistakes, make new friends, share your journey, grow, and learn on the way towards becoming fully embodied and a beautiful woman.

Love yourself, sleep, drink your water, eat your protein, and as Aj would say

"Sing your soul song."

Love,

Ayesha

Curiosity is the sister to vulnerability. You can't be curious if your shields are up. Let curiosity guide you into a deeper life of discovery, growth, and truth.

FURTHER EXPLORATION

What has been a spark of curiosity in your life that you haven't allowed yourself to look at lately?

What were you curious about as a child? As a teen? Did you stop being curious? Why or why not?

What are you curious about in this book or this chapter after getting this far?

BOOK RECOMMENDATIONS:

The Fire Starter Sessions by Danielle Laporte
The Sin of Certainty by Pete Enns
Walking on Water by Madeleine L'Engle

Curiosity Red Tent

Five minutes before the Tent Begins:
Leader: Lovelies, please put your phones on silent or off, grab your water, snacks, journal, and token and join me in the circle.

Opening:

Leader: Before we begin, I would like to state that this is a safe space. In order to make it so, there needs to be agreement around keeping what is said in circle, in the circle. I'm asking you all to agree to only speak of your own experiences, and only give advice when asked. We will be talking about deeply personal things in the Red Tent. A gentle reminder that we can disagree and still accept each other. Can I have a show of hands for everyone willing to keep this space confidential, for themselves and everyone here tonight?

Shakeout and Grounded Breathing:

Leader: Let us take a minute to stand up, shake out any worries, or frustration from your day. Twist your body, shake your booty, kick your legs, jump up and down. Audibly make sounds while relaxing your jaw. Stretch, or move in a way that feels supportive.

Please have a seat in this circle, and let's do some ground breathing. You can close your eyes, start to relax your shoulders. You can roll your neck from side to side, rest your hands on your stomach, knees, or the ground, whatever is most comfortable for you. Start breathing in from your belly. Take a deep breath. As you exhale, release anything that came before tonight that is on your mind.

Breathe in again, releasing anything to come in the future. Keep breathing, focusing on the sounds around you,

the breath of other women, and your heartbeat. As you release your breath, feel your body settling into this space. In this moment, here with us. You are safe. You are loved. We are glad you are here with us.

Call in:

Leader: We are gathered in our Red Tent, as women, as daughters, as mothers, as workers and dreamers. We come here to speak our heart's desires, our mind's thoughts, and share the song of our souls. We see with our eyes, hear with our ears, and will hum along in our hearts. May this space be open, sacred, and grounded for us here tonight. Let us hold hands as we travel deeper together, learning to better love ourselves, each other, and the world.

Gender Neutral Option:

We are gathered in our Red Tent Tent as humans, as explorers, as workers and dreamers. We come here to speak our heart's desires, our mind's thoughts, and share the song of our souls. We see with our eyes, hear with our ears, and will hum along in our hearts. May this space be open, sacred, and grounded for us here tonight. Let us hold hands as we travel deeper together, learning to better love ourselves, each other, and the world.

Song:

Leader: Close your eyes and think of what you want from this night and this week. It might be friendship, laughter, wisdom. We'll pass the bowl around one person at a time, and you'll say your blessing request, we'll sing the song with your word inside of it, and then after we sing over you, pass the bowl to the next woman. She'll share her

blessing word, and we'll sing a blessing over her until we reach the end of the circle.

Call down a blessing x3, Call down, ____before you, ____behind you, ____Within you, and around you
Repeat for each person in the group, end with three call downs.

15: 1st Circle:
Leader: When speaking, please use the talking light, and when you finish, please say "I have spoken," so we know you have completed your thought. You can react with hand snaps, hand on your heart, and facial expressions. Please speak only of your own story, and don't give any advice unless asked.

For our first circle, please share your name, pronouns, your intention for tonight, and your relationship to curiosity.

25: Quote and Response: *Depending on the size of the group, you can have only a few people share, or have a minute per person.*
Leader: I'll share the quote of tonight, and after, share how it makes you feel, or your thoughts on it.
"Your curiosity is a gift, not a burden."

35: Activity 1: Curious Questions
*Leader:*Grab your journal and a pen and Free write the finishing of the questions:
Take one to two minutes between each question. You can usually tell as pens slow how people are doing on a question.
What would it be like if....
What are things in the past that have made you excited?
What would you try if you couldn't fail?
What is something you have secretly always wanted to try?

What fascinates you lately or has fascinated you in the past?

What have you always wanted to know more about?

Pause for them to finish writing.

Curiosity is a scout. A lot of times we feel like if we have an idea we can't act on it at all, and maybe that is true and we have to wait a year, or a month to tackle something full on, but a dream on the back burner is still acknowledged. For example, you may have always wanted to be an archeologist, maybe you can't go on a giant trip, but you could listen to a podcast about dinosaurs, or read a book or an article about it. Getting curious is about giving yourself permission to hope and wonder, "What could go right?"

Grab a different color marker or pen if you have one available:

Circle questions or ideas you wrote down that you need more answers on.

Put a squiggly line underneath playful exploring ideas, you'd love to explore more.

Put a square around big life questions.

Pick one from each category of circle, squiggle and square and write it out on your journal. Next to it, write the next step in exploring this idea. Maybe it's a podcast, or reading a book, or having a conversation.

Give a couple of minutes to journal these questions.

Maybe it's not the right time for some of your curious questions and that's okay too. Sometimes not now becomes not ever, so we want to give ourselves the chance to explore if it is something we truly desire, and then we know what we want to do with it.

. . .

50: Second Circle: Share what you would like from the Curious Questions activity.

1:05: Womanhood story:
  Leader: Womanhood stories are a core part of Red Tent, sharing our stories is a brave act. Sometimes they are joy filled, sad, frustrating, or a mix of all of it. The story may include periods, sex, birth, or any part of the woman and human experience. ____ has offered to share her story tonight. _____ the floor is yours.
  *See the appendix of the book for reaching out to your women to see who would like to share before the tent day.

After her story:
  Leader: Thank you ___ for sharing your story. Is there anything you need from us? Hug, encouragement, a listening ear during break?
  *If they say yes, do what you can to fulfill that need if possible.

1:15: Soul Care Time:
  Leader: Now is our soul care time. This is 20 minutes to stretch, nap, chat, get food, go to the restroom. We do ask that you don't use this time to be on your phone. I'll give us a five-minute heads up to tent, and a one minute come to circle heads up.

1:35: Activity Two: Curiosity meditation
  Meditation is at the end of this script.

1:50: Journal:
  What was your first path like? What did it represent?

What did your second path represent? What was on your second path? How do you feel after doing the meditation? Did anything surprise you?

1:55: Circle:
Anything you would like to share from the meditation.

2:10: Closer *Grab your red thread (yarn) and make sure scissors are within reach.*
Leader: Red thread represents our connection to the women around us and those who have come before us. You will take your red yarn and wrap it around your wrist. You can wrap as many times as you want, as you recite your matriarchal spiritual lineage. Your lineage are the women and people who have influenced and loved you.

They don't have to be biologically related, you can claim or not claim anyone you would like. You can say your name, mother of (any children), daughter of x, daughter of y, daughter of daughters, daughter of whatever resonates (Eve, Spirit, the moon, etc). You can also say descendent instead, or daughter of those who ____ instead of names.

When you have finished wrapping, pass the thread to the next person until it has gone all the way around the circle.

You can start the process and do your lineage and wrap and then pass it to the person on your right.

After the Red Thread has come back to you.
Leader: As we are connected, let us sing our song, we'll sing it three times, it goes flow, ebb, weavers, thread, weavers, thread, spiders, web. Sing it with me:

Song: We are the flow we are the ebb,

We are the weavers we are the thread,
We are the weavers we are the thread,
we are the spiders we are the web.
x3

Leader, pick up the scissors, and cut your thread, and as you explain the below, you can have the person to the left tie your thread.

Leader: When cutting the thread to tie bracelets, share your favorite moment and a takeaway. Have the lady to your left tie your yarn, twice in a square knot, and one slip knot, and this way, your thread will not come undone. After you have spoken, pass the scissors to the right, and the next person can go.

After the scissors make their way back to you, and everyone has tied their thread, you can hold hands if you'd like.

Invitation to curiosity

Leader: Explore your next steps from your Curious Questions activity and see what inspiration is sparked. Thank you for being a part of tonight's Red Tent. You are all a treasure, and I'm glad you are here. Our Red Tent is now closed.

Curiosity Meditation

This is a meditation to explore a decision or two different ideas you are mulling lately.

Take a deep breath and let your shoulders relax.
Let your forehead release.
(pause)
Let there be space in your jaw and between your shoulders. You've been holding onto a lot. It's okay to let it be. You are safe.
Let your body root down in rest.
(pause)
Feel warmth through your body almost as if you were laying out on a summer's day
Let your breathe swirl through your toes, your body, your hands.
With each breath feel your body sinking deeper into the couch, or chair, or bed.
(pause)
Imagine, a path in front of you.
The path is safe, and you start walking.
What is this path made of? Could be made of gravel and you can hear the crunch underneath or soft grass as you wade through. Or a creek you follow.
(pause)
As you walk this path you start walking towards the forest.
It's a good forest, and next to you is your helpful scout: Curiosity.
(pause)
What do they look like? Curiosity could be in animal form, human, or a spirit.
How do they make you feel?
(pause)

Keep walking on your path, into the forest.

The forest may have a few twist or turns and maybe the scout comes ahead and comes back but keep walking.

What time of day is it?

What kind of forest are you in?

A rain forest, pine forest, rainforest, red wood forest or a fairy forest?

Take in the smells and sounds around you, you are in no rush.

You go around a curve and you notice ahead that there is a fork in the road.

You take a look at both paths. But you just aren't sure.

(pause)

Instinctively you have an idea of what this path of 'what if' is. Maybe it's a decision you are trying to make in life right now. It could be light hearted or it could be kind of difficult right now, but your curiosity is with you and they are your scout. Which path are they going to go down first to explore?

(pause)

Maybe they have a camera with them, so you can see what they can see as they explore.

When you are ready, send Curiosity down the first path. Maybe you have a horse with you, or you will be by yourself in this fork for a bit, and that's okay. You are safe.

Send your curiosity ahead.

(pause)

What does your curiosity see? What is on this first path?

What is this path like in six months? Who is beside you in helping in this path in six months? What about a year?

As Curiosity looks around they might notice a few brambles, or thorns or things to look out for. What are those? What are things to look for on this path that might cause issues if not noticed?

Is there any food on this path? What is nourishing on this journey?

Maybe your Curiosity can't go any further, or maybe it sees ahead a little to five years? What do they see?

Have Curiosity look around another minute to see what they notice on this path

(Pause)

When Curiosity is ready they come back to you in the fork in the road to share insights, possibilities and ideas about the first path.

(pause)

After Curiosity has told you all they have to say about that path right now, send them down the second path.

Does this path look any different than the first one? They might look similar and that's okay. There's no right or wrong, they just are.

(pause)

As Curiosity looks around, what do they see on this path? Are there any rocks they stumble over, or is it smoothly paved?

(pause)

Does anything surprise Curiosity on this path? What about in six months?

Something might catch Curiosity's excitement and they might notice something, a small benefit of this path. Maybe it's extra shade or water. What do they find nourishing about this path in a year or two?

(pause)

Curiosity takes a long look to see if they can see anything else further or back on the path and they start to make their way back to you.

And as they finally return, what do they have to share about this second path? About this possibility? What is the good, the bad and the unknown?

(pause)

Tonight is not the night we will go any further down either path. You can make a cairn or a sign or a rock so you know this is where you paused your path. So you can make your way back here in the future and decide where to go. Maybe you tie a ribbon around a tree or draw in the sand.

(pause)

When you are ready turn around with curiosity and make your way back to the open path.

Keep walking.

Maybe you notice the time of day has changed. Is there wind? Keep walking on your path.

(pause)

Walking back to you, the sound of my voice, and the feel of your body in the chair.

(pause)

You can almost feel where the path was beneath your feet to where the ground now is.

When you are ready you can stretch, wiggle, yawn and make your way back to circle.

CREATIVITY

"*J*'m not creative."
 I can't tell you how many times I hear this.
 From Red Tent ladies, friends, and even family, many of us believe we are not creative. Saying "I'm not creative" is the same as saying, "I'm not human." We all have creativity woven into the marrow of our bones—it simply looks different for every person. Earl Nightingale states, "Creativity is a natural extension of enthusiasm."[1]

We compare our creative capabilities to others by saying, "Oh, I do this little thing, but I could never do *that*." Maybe we think creativity looks like gallery-ready art, professional acting, or being a world-famous musician. While art and creativity are lovers, art is not central to your soul; creativity is. It's a slippery slope to limit ourselves out of fear of feeling like our art is for the consumption of others.

My friend, creativity is the expression of our souls.

The first time I shared the concept of cultivating creativity in our souls in Tent, I got some pushback as some women felt they weren't creative enough in their preferred expression. Others thought because they weren't flashy, it was somehow proof they weren't creative. Loud actions and colors aren't the center points to creativity. The warm embrace of a hug, the smell of delicious home-baked cookies, or a cozy home are all ways of showing creativity and love.

As you read this chapter, please don't let the idea of what creativity should look like freeze you from exploring what it looks like in real time in your life.

When we embrace a soul-rooted view of creativity, we free ourselves from the constraints holding us back from our embodied expression. Brené Brown shares my perspective and says, "Creativity is the way I share my soul with the world." Sometimes we just need someone to hand us a key to help us realize it.

> Ayesha shares her thoughts on creativity, "'Creative soul' to me means seeing things in a different way. You create your joy, path, and life by looking at those moments as possibilities for what you can do to continue growing and learning. It doesn't mean you are physically creating something or that you are an artist (although you are an artisan of life); creativity is your ability to see the possibilities that life has to offer."

I love the idea of creating moments to see life differently. According to Marion Woodman, "If we fail to nourish our souls, they wither, and without soul, life ceases to have meaning...The creative process shrivels in the absence of continual dialogue with the soul. And creativity is what makes life worth living."[2]

I could not agree more, but I didn't always believe I was creative.

In college, I was a camp counselor and loved every minute of it. Two years later, Jer was enlisting in the military and had to train for seven months. During those seven months, I had time to work, travel and explore. I decided to spend my summer at the Des Moines YMCA Camp as a camp counselor. They were thrilled I was returning and asked if I would be the Art Program Director.

I said no.

I wanted a fun, "relaxing" job.[3]

A month before I arrived, they told me I'd be working as the Art Program Head. I frantically rejected the offer, "No! I'm not creative! I could never be the Art Head!" I was introduced at camp to the other employees as the Art Program Head. My face went stone, and I spoke through clenched teeth, "I. Am. Not. The. Art. Person." Completely blaise, my director pointed to a 16-year-old camp counselor and asked, "Do you want him to do it?"[4] I rolled my eyes and grudgingly mumbled, "No." Enthusiastically, he replied, "Congratulations, you're the new Art Program Head!"

I was frustrated with this new job title. I wasn't artsy; I was a creative performer in theatre but was devoid of artistic talent, except for my kindergarten-level stick figures. I had spent zero time preparing and felt behind as the first set of kids would be coming in two weeks. I had to prepare for nine weeks of camp. Over 300 children would come through the program each week, not to mention day campers, weekly tie-dye, and an extra art class. I was overwhelmed.

Where my director saw potential in me, I only saw disaster.

I took stock of my skill set. Once I figured out ideas that would combine a little theatre and a little art, I bought what I needed: bulk tie-dye, sheets, clay, rubber, and powdered paint.

One week I was a Master French Painter with a blue mustache, and we used flat bedsheets as our canvases. We listened to music and painted how the music made us feel. I would later cut up the sheet, and their cabin mates would write what they loved or noticed about them from the week.

Another week I donned a toga as an Ancient Princess

and taught the kids about seals, and we each designed and carved our stamps so people would know it's genuinely us and not an impostor.[5]

Once I figured it out, I found a groove. This job made me realize I didn't need to limit my creativity to one thing. I started thinking, "If I could do this project, then maybe I could try this other thing." When we allow ourselves space to explore, we may surprise ourselves where the path leads.

The key to trying something new is to keep growing and to be flexible. Anytime we learn something new, we do it 'badly' the first time, and we keep getting better. Remember, anything worth doing is worth doing imperfectly...except surgery.[6]

Be willing to stretch! Make those mistakes! Don't let scarcity and fear keep you from enjoying the possibilities that are around you. I know this is hard, but discovering something new is worth the discomfort of trying.

I don't think my growth into creativity would have been possible if my director had let my fear win. He saw possibilities in me, and he spoke into them. He said, "I see you, Aj. I see what you are capable of, and you can do this."

When you can, speak into someone's capabilities. Tell them you see them. Appreciate and believe in them. Then root them on.

They may fail or learn new skills (or, more than likely, both). Lives can shift because of exploring one possibility.

The voice of fear in our heads has a name—it's the Inner Critic, and as loud as it can be, I've found some excellent tools to learn to work through it.

INNER CRITIC

Listening to encouragement can be difficult when our Inner Critic (IC) doesn't give us any space to play. You know that voice inside our brain that says, "You will never be good enough," "Why are you even trying?" and "Who do you think you are?" That is your Inner Critic. When we talk about the Inner Critic in our heads, we brush over it by saying, "it's not a big deal," and "I'm just tough on myself. I push myself because I have to."

But lovely, you don't have to listen to or be limited by the voice that whispers you'll fail at everything you do.

 In her book *Playing Big,* Tara Mohr talks about the Inner Critic and lists eleven qualities your Inner Critic may have. A few stuck out to me.

One is Binary: "The inner Critic is a black-and-white thinker. You are awesome or you are pathetic. You are gorgeous or ugly. You are a fabulous friend or a horrible one. Your dreams are possible, or they aren't. When the inner Critic speaks, there's usually no room for gray."[7]

She also mentions how cruel the Inner Critic can be, "When you hear a voice in your head saying harsh things to you that you would never intend to say to a person you love, you're hearing the Inner Critic."

We tend to label this voice perfectionism, a play on anxiety's behalf, to say, "this is just who I am." Your authentic Inner Voice is one of grace and patience. Other times we say the shaming voice is God, but God's voice isn't a shaming one. We often use shame as a weapon regardless, preferring to label it God as we beat ourselves with it to "be better."

Remember, having an Inner Critic doesn't mean you are broken. It means you are human.

Tara shares, "The inner critic is an expression of the safety instinct in us—the part of us that wants to stay safe from potential emotional risk

—from hurt, failure, criticism, disappointment, or rejection by the tribe."[8]

Just as our fear is not trying to control us but pointing out possible issues that could arise and alert us with the only tool it knows, the IC believes adrenalin and worry are the best tools to save us.

When we can look at the Inner Critic through a compassionate lens, we can see why it is trying to protect us. Maybe you are secretly worried about sharing an idea, having it shot down, or are privately concerned about disappointing your parents when you want to change your major. Maybe your IC tells you no one needs your idea because it's already been done, and you feel like your work would be a waste.

If you can point to the protection and fear behind the thoughts, you can tell your Inner Critic that you can see what's going on and then decide your next steps.

If we call our Inner Critic our authentic Inner Voice, we push ourselves and strive until we break or get near our breaking point. Something breaking is a sign of a weak point, of too much pressure. Breaking down doesn't mean you can't take the pressure in the future, but you'll have to grow a new muscle: resiliency. You may have to rearrange things, such as your schedule, commitments, or the amount of work you'll need to do.

In his book, *Do Over*, Jon Acuff mentions how a friend starting up his business put his nose to the grindstone and did not apologize for it. He called it his 'med school season.' The idea was that people wouldn't tell him to slow down or relax if he was in actual med school. They'd understand why he was hustling. The idea here is that 'med school' season is just that: a season. There may be times in your life where you have to focus on one thing, but if that one thing takes over entirely and causes wreckage, take it as a sign that something is not sustainable long term.

Your Inner Critic will tell you this is the price of admission. Yes, growth can be painful, and hard work and diligence are often the way forward, and we will mess up royally sometimes, but utter exhaustion and burnout shouldn't be normalized as 'the way it always is.' A season is a season for a reason. If a burnout season becomes the way of living — something is broken — whether a system, process, or organization.[9]

If you fill your tank with the 'fuel' of shame, guilt, pressure, and worry, you will have a life filled with shame, guilt, stress, and fear. If you can give yourself grace as you explore and go after a dream, the journey will still happen, but you'll be able to sleep better. See if you can't replace angry self-loathing thought with even a 1% better feeling thought. As counter-intuitive as it may seem, you might be surprised how much you flourish with a bit of TLC.[10]

INNER VOICE VS. TAUGHT VOICE

Imagine a toddler who paints a picture of an elephant and brings it to you, exuberant with excitement. They share their elephant, which looks a lot like a sideways tree. You compliment their drawing, and their next drawing is a blue horse on the moon. In a different scenario, you disparage their elephant, and they may think you don't understand or start double-guessing their work.

If these discouraging words add up, they begin to auto-play the tape in their heads with other people's opinions and stop drawing before anyone can say anything of note about their abilities. Fixating on how we should be different, more or better, is how the Inner Critic is born: when you hear enough criticism that is too vague to be fixable but feels true.

The Inner Critic is a taught voice we pick up when we are young. It reminds us of what we think we need to do to be the best, belong, get ahead, and not get left behind. That voice is formed from creativity scars and Heart Wounds —

places we are incredibly vulnerable—and those heart wounds shape how we hear feedback.[11]

> Brene Brown shares, "When I started the research on shame, you know, 13 years ago, I found that 85% of the men and women who I interviewed remembered an event in school that was so shaming, it changed how they thought of themselves for the rest of their lives. Fifty percent of that 85% percent, half of those people: those shame wounds were around creativity. So fifty percent of those people have art scars. Have creativity scars."[12]

These scars lead to beliefs we hold about ourselves, which can hold us back. When we transform these ideas into core truths about ourselves and believe the story shared from those, they become Heart Wounds. Heart Wounds create a feedback loop that is difficult to get out of. We have to rewire our brains and name our Critic. We need to make at least an inch of space between the Critic's voice and our own.

The Artist's Way book encourages us to name our Inner Critic, and this alone has been a game-changer for me. Your Critic could be a cartoon-esque villain, a teacher from middle school, or a caricature of a family member. The point is to create distance. Imagine if some random person belittled you in a store; You wouldn't take it seriously because you know your worth and what you are doing.

I named my Inner Critic Brenda,
    and
    She.
    Is.
    Fancy.

She's a 70-year-old lady with a perfectly coiffed bun, has a verse for everything, and dresses me down for my red lipstick, purple hair, and side-eyes me for questions I ask at Bible Study. I have met many fancy ladies whom I absolutely adore and who love God fiercely. Our IC often shows who we are afraid of being judged by and for what.

As you personify your Inner Critic, journal about their traits: what they look like, what they say, what they love, and what they hate. What is their name? Something simple, like Bob, or more absurd like Reginald "Reggie the Mouth" Reggington the 5th? The more particular you can make it, the better because it creates even more distance between you and your Inner Critic.

Here is where the rubber hits the road. You now have a name for the mean voice in your head. It's not you, but it doesn't mean it is any less loud or feels less accurate. The weight of the Critic may still ring in your head. I have two tools I'd love to give you so you can look at a statement being made in your mind and say, "Actually, this isn't true for me" or "I see this, and I'm going to proceed anyway. It might fail, and that's okay." One is making your Inner Critic ridiculous, and the other is cultivating an Inner Defender. One idea may resonate more than the other, but try both and see what works for you.

ISN'T THAT RIDICULOUS?

If you've ever seen or read Harry Potter, you may know of a creature called a Boggart. Upon seeing you, Boggarts transform into your worst fear. The way to conquer them is to cast the spell *Riddikulus*, which transforms the Boggart from your scary fear into something silly. (For example, a giant spider turns into a spider on roller skates.) We are going to do the same thing to our Critics.

Take a minute and figure out who or what your Inner Critic transforms into. Maybe they shift into an overly dramatic cartoon character or a feisty squirrel who is distracted by everything, and you can respond with, "Really? You're going to give me advice?" Make them absurd.

Even if you feel like this is dumb or won't work, remember it's about small steps we can take to rewrite our brains slowly. The resistance is part of the process. Resistance may also be more challenging if your Critic is a close family member in your brain. If you are hesitant to make them ridiculous, you can uncover their motive and where they are coming from with the words they say. So you can respond with, "I understand your perspective. Thank you for sharing; I'm moving in this direction."

When I make my Inner Critic Brenda ridiculous, she turns into a woman who only watches 90's reruns of Jeopardy. She has 3,392,393 emails in her inbox, gets spam viruses all the time, and her favorite party dish is stale fruit cake because it's the only dish she can make. So now, when Brenda, my rediculoused-Inner Critic, screeches, "Aj, you look ridiculous, you can't wear that!" or "That's a absurd goal, who do you think you are?" I can laugh and respond with, "You know what, Brenda? This flower crown makes me feel fabulous, and you are right, this book does feel like an undertaking, but it's an adventure I'm going on with red lipstick and glitter. Doing life in this way might not be for you, but let me know if you want to have fun soon. Otherwise, I'll leave you be."[13]

Take out your journal, or write a dialogue with your Inner Critic here in the margins. Putting their words on paper can help create some distance and help you see where the twists in logic are. When we write down what our IC says, there may be parts of us that see it and say, "Oh, that's cruel or not always true," which can help us be more generous with ourselves.

INNER DEFENDER

Another way to create space between our critics and us is by having an Inner Defender who can hold their own with your Inner Critic. My Inner Defender's name is David. He's a real man I met at a conference I spoke at, and he loved my work. He has white hair, owns his own successful business, and thought I was the bee's knees.

I adopted him as my Inner Defender, and anytime Brenda says something along the lines of, "Aj, you're too much. God would be disappointed. This idea is absurd!" David responds with, "Brenda, Aj's work is astounding. She cares deeply, and you can see her faith in the way she speaks and responds to people." It feels like the moment in *Aladdin* when Jafar's staff breaks, and the Sultan's gaze refocuses on the present. When I hear my Inner Defender, I remember, "Yeah, my work is good. It's doing good things."

We almost don't realize we listen to our Inner Critic until we name it and understand it for what it is.

Who is your Inner Defender? It might be a six-year-old girl who won't take crap from anyone. It could be your mom or someone you've never met in person, but you know they would speak up for you.

> For Brooke, her defender changes based on what she's coming up against, "My sister is my defender when my aunts are my critics, they cackle and talk, and my sister comes in and cracks jokes to make them uncomfortable. Another defender is Aj with her maracas and jewelry, and sometimes my Inner Defender is me."

If you can't pull anyone to mind, I volunteer to be your Inner Defender for you because you are worth protecting.

Faith is also a beautiful way to find refuge from your IC.

I can't tell you how often I remind myself of the verse telling me God will never leave nor forsake me when I feel terrified about trying something new. Taking solace in knowing the universe has your back, and you aren't a mistake can help guide you through a dark night of the soul.

The difference it creates to make space is illuminating because you can judge the critique it gives you.

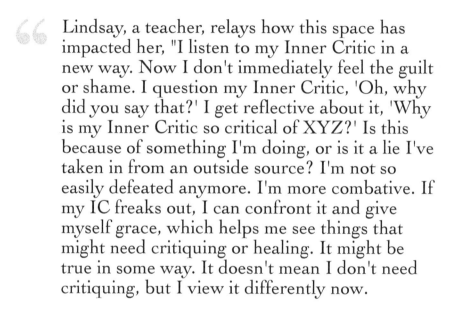 Lindsay, a teacher, relays how this space has impacted her, "I listen to my Inner Critic in a new way. Now I don't immediately feel the guilt or shame. I question my Inner Critic, 'Oh, why did you say that?' I get reflective about it, 'Why is my Inner Critic so critical of XYZ?' Is this because of something I'm doing, or is it a lie I've taken in from an outside source? I'm not so easily defeated anymore. I'm more combative. If my IC freaks out, I can confront it and give myself grace, which helps me see things that might need critiquing or healing. It might be true in some way. It doesn't mean I don't need critiquing, but I view it differently now.

It's shifted how I relate to others too. I'm more aware of whether or not my words sound like an Inner Critic to others. If I say something harsh, my Inner Voice nudges me, 'Why don't you think about what you just said and how you said it.' I can then go back and say, 'Oh babe, I'm sorry for how I said that. Naming my Inner Critic has created a whole new relationship dynamic with myself and others."

GREMLINS

Alongside our Inner Critic, we house tiny gremlins—no water required.

These are bits of shame, accusations, memories, and

comments others make that can throw us off our rhythm when we are in the flow. One of the gremlins is, as Rachel Hollis calls it, 'other people's opinions. These can be spoken or unspoken, and frequently these opinions we think they have are implicit assumptions of what they would say, should they find out what we are doing. We get so wrapped up in playing the tape forward of what will happen and being stuck in that possible reality that we forget to show up for the present.

Guilt, Should, and Shame are three of the main gremlins we wrestle. We wear our guilt like its clothing.[14] You may be beating yourself up for an idea that didn't work, or a plan you can't do yet, or a dream that flopped. Perhaps you said the wrong thing and keep replaying it in your mind as proof you aren't worthy of taking the next step towards your goal.

'Shoulds' are often revealed in words others say coming from wanting to protect you from failure (which is a part of learning anything new) or how they didn't allow themselves or feel allowed to follow their dreams. So they inadvertently try to impose the same on you.

The way you live your life may be different from those around you, but lovely, you are living your life, not them. You have to live with your choices instead of letting the Gremlins and Inner Critic in your mind take ownership of your dreams.

Gremlins love to keep your face down in the dirt, while curiosity realizes we're in the dirt and that this is as good a place as any to figure out the next step. Creativity uses the soil to help you grow from it.

So you screwed up and double-booked yourself at an event. *Not that I'm speaking from personal experience here.* Do you know what you're going to do better from here on out? Your booking process.

Shame is not conducive to growth; it merely freezes us and adds to the guilt we are already carrying, making it harder to see the good in and around us.

So let's stop bathing in shame and start walking in freedom.

Critics and gremlins wither in the light of the three C's: creativity, curiosity, and compassion. These are the things that make us most human. These three things help us recognize the image of God in the souls of the people around us.

> Mary Daly says, "It is the creative potential itself in human beings that is the image of God."[15]

When our creativity is gone, the world exists in black and grey.

When our curiosity is gone, we don't see a new opportunity or a new adventure around each corner.

When our compassion is gone, we use ourselves and dehumanize others until nothing is left but vitriol and hate.

> Author and Theologian Matthew Fox says, "Creativity and imagination are not frosting on a cake: They are integral to our sustainability. They are survival mechanisms. They are of the essence of who we are. They constitute our deepest empowerment."

Although these things may seem like non-essentials for the way you run your business and life, we can very clearly see without these things, the life you are living can quickly become one devoid of joy and wholeness.

We often withhold creativity from our lives because we believe it's separate from us and believe we don't deserve it. But if creativity is the expression of our soul, then it isn't a treat to be strung onto a stick just beyond our to-do list. Instead, it needs to be an interwoven part of our thriving lives. When play is threaded in, our ideas, energy, and possibilities will become brighter and more vivid. You might be wondering, "Sure, but Aj, I don't know how to play. I don't know what I even like anymore." Lovely, what a wonderful place to start, with fresh eyes and new curiosity!

One of my favorite ways to play with my curiosity is to take it on an Artist Date. In *The Artist's Way* by Julia Cameron, she talks about Artist Dates. Artist Dates are a date with yourself and your inner child to play and explore the world. Maybe this looks like writing a letter and adding stickers to it, dancing down by the lake, or sculpting with Play-doh. Keep your eyes and ears open for what perks you up.

Have you ever had an idea you think would be fun, but then your Inner Critic said, "No, that sounds dumb!" Is there a way for you to explore that idea? Maybe you always wanted to be a chef but never went to culinary school. Could you take a cooking class or find a fun recipe and make it for your family or friends? Start taking small steps towards what feels fun and freeing, and perhaps a little silly and ridiculous.

Maybe as a mom, you think you 'shouldn't have time for yourself because that's selfish." Or "It doesn't matter, because I have kids now." These limiting shoulds are often your Inner Critic trying to keep you small and convincing you to conform to what other people want, EVEN IF THEY DON'T WANT YOU TO BE SMALL IN REALITY. In the past, I've assumed others would be uncomfortable with who I've become in my 30's, but when I showed my soul, they were thrilled to meet my whole self.

Let's stop playing for a real or imagined peanut gallery that doesn't even have a vested interest in our flourishing. Bad-faith critics will never cheer you on, even if you do things their way. They will always try to find flaws, so trust your path.

The more steps you take towards playful living, the more nudges you'll receive from your Inner Voice on what you would make your soul sing. Singing your soul song means living a life brimming with Spirit and creativity.

QUESTIONS FOR FURTHER DISCOVERY:

What has creativity looked like in your life?

When was the last time you allowed yourself to play?

What could an artist date look like for you this week or month?

BOOK RECOMMENDATIONS:

The Artist's Way by Julia Cameron
Creatrix by Lucy Pearce
Big Magic by Liz Gilbert

Creativity Red Tent

Five minutes before the Tent Begins:

Leader: Lovelies, please put your phones on silent or off, grab your water, snacks, journal, and token and join me in the circle.

Opening:

Leader: Before we begin, I would like to state that this is a safe space. In order to make it so, there needs to be agreement around keeping what is said in circle, in the circle. I'm asking you all to agree to only speak of your own experiences, and only give advice when asked. We will be talking about deeply personal things in the Red Tent. A gentle reminder that we can disagree and still accept each other. Can I have a show of hands for everyone willing to keep this space confidential, for themselves and everyone here tonight?

Shakeout and Grounded Breathing:

Leader: Let us take a minute to stand up, shake out any worries, or frustration from your day. Twist your body, shake your booty, kick your legs, jump up and down. Audibly make sounds while relaxing your jaw. Stretch, or move in a way that feels supportive.

Please have a seat in this circle, and let's do some ground breathing. You can close your eyes, start to relax your shoulders. You can roll your neck from side to side, rest your hands on your stomach, knees, or the ground, whatever is most comfortable for you. Start breathing in from your belly. Take a deep breath. As you exhale, release anything that came before tonight that is on your mind.

Breathe in again, releasing anything to come in the

future. Keep breathing, focusing on the sounds around you, the breath of other women, and your heartbeat. As you release your breath, feel your body settling into this space. In this moment, here with us. You are safe. You are loved. We are glad you are here with us.

Call in:

Leader: We are gathered in our Red Tent, as women, as daughters, as mothers, as workers and dreamers. We come here to speak our heart's desires, our mind's thoughts, and share the song of our souls. We see with our eyes, hear with our ears, and will hum along in our hearts. May this space be open, sacred, and grounded for us here tonight. Let us hold hands as we travel deeper together, learning to better love ourselves, each other, and the world.

Gender Neutral Option:

We are gathered in our Red Tent Tent as humans, as explorers, as workers and dreamers. We come here to speak our heart's desires, our mind's thoughts, and share the song of our souls. We see with our eyes, hear with our ears, and will hum along in our hearts. May this space be open, sacred, and grounded for us here tonight. Let us hold hands as we travel deeper together, learning to better love ourselves, each other, and the world.

Song:

Leader: Close your eyes and think of what you want from this night and this week. It might be friendship, laughter, wisdom. We'll pass the bowl around one person at a time, and you'll say your blessing request, we'll sing the song with your word inside of it, and then after we sing over you, pass the bowl to the next woman. She'll share her blessing word, and we'll sing a blessing over her until we reach the end of the circle.

Call down a blessing x3, Call down, ____before you, ____behind you, ____Within you, and around you

Repeat for each person in the group, end with three call downs.

15: 1st Circle:

Leader: When speaking, please use the talking light, and when you finish, please say "I have spoken," so we know you have completed your thought. You can react with hand snaps, hand on your heart, and facial expressions. Please speak only of your own story, and don't give any advice unless asked.

For our first circle, please share your name, pronouns, intention for tonight, as well as what your relationship with creativity has been like?

30: Quote and Response:

Leader:I'll share this quote and after you can share what resonates with you about it.

"Creativity is the way I share my soul with the world". - Brené Brown

40: Activity One: Creativity Titles

Leader: I want you to write down 5 things that light you up. That spark joy, and make your soul sing. These could be big things like running a marathon, or it could be making chocolate chip banana bread, swinging in a swing set, going on a hike or forest bathing. Things that are semi repeatable.

(Pause for them to write)

On the next line, I want you to write a fancy title. Perhaps it's Professor, Duchess, Queen, Marquis?

Next, write an over the top positive adjective. Something like fabulous, or outstanding, splendid, or extravagant!

(Pause)

Then on the next line, I want you to do a mad lib by filling in the blank:

I am the Adjective Title, Name, doer of your five soul lighting choices.

Example. I am The Splendid Marquis Kayla, creator of great meals.

Or I am the astounding Duchess Aj, reader of fabulous books.

(Pause)

Once you have your title, I want you to introduce yourself to the group. Don't share where you work, or what you 'really do' for your job. Let your creativity title be enough for the moment, and meet the people around you by introducing yourself creative title first.

You can start first, and then have the women go around the circle. When it comes back to you, share the below.

We forget these parts of ourselves and don't often bring them first to the conversation because they aren't usually useful to anyone. People don't profit from it, or we often can't sell the lusciousness that is us enjoying life without exploiting it, so we ignore it in others and ourselves. It's seen as a luxury, something we allow ourselves when we've been good, but we can start weaving our creative souls into our conversations.

55: Womanhood story:

Leader: Womanhood stories are a core part of Red Tent, sharing our stories is a brave act. Sometimes they are joy filled, sad, frustrating, or a mix of all of it. The story may include periods, sex, birth, or any part of the woman and human experience. ___ has offered to share her story tonight. ____ the floor is yours.

See the appendix of the book for reaching out to your women to see who would like to share before the tent day.

• • •

After her story:

Leader: Thank you ___ for sharing your story. Is there anything you need from us? Hug, encouragement, a listening ear during break?

*If they say yes, do what you can to fulfill that need if possible.

1:05: Soul Care Time:

Leader: Now is our soul care time. This is 20 minutes to stretch, nap, chat, get food, go to the restroom. We do ask that you don't use this time to be on your phone. I'll give us a five-minute heads up to tent, and a one minute come to circle heads up.

1:25: Activity Two: Inner Critic

When we move towards creativity, we usually have an inner voice that pops up who tells us we are not allowed goodness. This voice asks us "Who do you think you are?" We believe we don't deserve this. We think we aren't smart enough or good enough. This is not your true voice, this is the voice of your Inner Critic. So often we say it's us, but when we do this we create a limiting belief of what we are capable of.

Because this is learned we have to rewire our brain and name our Critic, by doing this we are creating at least an inch of space between the Critic's voice and our own. Your Critic could be someone either like a cartoon-esque villain, or a teacher from middle school, or a caricature of a family member. This person may have held a lot of power over us at some point, but we need to start taking back control from our inner monologue.

Write down the name of your Inner Critic. Who are they? What do they look like? What do they wear?

Pause for them to write

. . .

Here is where the rubber hits the road. Great, now you have a name for the mean voice in your head. It's not 'you', but it doesn't mean it is any less loud, or feel less true. The weight of the accusations still ring in your head. I have two activities I love to give you the space to look at a statement being made in your mind and say, 'actually, this isn't true for me' or 'I see this, and I'm going to proceed anyways. It might fail, and that's okay'. One is making your Inner Critic ridiculous, and the other is cultivating an Inner Defender. One idea may resonate more than the other, but try both and see what works for you.

Idea 1: Cast a *Riddikulus* spell on your Inner Critic
If you've ever seen or read Harry Potter, you may know of a creature called a Boggart. The power of Boggarts is that they transform into your worst fear. The way to conquer them is to cast the spell Riddikulus which transforms the Boggart from your scary fear, into something silly. For example a giant spider turns into a spider on roller skates. We are going to do the same thing to our critics.
Take a minute and figure out what your ridiculoused Inner Critic might look like. Maybe they shift into a cartoon character that's overdramatic, or a feisty squirrel who is distracted by everything and you can respond with, "Really? You're gonna give me advice?" Make them absurd. Even if you feel like this is dumb, or this won't work, it's about small steps we can take to slowly rewrite our brains. This may also be harder if your critic is a closer family member in your brain. If you are hesitant to make them ridiculous, you can look for the human parts of them, and uncover their motive for why they are saying the things they are, (examples: trying to protect you, they are jealous, they never went after their dream).

. . .

Give a minute or two for them to create their rediculoused Inner Critic.

The second idea is to give space between us and our critic is by having an Inner Defender. This is someone who can hold their own with your Inner Critic. We almost don't realize we are listening to our Inner Critic until we name it, and understand it for what it is. Who is your inner defender? It might be a six year old girl, who won't take crap from anyone, it could be your mom, or a pet, it could even be someone you've never met in person but you know would speak up for you. Draw them on your page. Write down their response to the things your Inner Critic says.

Give a minute or two for them to create their Inner Defender.

1:40: Circle:
    Share as much or as little as you would like from the Inner Critic exercise.

1:55: Closer *Grab your red thread (yarn) and make sure scissors are within reach.*
    Leader: Red thread represents our connection to the women around us and those who have come before us. You will take your red yarn and wrap it around your wrist. You can wrap as many times as you want, as you recite your matriarchal spiritual lineage. Your lineage are the women who have influenced and loved you.
    They don't have to be biologically related, you can claim or not claim anyone you would like. You can say your name, mother of (any children), daughter of x, daughter of y,

daughter of daughters, daughter of whatever resonates (Eve, Spirit, the moon, etc). You can also say descendent instead.

When you have finished wrapping, pass the thread to the next person until it has gone all the way around the circle.

You can start the process and do your lineage and wrap and then pass it to the person on your right.

After the Red Thread has come back to you.
Leader: As we are connected, let us sing our song, we'll sing it three times, it goes flow, ebb, weavers, thread, weavers, thread, spiders, web. Sing it with me:
Song: We are the flow we are the ebb,
We are the weavers we are the thread,
We are the weavers we are the thread,
we are the spiders we are the web.
x3

Leader, pick up the scissors, and cut your thread, and as you explain the below, you can have the person to the left tie your thread.

Leader: When cutting the thread to tie bracelets, share your favorite moment and a takeaway. Have the lady to your left tie your yarn, twice in a square knot, and one slip knot, and this way, your thread will not come undone. After you have spoken, pass the scissors to the right, and the next person can go.

After the scissors make their way back to you and everyone has tied their thread, you can share the invitation below. Feel free to hold hands if you'd like.

Invitation to curiosity

Leader: When your inner critic raises their voice this month, use either Riddikulous or your Inner Defender to create some space between you and them. Thank you for being a part of tonight's Red Tent. You are all a treasure, and I'm glad you are here. Our Red Tent is now closed.

VOICE

"*C*an I trust myself?"
This question is one many of us have asked
ourselves. We run the gambit of wondering 'what if' while
replaying past events to discern the future. While we do this,
we feel a little voice inside saying, "Take the next step. You
are on the right path." Do you trust the small Voice? Or
replay past mistakes and the words of others saying it might
not work out?

The outside world is overflowing with opinions, but so is
your inside world. You can take other people's thoughts and
weaponize them against yourself in your mind.
Overthinking can take every possibility and twist it until
you can't think straight about what's real and what's not.
When you sort through the different thoughts in your head,
you can get clarity on your next steps. Instead of stopping
and starting, wondering if you'll ever be able to trust
yourself, you can listen to Your Inner Voice.

As loud and over the top I can be, I have spent a lot of
time over the years double guessing my Inner Voice and
asking other people what they thought before thinking,
"Okay, yes, I'm okay. I thought that too." The Voice of doubt

and my Inner Critic made me question myself at every turn. I learned the still small Voice was Spirit and was the only Voice I could trust. So I listened and was approved by others, but then the Voice of Spirit led me to new ideas and places others doubted. In turn, I doubted myself and my Inner Voice.

As I've gotten older, I realized my Inner Voice is made up of the ideas and dreams I was given when I was born. I believe each of us is God-breathed. The still small Voice is the Voice of Spirit, urging us to live genuine lives steeped in love.

So, what is your Inner Voice?

It's the Voice who asks, "What if there was a better way?" Who sees new possibilities and hope in complicated situations. Maybe you haven't listened in a while or don't feel you have the time to listen. It's hard to listen to your Inner Voice when the kids are screaming, the TV is on, emails are pinging, and the dogs are barking at the construction going on across the street. The world can be pretty loud. It's essential to find ways to listen through the noise, so you can find it when you need to know the next step. Acknowledging and listening to your Inner Voice is necessary if you don't want to feel like you are being split in half.

Our Inner Voice guides us to where we need to go while urging us to live our life with more kindness and grace towards ourselves and others.

 Lindsay has been exploring this concept: "Following my Inner Voice goes along with things that are bringing me joy, like yoga, intentional learning, and being outdoors. My Inner Voice reminds me to take part in them and not deprive myself. I can tell the difference from Red Tents; I notice my Inner Voice gets louder, like, 'Hey! This is me!'. My Voice is me, and I'm

allowed to listen to my Inner Voice. I don't have
to ignore it; I can act by it. It's been a weird
shift. I'm much more attuned to it now. It's just
me, my Inner Voice. It's my desires, not like
fleeting desires, but my goals, my longings, and
now it's all just me. It's different now, and I can't
put my finger on it. I think about where I was
before Red Tent, and it's like I was in a room,
and my Inner Voice was around the room, but
now it's like we're doing life together, and there
are no walls anymore."

One of my mentors, Jenn, always reminds me to listen to
the 'first voice' (what she calls the Inner Voice). Our first
Voice might say, "Oh, I would love to do that," but our
second Voice (our Inner Critic) pipes in with, "You don't
need that. What a waste of time." She told me our second
Voice gets more air time because we don't cut it off. If we
can respond with, "Wait. Second voice, you interrupted.
First voice, what were you trying to say?" we can then tune
in to what our Inner Voice is trying to tell us without the
Inner Critic harping about why we can't have any joy in our
lives.

This Inner Voice can feel like a whole-body knowing or
instinct. You might feel a nudge, hear your Inner Voice
during meditations, journaling, or by feeling it in your body,
like your 'gut instinct.' You may feel it in different places in
your body depending on how you were taught to recognize
it: through your hearts, your guts, or in your heads. Perhaps
you get that feeling in the pit of your stomach.
Unfortunately, many people do not recognize their Inner
Voice at all. Let's dive into what your Inner Voice sounds
like for you and the different ways you might tune in to hear
it, feel it, and use it well.

YOUR INTUITION

Your Intuition is what I call the feeling when you have two or more options in front of you, and something inside tries to help guide you — others call this the gut instinct. I feel it in my gut, of 'yes' or 'no.' When you have different options and are both good independently, your Intuition can tip the scales one way or another. When we tune in to feel our Intuition, we can get a sense of our next step regardless of what everyone else says we should do. According to Einstein, "Intuition, not intellect, is the 'open sesame' of yourself." Allowing space for Intuition to be honored and not sidestepped for what may feel more logical can help us stand by our decisions from a place of strength.

It's hard to stand by your decisions when you aren't sure if you can trust your Intuition. I was taught early on that my Intuition and longings were temptations in disguise. Which is one reason I have found it hard to trust myself, because 'anything I want or yearn for is most likely bad and needs to be double-checked (by someone else) to make sure I'm choosing correctly.'

People give into or seek out temptation out of urge or addictions because it silences their Inner Critic temporarily, or feeds a surface desire. Giving into temptation is a bandaid and doesn't heal you at all. It usually does more harm than good. Listening to your Intuition and Spirit is a salve for your heart and treats the inner desires. Temptations are habits and pitfalls we make when we forget we are made with purpose and aren't honest about what we genuinely need: love, rest, peace, or understanding.

It's NOT your Intuition if it causes destructive harm to others or yourself. By discerning your Intuition, you can make healthier choices.

Your Intuition CAN tell you to leave a dangerous situation, and leaving may be destructive to a relationship or situation. Sometimes old habits, relationships, or toxic situations need to be destroyed or left behind for the healing of those in the situation. Your Inner Voice moves you towards the next right step to wisdom. If you feel cloudy, talk to friends or loved ones who are on a similar path or that you trust. Always take everything with a grain of salt *and* acknowledge what your body is saying too.

> You may feel your Inner Voice in your heart like Ayesha does: "My mom always told me to listen to my gut, but I could never sense my Intuition there. I always felt my Inner Voice in my heart, not necessarily that something was good or bad. I could feel the situation empathetically and know in my heart what the right decision was for me at that moment."

Our Intuition whispers the steps we long to take, even when we don't acknowledge them. Each time we listen, it gets easier to hear. Whether or not you can trust the Intuition depends on your relationship with trusting yourself. It can feel terrifying and/or transforming. If we don't ask our Inner Voice until it's pointing us toward life-altering choices, we wonder if we can trust it. Trust forms over time from small moments.

I encourage you to check in when it's the little things, where you think, "Oh, I don't care where we go out to eat or what E-book to read." You most likely do, but we've been trained not to care or speak up. As we grew up, we learned to ignore Intuition because our wishes weren't always welcomed or wanted. Internalizing this, we squash down our Inner Voice, and over time we forget how to listen.

> Arianna Huffington says, "Sometimes what your intuitive response signals is that you need more information. But our modern, hyper-connected world throws up roadblock after roadblock

between us and our Intuition. It can get buried under a groaning email inbox, the constant chirping of our smartphones, or our running from appointment to appointment, stressed and burned out. If our intuitive Voice had the same strength-of-signal bars our phones do, we'd often see that we're out of range of our wisdom."

To return to the range of our wisdom, we have to start listening to the still small Voice when it speaks up. Start small, like the choice of a blue pen or purple pen, to learn to listen for the Inner Voice when it speaks up for big decisions. With practice, you can hear it, trust it, and listen. The more you tune in and respond from that grounded place in your body where you can listen and take the next right step, the more you'll be able to trust yourself when situations or life feels out of control.

KNOWING

Intuition helps you figure out the following steps, and your Knowing helps you know when things are right or wrong where you are. I believe a Soul Song is placed in your heart when you are born. Your Soul Song is your Knowing that leads and guides you—the whisper of spirit echoing through your body, leading you closer to wholeness. For me, Knowing is when everything feels aligned, and the world stands still. I know I'm right where I need to be in the moment; I feel it in my soul. I am at peace with my choice when my Knowing resonates within me.

 For Bruna, it's when she doesn't look to anyone else for the answer, "For example, with conversations with my doctor, and they completely oversimplify what I just explained. And I say again, 'No. THIS is what's happening to my body.' That's my Knowing I don't even turn to see if my husband agrees...I know my body, and that's my Knowing."

Maybe your Knowing feels accessible with work but less accessible with relationships. An example of my Knowing is when I was becoming a mermaid. I knew I needed a name, and I came across the name "Harmony" in a book I was reading. I gasped, "Oh, that's my name!" It was this revelation inside where it felt as if a piece that was missing just clicked into place. I also call my Knowing "bone resonance." I can feel if something is right in the moment, almost like it's a whole-body exhale.

Can you remember when you felt your Knowing, where it felt like your entire body lit up? Maybe it's when you held your baby for the first time or when you put your feet in the ocean. If you don't recognize a time in the past, do something you know makes you smile or go to a place where you feel calm and rested. For me, this is going into the clearing by my house. As I walk the path in, I feel my body relax, my brain quiet, and I can figure out my next steps more easily.

The key here is figuring out how it feels in your body, so you can start tuning into it when you need it. If you are in a situation where you wonder what's going on, you can tune into your Knowing and ask, "What's happening here? What do I need to do next?" You'll be able to listen better to your Intuition when it comes up because you're in tune with your Knowing, and you know what to notice. We can't control everything, but we do have control over leading from our Inner Voice. Intuition and Knowing may feel the same for you, and that's okay. Every person is different. It's important to note that sometimes our feelings about a situation may be more subtle than others, so understanding the different ways it can feel is vital.

Obbie's Inner Voice shows up as a deep feeling of trust. "I'm very good at listening to my Inner Voice. I run all of my life on my Inner Voice. If I feel any sort of way about anything, I trust myself to know that there's a reason why and it's never failed me. I've been in tune and paid attention to it. I feel like a lot of people ignore their Intuition. They don't trust themselves, and so they question everything. I'm the opposite. I do trust myself, more than I should, maybe. I'm fond of my Inner Voice. She knows things. Sometimes more than I even do."

I like to surround myself with women like Obbie who listen to their Knowing. In a culture that teaches me to second guess and please everyone else first, it can be hard to quiet myself and know what is in my heart. Women like her remind me it's possible to listen even if it feels difficult. We can be encouraged by others who brave the unknown and step out to claim their sovereignty and Voice in their everyday lives.

Your Knowing might feel different. You might feel light, heavy, relaxed, joyful, or calm. You can start fine-tuning your life towards what resonates and lights you up by acknowledging and responding to your Knowing. Embrace it, grow into it, love it, and do what you need to do in this lifetime. You can choose to live authentically. Although this may feel daunting, it is worthwhile. Writer Glennon Doyle says, "Brave does not mean feeling afraid and doing it anyway. Brave means living from the inside out. Brave means, in every uncertain moment, turning inward, feeling for the Knowing, and speaking it out loud."

As you speak your Knowing out loud, people around you will shift because they will realize there's a different way to be. Even when no one else around you trusts themselves, it doesn't mean you can't. Permit yourself to be the first and lead from right where you are. When you do this, you become an example for others to trust their Knowing.

And that, my friend, is when the world starts to shift.

REPLAYS

Our Inner Voice pulls from our experience to protect us, and so sometimes your instincts can go into overdrive. One of the ways instincts come out is through replays. Replays are past events and memories that are repeating in your life. Elizabeth, a graphic designer and Tent lady says there's a chance for her to get it right anytime a replay happens.

Let's say you were codependent with a significant other, and you eventually broke up. Now, you are with a new partner, and you see the tendencies of codependency creeping in. Fear bubbles to the surface with worries of you breaking up soon. When replaying the past in your mind, you might unfairly anticipate what will happen because of the past.

But being in a replay situation doesn't mean it's going to happen the same way again. A replay, using the above example, might look like this:

Because your significant other was difficult to communicate with in the past, you questioned yourself and eventually broke up out of exhaustion. With your new partner, you find you're walking on eggshells and are hesitant to bring up new conversations, even though your new partner is much kinder and easier to be around than your previous relationship.

Instead of projecting your old learned fears and apprehensions and bringing unnecessary baggage into a new relationship, you can ask to have a sit-down conversation about how you both can navigate feeling safe and secure in this new relationship. You set guidelines, ask for more clarity around expectations of schedules, and plan weekly walks to catch up and talk about what is on both your minds, so you feel like you get time to connect one on one without feeling guilty for having time by yourself throughout the week.

If you can catch a replay in action, you can change your next steps with awareness. If you don't realize what's going on in your brain, you can't change anything because you don't recognize the pattern. When you see the replay happening and identify it in your mind, you can process in real-time what is happening instead of having echoes of your past emotions impact the new situation.

I want to encourage you to allow yourself to make mistakes. Everyone I know has made many mistakes getting to where they are now. Mistakes happen when you are challenging yourself, and that means you are growing! We can ask new questions when a replay shows up; here are some examples:

What are some ways I can bring joy into my life?
What would I like to do now, since I don't have this partner in my life?
How can I discuss a complex topic and still show my partner I care?"
This job didn't work out; what would be thrilling to try next?

When replays come up, create an inventory of your options. You can brainstorm new ways of interacting. Replays help you navigate in a new way so you can learn a lesson. If something is repeatedly happening with different people, the problem may not be with them; it might be an issue with you. Maybe you need to set better boundaries or find new friends. [1]

As you examine the story you have about past situations, keep an eye out for lessons you learned and good things that happened. It's easy to broad-brush paint a past situation that ended poorly as wholly bad, but maybe there were some joyous moments too. Replays can remind us we got through the past, both the good and the bad, and will get through whatever is in front of us. The more honest you are with yourself, the more you can move forward in a situation with a clear vision.

As your brain is processing in real-time, it's trying to move faster by matching the present to the past to see and anticipate what will happen next. If you have trauma in your background, if you have memories of being yelled at, ignored, or manipulated, these memories can impact how your body anticipates what happens next. As we talked about in the Creativity chapter, your Inner Critic is an imposter that uses shame as a weapon instead of treating the wounds of your heart. Your authentic Inner Voice is one of love, grace, and nurturing.

Trusting your Inner Voice and Spirit is a process of listening, and trust is the first step. Because once you know what you need, you can't unknow, and that in-between may feel terrifying as you trust, because you are choosing to listen to your Intuition over other peoples' opinions, maybe for the first time.

May you tune in to all the different ways your soul and body are trying to help and speak to you to show up as the fullest embodiment of who you were created to be and using your Voice for life, growth, and encouragement.

SCARY DANGEROUS VS. SCARY NEW

We know our gut instinct uses replays of our past to protect us. Our spidey sense lets us know something is wrong. "That guy is a creep, and you need to leave immediately." Trust your instincts AND understand that our body can't always differentiate between something harmful and scary vs. something new and scary.

I've learned in Tent that sometimes when we want to use a 'but,' we can use an 'and' instead. Just because it's scary doesn't mean it's the wrong thing. Roller coasters can be frightening and fun. Nerves and excitement get processed the same way in the body via adrenaline.[2]

When you challenge yourself in a new way, you can help your body identify what is scary AND could also be cool. You can question thoughts like, "I've never spoken in front of people before, and I'm going to die." Questioning your thoughts doesn't mean you won't still feel a little scared. It means you allow space for both sides to be heard instead of repressing the fearful feelings.

We can hold the duality of being nervous and choosing to move forward anyway.

We often run the gambit of "What if!?" questions in our worried state, but what would happen if we started asking, "What would it be like if...." instead? There's an anticipatory excitement we can see and acknowledge by considering how it makes us feel. We can notice how our body wants us to protect ourselves from scary-bad, even if a situation is scary-new. It might feel dumb when you realize your body is pulling up memories from middle school and making friends, but the layers run deep. They impact us whether we examine our Heart Wounds or not.

Listening to your Instincts helps you to know when you go into defense mode. In defense mode, we start putting up walls before anything terrible can happen. Our Instincts want to keep us safe, which can be unhealthy in pushing others away or not letting anyone in. Our instincts can range from wrapping us in a soothing bear hug or over-protective bubble wrap. One comforts, the other suffocates.

Your Instincts are trying to help, so take a step back and ask, "Is this a situation where I'm in trouble?" Maybe you are, and your Instincts are going to save you from something terrible. However, the situation may also be one where you need to take a deep breath and trust you are doing it for a reason, like the first time you lead a Red Tent, go on a first date, or ask for a raise. The most important thing you can do is honestly ask yourself, "Which kind of scary is this?" so you can make the choice that most aligns with your values.

SPEAKING YOUR INNER VOICE OUT LOUD

Words can speak life or death.[3] It's easy to remember to be kind to other people, but it's harder sometimes to have compassion for ourselves. We have to go against the grain to give ourselves as much patience as we give everyone else. Everyone else can take a break, but us taking one? *How dare we, right?* Our Inner Critic leaps at the opportunity to thwart us, yelling, "Woah, you haven't done enough to earn this yet. What do you think you are doing?"

There's a protective aspect of putting ourselves down before other people can; we think, "Oh if I can get to it before they do, I won't feel as bad." We focus on the negative things, but what if we got excited about ourselves before anyone else did? What if we switched it? What if we were our own hype man?

I got chalk markers to write encouragement on my mirrors, and I have friends who have favorite verses or quotes written on post-it notes around their house for them to see. What is the boost you need, and what is a way to give that to yourself, so when you walk out your front door, you are overflowing instead of desolate? Maybe this looks like sacred time, a workout, good food, jamming out to your favorite song, or journaling why you are worth taking care of today.

When you speak life, you are sowing seeds of goodness into the world. There is so much anger and divisive manipulation happening all around us. *The Social Dilemma* is a useful documentary about how technology impacts our relationships, cognitive thinking, and community. When we actively speak life and weave kindness and truth into our community, it brings us together.

Even if you aren't speaking aloud, the energy you walk

into a room with says more than you think. When someone walks into a room, and it lights up, the place is better for them being in it. You may notice if someone is bringing a dark cloud of angst and fury with them. There's a difference between being Eeyore and being toxic and harmful. You don't have to have the best-day-ever-attitude every day, but it is a worthwhile experiment to ask what kind of energy you bring to the table on your average day.

We can have a bad day and be able to face the problems head-on without lashing out at everyone around us. We can be calm in the midst of a storm or just getting by. All of these are okay. We aren't machines, and our emotions aren't the same every day. If we can remember how our cycles impact our hormones and bodies, we can notice how we show up.

Emotional awareness gives us the ability to shift to what would feel most supportive to ourselves and others at the moment. Some people believe no one notices when they walk into a room, but they keep the waters calm. They bring everyone together and keep the energy smooth. Tune in during this next week to see your energy tendency when you walk into the room.[4]

There's so much hurt and woundedness already going around; we don't need to add to it. Misery makes company, and sharing in suffering may feel like the only path to join for some people. Suffering is a part of life. That said, we don't have to heap additional despair on top of ourselves to *prove* we can have joy.[5] You don't have to say how much you suffered when explaining why you have joy now.

What does it look like to enjoy life and not make it harder than it already is? Sometimes we might think, *oh my gosh, this is impossible*. But is it, though? Or are you putting the word impossible on it? What are the words you are using for a situation? Because if you keep repeating to yourself, "This sucks, this sucks, this sucks," you'll keep replaying it on your brain, and that's the only thing you'll see.

If you are in a broken situation, being honest about its reality can reveal your options. Figuring out tangible steps can help keep you from spiraling. As scary as it may feel to be honest about how bad it is, it'll help show you what is under your purview of control. Hopelessness can easily pull you under, so try to find a community of those in a similar boat to be around people you can be honest with and understand the difficult path you are on. Not only are there support groups for almost anything, but online forums can be a lifeline when you don't know anyone personally you can go to for help.

Sometimes we also need to speak up for others. There's a quote about speaking for those who have no voice, but everyone has a voice. Some voices are oppressed and silenced. Whose Voice are you lending yours to? Who are you advocating for or encouraging? We discussed speaking life or death over ourselves, but what about through an idea? An organization? A community?

Are you speaking up to manipulative people? To underhanded comments? To stop the water cooler talk about a coworker? Your Voice has weight, even if you don't realize it. Where are places you can practice using it? Give yourself some credit: If your Voice can be a wrecking ball to your self-esteem, can you imagine the power it has when put to good?

What is your good?

What are you speaking life into?

QUESTIONS FOR FURTHER DISCOVERY:

What does your Knowing, Inner Voice, or Instincts feel like to you?

How do you use your Voice?

When was a time you listening to your Inner Voice or Knowing? What happened? What about a time when you didn't listen? What happened?

BOOK RECOMMENDATIONS:

A Year of Yes by Shonda Rhimes
Raise Your Voice: Why We Stay Silent and How to Speak Up by Kathy Khang
Daring Greatly by Brene Brown

Voice Red Tent

Five minutes before the Tent Begins:
Leader: Lovelies, please put your phones on silent or off, grab your water, snacks, journal, and token and join me in the circle.

Opening:
Leader: Before we begin, I would like to state that this is a safe space. In order to make it so, there needs to be agreement around keeping what is said in circle, in the circle. I'm asking you all to agree to only speak of your own experiences, and only give advice when asked. We will be talking about deeply personal things in the Red Tent. A gentle reminder that we can disagree and still accept each other. Can I have a show of hands for everyone willing to keep this space confidential, for themselves and everyone here tonight?

Shakeout and Grounded Breathing:
Leader: Let us take a minute to stand up, shake out any worries, or frustration from your day. Twist your body, shake your booty, kick your legs, jump up and down. Audibly make sounds while relaxing your jaw. Stretch, or move in a way that feels supportive.

Please have a seat in this circle, and let's do some ground breathing. You can close your eyes, start to relax your shoulders. You can roll your neck from side to side, rest your hands on your stomach, knees, or the ground, whatever is most comfortable for you. Start breathing in from your belly. Take a deep breath. As you exhale, release anything that came before tonight that is on your mind.

Breathe in again, releasing anything to come in the future. Keep breathing, focusing on the sounds around you,

the breath of other women, and your heartbeat. As you release your breath, feel your body settling into this space. In this moment, here with us. You are safe. You are loved. We are glad you are here with us.

Call in:

Leader: We are gathered in our Red Tent, as women, as daughters, as mothers, as workers and dreamers. We come here to speak our heart's desires, our mind's thoughts, and share the song of our souls. We see with our eyes, hear with our ears, and will hum along in our hearts. May this space be open, sacred, and grounded for us here tonight. Let us hold hands as we travel deeper together, learning to better love ourselves, each other, and the world.

Gender Neutral Option:

We are gathered in our Red Tent Tent as humans, as explorers, as workers and dreamers. We come here to speak our heart's desires, our mind's thoughts, and share the song of our souls. We see with our eyes, hear with our ears, and will hum along in our hearts. May this space be open, sacred, and grounded for us here tonight. Let us hold hands as we travel deeper together, learning to better love ourselves, each other, and the world.

Song: Call Down a Blessing

Leader: Close your eyes and think of what you want from this night and this week. It might be friendship, laughter, wisdom. We'll pass the bowl around one person at a time, and you'll say your blessing request, we'll sing the song with your word inside of it, and then after we sing over you, pass the bowl to the next woman. She'll share her

blessing word, and we'll sing a blessing over her until we reach the end of the circle.

Call down a blessing x3, Call down, ____before you, ____behind you, ____Within you, and around you
Repeat for each person in the group, end with three call downs.

15: 1st Circle:

Leader: When speaking, please use the talking light, and when you finish, please say "I have spoken," so we know you have completed your thought. You can react with hand snaps, hand on your heart, and facial expressions. Please speak only of your own story, and don't give any advice unless asked.

For our first circle, please share your name, pronouns, your intention for tonight, and your relationship with your Inner Voice.

30: Quote and Response: *Depending on the size of your group, you can have a few people share, or have people share for one minute.*

Leader: I'll share the quote below and then you can share your response of how it resonates.

Author Glennon Doyle says in her book *Untamed*, "I will not stay, not ever again, in a room or conversation or relationship or institution that requires me to abandon myself. When my body tells me the truth, I'll believe it. I trust myself now, so I will no longer suffer voluntarily or silently for long."

40: Activity 1:
Listening to your Intuition

When are times where you aligned your behavior to your Intuition or Inner Voice, and it benefited you? Take 60 seconds to remember how that felt in your body.

How did you know? How did it feel?

(Pause)

Learning to trust yourself takes time, but when we can remember how it feels in our body we can recall it when we face a new problem.

Was there a time you didn't listen to your Inner Voice and you knew you should have?

(Pause)

If your Intuition tells you one thing, and your Inner Critic flares up, you can say, "Thank you, but you interrupted", and tune back into what your Intuition was trying to say. Write down a few times you've listened to your Intuition and what it felt like.

If there is time, you can go around the circle and have each person share what their intuition feels like.

1:00: Womanhood story:

Leader: Womanhood stories are a core part of Red Tent, sharing our stories is a brave act. Sometimes they are joy filled, sad, frustrating, or a mix of all of it. The story may include periods, sex, birth, or any part of the woman and human experience. ___ has offered to share her story tonight. ___ the floor is yours.

*See the appendix of the book for reaching out to your women to see who would like to share before the tent day.

After her story:

Leader: Thank you ___ for sharing your story. Is there anything you need from us? Hug, encouragement, a listening ear during break?

*If they say yes, do what you can to fulfill that need if possible.

1:10: Soul Care Time:

Leader: Now is our soul care time. This is 20 minutes to stretch, nap, chat, get food, go to the restroom. We do ask that you don't use this time to be on your phone. I'll give us a five-minute heads up to tent, and a one minute come to circle heads up.

1:30: Activity Two: Speaking the Truth *Depending on the size of the group you can do this in pairs or go around the circle. If in a circle Person B becomes Person A as they turn to their left with a new partner.*

Sometimes the things we want or want to say and the way we say things are two different things. It can get lost in translation, or we expect others to understand without us saying what we need. We say we're fine when we're not. We're going to listen to how we are actually feeling and try asking for what we need. We're going to do something that you can't always do in the moment, but you can tonight.

Pull out your journals and write, I feel _____ because _____, and I need _____.

You can write multiple versions of this if you would like.

Choose one sentence you feel comfortable speaking aloud.

Find a pair, and together you will go through the questions below asking how you are really feeling. I'll read through the questions and responses and then you can try it out with each other.

Take your time, this is a confidential and brave space to explore your truth.

Person A: How are you?

B: I'm fine.

A: How are you really feeling?

B: I feel _____ because _____, and I need _____.

A: I hear you. Thank you for sharing that with me. Would you like a hug, or anything else?

B: *Can respond accordingly to that question for their needs. Switch partners*

1:45: Circle

How was the experience of asking for what you needed?

2:Closer *Grab your red thread (yarn) and make sure scissors are within reach.*

Leader: Red thread represents our connection to the women around us and those who have come before us. You will take your red yarn and wrap it around your wrist. You can wrap as many times as you want, as you recite your matriarchal spiritual lineage. Your lineage are the women and people who have influenced and loved you.

They don't have to be biologically related, you can claim or not claim anyone you would like. You can say your name, mother of (any children), daughter of x, daughter of y, daughter of daughters, daughter of whatever resonates (Eve, Spirit, the moon, etc). You can also say descendent instead, or daughter of those who _____ instead of names.

When you have finished wrapping, pass the thread to the next person until it has gone all the way around the circle.

You can start the process and do your lineage and wrap and then pass it to the person on your right.

After the Red Thread has come back to you.

Leader: As we are connected, let us sing our song, we'll sing it three times, it goes flow, ebb, weavers, thread, weavers, thread, spiders, web. Sing it with me:

Song: We are the flow we are the ebb,
We are the weavers we are the thread,

We are the weavers we are the thread,
we are the spiders we are the web.
x3

Leader, pick up the scissors, and cut your thread, and as you explain the below, you can have the person to the left tie your thread.

Leader: When cutting the thread to tie bracelets, share your favorite moment and a takeaway. Have the lady to your left tie your yarn, twice in a square knot, and one slip knot, and this way, your thread will not come undone. After you have spoken, pass the scissors to the right, and the next person can go.

After the scissors make their way back to you and everyone has tied their thread, you can share the invitation below. Feel free to hold hands if you'd like.

Invitation to curiosity
   Leader: This month, *when possible,* when you need or want something, ask for it. Speak up. Use your voice when needed. When you realize you are about to say I don't know, pause for a moment check In. See how you actually are doing, and respond.
   Thank you for being a part of tonight's Red Tent. You are all a treasure, and I'm glad you are here. Our Red Tent is now closed.

VALUES

Growing up in the 2000's evangelical church meant I was madly in love with God, wore my True Love Waits ring all of the time, and took any inclination anyone was disappointed in me straight to my core. I found my value in doing what was expected of me: from the church, teachers, and family, and aligned my values as such. I trotted along seamlessly, earning A's and B's and performing my heart out in the dance team, theatre, and show choir. I thought I would go to college, get married, have children, and live happily ever after.

Sometimes things go as planned.

Sometimes they don't.

Jer and I met each other freshman year of college as he strolled into my friend's dorm room. I thought he was handsome and kind, and he thought I was cute. Hilariously enough, he had come to hit on my friend, and I was in the room complaining about a current boyfriend. Throughout the semester, we bumped into each other (both forgetting each other's name so couldn't find one another on Facebook. I thought his name was Kyle...it was not). We were cast together for the spring show of Romeo and Juliet, I was Juliet, and he was Paris.[1]

We became casual acquaintances as we were on and off dating other people but saw each other in theatre, and our circles mixed as we went to the same church and Bible study, so I knew our values were aligned. Later during the summer, we started texting and flirting more, and we set a date for when we would meet back at college and see if our feelings were also real in person.

He showed up at my dorm room with a half-pound bag of gummy bears and *Settlers of Catan*.[2] I melted. I wanted to marry him on the spot and have all of his babies.[3]

Mom and Dad drove up the following weekend to bring me a few things I had forgotten at home. I complained to my mom that my arm was hurting. I was pretty active, and I thought nothing of it, just a sore muscle, but she felt like something was off and took me to the hospital when I kept complaining. Because I was sick on and off throughout high school, going to the hospital felt like no big deal, but it turned out it was a big deal. I had a blood clot in my left arm —a side effect of the Estrogen birth control I was taking at the time.

I was prescribed shots of a fast-acting blood thinner called Lovenox to treat the clot. As I stayed overnight, the nurse gave me my first dose, and instead of going into my fat cells, she put it into my ab muscle, where the medicine burned for hours.

The next day the doctor told me that if I were ever to become pregnant, I would have to take daily injections of Lovenox,[4] and my pregnancy would be high risk. As much as modern medicine has progressed, being pregnant is risky for all women, with one in four pregnancies ending in miscarriage. I was terrified about my risk being significantly higher after seeing my cousin lose her daughter via a miscarriage. I decided I would do whatever I had to avoid the pain of both Lovenox and the profound loss of a miscarriage.

Jer drove and surprised me in the hospital later that morning, and I realized he fulfilled my fairy tale romance dreams. (Here I had on a blue backless gown, and between the Lovenox and the pregnancy-risk news, I was in distress. Doesn't the damsel in distress always wear a beautiful gown? *I nailed it!*)

We had a whirlwind relationship; were promised a month later, and another month after we were engaged. We set a date nine months later to be married before the start of our Junior year. We planned to have a few kids in a few years, when it would be less risky.

We were as safe as we could be and explored various non-hormonal birth control and low-hormone options. I had Paragard placed, an IUD that made cramps worse, although the 99% safe-odds helped me sleep at night. As each month's cycle drew closer, the panic rose to my chest as I feared whether or not it worked. Ectopic pregnancies (a high risk caused by IUD pregnancies) were an entirely separate nightmare I also didn't want to experience.

I know many people get pregnant even while on birth control, so I knew it was possible every month despite our best safety measures. I would usually message a few of my closest friends and wish them a Happy 'National Aj's Not Pregnant Day' as relief flooded my body when I got my period each month. It was the easiest way I knew how to make a light-hearted joke out of something I dreaded each month.

Other women whose infertility is a constant struggle also send texts, but these are with tears of grief instead of relief. I've found the hyper-awareness around being able to (or not able to) have children leads to many of us being frustrated with and hating our bodies, wondering, "why me."

The things we value can drastically impact our experience of a moment, whether seeing blood or taking a pregnancy test, but we might be more alike than we think at the same time with the depths of the emotions we feel.

After college, Jer decided to enlist in the Air Force, and our first base was Hawaii which was astounding and beautiful. I was busy working as a mermaid and didn't want to be pregnant as we enjoyed our time on the island—I also needed to fit into my tail to work. At 23, we decided to check back in at 25 on whether or not we wanted children. By this time, we'd been married for five years, so the baby questions and unsolicited advice kept pouring in.

When sharing the danger of being pregnant for me with a close family member, she asked, "Isn't it worth the risk?" I felt rejected, with her being so willing to gamble my life on a hypothetical child.[5] Once a woman (without asking) placed her hands on my lower stomach and started praying for God to grant us a child in my womb. I have never interrupted someone so quickly in my life. We faced constant pressure from people wondering why we didn't have children yet. It felt exhausting to have to defend our choice not to have any children now or maybe ever.

When we turned 25, we received news that we were about to move to Germany. All the travel possibilities had us excited. We chose to use our extra money and time traveling through Europe. After all, we could always explore having a baby or adopting after we returned to the US. So we decided to check back in at 27.

I remember the day our 27-year-old Are-The-Risks-Low-Enough-Yet-For-A-Baby chat day happened. It was a warm spring day, and Jer and I sat around the fire pit in the backyard in our house in Germany. We talked about our dreams, traveling, and kids. We had made friends with and without babies and saw how children impacted their lives from an outside perspective.

Weighing all of the stories and possibilities in my mind

while sitting around that fire, Jer asked me a question I will never forget. "We keep putting off kids for two years and two years. Next time we chat, we'll be 29. Do we even want kids? Are we just continually bringing this up because it's what we think we are supposed to do?"

The question completely took me off guard.

In quiet shock, I whispered, "Are we allowed not to have children?"

I hadn't thought about that possibility at all. More often than not, I felt grateful we didn't have kids in that specific season. Looking back at our time in Hawaii and Germany, we realized how much we loved our lives and didn't want them to change, even for cute, tiny humans. We decided against having any children, and if we changed our minds, we could adopt. At that moment, I shifted from placing my value in living the life others thought I should to prioritizing the values and life choices Jer, and I wanted to lead.

Shortly after our backyard conversation, I saw a meme on Facebook and shared it. It said, "People having babies, and I'm like, what country am I going to next?" I shared it because it was precisely our thought process at the time of, "No time for having babies right now, we have Europe to see!"

To say my friends and family overreacted is an understatement.

Instead of seeing this as a statement that reflected my values and choices, people defended their values and preferences. Some wrote strongly-worded paragraphs about how they could travel with kids and didn't understand why the post said you couldn't have kids and travel simultaneously. (Which was not what the post said).

Others listed their next travel spots with excitement. Some agreed with the post's intention and said they brought their kids to travel, and it was more expensive, but it was worth seeing the world through their eyes. A few parents also chimed in that it's doable, but it is for sure easier and cheaper to explore the world without little kids. Other moms said they chose their kids and would travel later in life and were happy with their choice.

I thought there was room for all of it because children, life, and travel are deeply personal.

One friend of a friend who saw the post said I was a child-hating bitch who should never have children and other lovely things. I didn't know how to respond because I love being around and working with other people's children; I just didn't want any of my own. Thankfully, other friends let her know she was out of line, so I didn't have to respond. I eventually took the post down because everyone was playing defense and offense in the comment section and slamming others for their personal choices.

I wondered if I was crazy for valuing traveling and a life of just Jer and I over having kids. I started being quieter about our choice after this incident because if I brought up not having children (without explaining why), people began listing all the reasons I was wrong.

After realizing we wouldn't have any bio children, I looked into getting my tubes tied or getting a hysterectomy when I was 27. Still, the system fought me tooth and nail, not to mention I wasn't a fan of the early menopause that would come from a total hysterectomy.[6]

Four years later, when we moved to Texas, I heard about Bilateral Salpingectomies, a procedure where the tubes are cut out entirely instead of seared together. There were fewer risks than some of the other options available. The more I researched, the more I thought this was the best option for me, mainly since I would still cycle and keep all of my hormones. Waking up from my surgery was one of the top three best moments of my life. After checking to ensure there weren't complications, I asked if the surgery was successful, and they said "yes."

There's a moment in Disney's *Aladdin* where Genie's bracers break off, essentially freeing him to live his best genie life. That scene was all I could think about as I whispered through sobs, "I'm free. I'm free."

My brain was silent, and the fear was gone for the first time in twelve years since I had first found out the dangers. When I shared about my surgery, I had support from some, while others were stunned or felt betrayed by my choice. I feel like I'm living a life aligned with my values.

Flourishing, value-aligned lives can look like six kids, adopted children, solo traveling, focusing on a career you love, having no kids, or other countless possibilities. We live richer lives when we recognize we're all needed in the vast variety of our world and that each life is unique and valuable.

SHIFTING VALUES

If this is true, why do we get defensive when people hold different values than we do?

Our values and the choices we make (to honor them or not) can cause us to react negatively to others choosing different paths. Because we can build our structure of self-worth around our values, if others choose differently, it can feel like an attack on our choices even if it isn't. What other people choose is what is right for them in that moment, which may align with your values or not. As long as others' values are not actively harming other people, it is okay to believe or feel differently with one another.

Many of us learn a specific set of values is most important, and anything that veers off is wrong, meaning anyone who doesn't hold the same values as you can be dismissed as lesser or not as significant.

Ranking lives based on perceived value is supremacy at its core. Superiority creates a hierarchy placing the weight on one way of living, which is not ethical or valuable for our society. If your values require valuing some lives over others or controlling others' bodies, consider that they may not be values worth keeping, as they were born out of fear, power, and greed. We can see value ranking displayed via capitalism, white supremacy, and nationalism. All of these have a substantial impact on the lives of those who are deemed 'inferior.' Take note of where you have ranked yourself or others as more or less valuable in your social hierarchy, and see what may need to shift values-wise.

Values shift over time, which is normal because humans change.

What are your values?
What values do you hold close, and what values are more flexible for you?

There may be values you learned growing up that don't resonate anymore, and setting these aside can be incredibly difficult. Our values are often deeply connected to morals. So as our values shift, they can get tangled up in a "is this right or is this wrong" conversation. For me, the decision about not having babies isn't just "Do I want this?" "Do I value this? It's "is it moral and allowable for me to NOT want this?"

Being the best, faith, money, kindness, high-paying job, education, rest, growth, excitement, love, peace — these are all values. Each has something unique they bring to the table. We must examine the values we carry to see if they are healthy for our souls and lives.

Take a sheet of paper and lay out your values. Make a list of the ideas or standards you hold in your life.

When mulling over her values, DeLandrea shares, "My values are honesty, integrity, loyalty, and respect. I also value contentment. For the longest time, I thought I had to be happy, so it was always extremes, but sometimes this peace comes from being content. So I value the stillness of that sometimes. I also value laughter; I love laughing, I love making people laugh."

You may notice some values you wrote down don't resonate anymore or feel off as you write. Put a note by them to revisit them and wonder why. Noticing these small shifts allows you to take a step back and see what you still hold dear.

What brings you joy and enriches your life?
   What no longer serves you?

Think of this as Marie-Kondo-decluttering-vibes for your heart. Set aside what no longer belongs in your life. Consider how to focus more deeply on what resonates with you and helps you flourish. If you feel exhausted reading your values list, create a new one. While writing your new list, tune into your inner voice and ask, "What are my true values?" You might just be surprised at what comes up.

REMEMBERING YOUR VALUE

It can be hard to remember your worth in a world that tells you that your value comes from what you do, what you buy, and who you know. Our instinct as humans is to assess situations and judge how safe they are, so it should come as no surprise when we extend these assessments to others and evaluate how we stack up against them. Comparing ourselves can result in being overly proud or believing you are trash. Either way, the comparison game is not the best judge of your worth.

 Elissa struggles with this and says, "I can't say with certainty that I find value in myself every day. When titles and roles are boxed and stripped away, it becomes challenging to answer. I'd like to say that I have value because I'm a person; I'm living and breathing. I'm here. I place a lot of value on that answer. I've also started applying the idea of legacy to my value. In 100 years, will my children's children remember my name? Maybe not. But if I've taught someone else to be compassionate, if I've taught somebody else to be true to who they are, that is a value—a legacy long after I'm gone. Someone will have that. Maybe it's a letter to a friend or an email I wrote. Something small but tangible. In the end, we all have a value that we'll leave behind in that way."

A big part of my journey from being driven by the world's opinion to choosing to honor what I value has been learning about *Imago Dei*. This idea that all humans are made in the image of God directly challenges the deeply rooted hierarchy that allows supremacy to thrive. Embracing the fact that I am made in the Image of God, with or without having babies, helped me relax and remember that we are all loved. We're all here for a purpose and are not a mistake.

Remember, you have value simply because you are here.

When we view the world from a use-or-be-used perspective, it creates transactional relationships. We fall into the trap of using other people as boundary markers, believing, "Oh, I'm good because they like me." or "They called me, so they value me."

. . .

But what happens when other people don't?
   When we don't get the feedback, we desire from others?
   Does this mean our value becomes nothing?

> Jill relates to this on her faith journey, "There was always a measure of shame I felt for things. I'll be honest; I hated myself. I wasn't truly connected to my values grounded in my past faith, so I felt conflicted all the time. I had a crisis of identity. Moving forward in my new faith journey, I've noticed I'm easier on myself. I'm easier on others, and I'm very much less judgemental. I'm not constantly at war or in conflict. So when I think of my value, now I'm worthy of that love. And so are others. I feel like my values made a positive shift, and now my spirit is nurtured."

If you let other people define your worth, it can be as dangerous as a riptide. You think it'll be fine, but if you give yourself up to the tides of changing opinions, it will take you under at one point or another. We see this in teens and the rise in depression and anxiety in society with the online highlight reels and competition for likes and shares. The popularity game takes us out of our lives and into our fear. Fear is not a productive place to create our values. Fear is biased, scared, and creates manipulative values that don't serve our whole flourishing lives.

Comparison-based value often leads to feeling unworthy.

> Writer and dream worker Toko-pa Turner writes how we can reclaim our worthiness through belonging. "The habit of unworthiness

is a kind of splitting-off, causing us to show up only partially for life; worthiness is felt in direct proportion to our ability to live an integrated life. Rather than outcasting the parts of ourselves which were once rejected, we work to reclaim those parts of ourselves that are afraid of being seen, hurt, or left behind. We allow and include them, moment by moment, strengthening our capacity for inclusion for belonging. It is the practice of bringing the fullness of our presence to a moment, whether it's filled with rage or an upwelling of sadness, to say, 'This too belongs.'"[7]

When we get to the center point of knowing who we are, we can create space for ourselves and others to belong. We can choose from a more grounded place because our value is no longer up for discussion. Sometimes having a place where you can relax and don't feel like you have to be 'on' can allow you to explore the feelings you have wrapped around your worth.

 Lindsay shares, "After every tent, I felt like I meet more of myself. From there, I live my next steps. I decide each step as a more embodied me, with my confidence, self-esteem, and knowing. I didn't realize I questioned all of these so deeply before. It's almost like you don't notice you live with question marks around who you are. Now, each day I walk in my Knowing. It's a whole new dynamic of language and getting to dissect patterns that are not healthy or helpful for friendships. I'm not moving forward negatively because I'm moving forward in a positive productive-for-my-soul way now. Whereas before, I was so worried to share about things I loved, but now I'm not so much anymore."

When we remember we each are Spirit-breathed, and our full humanity deserves dignity, respect, and kindness, we can take our value out of the debate arena and use our authentic core values to make our decisions.

THE VALUE OF POSSIBILITIES

Sometimes you have to choose between two things you value, like your health or your way of living.

In no small words:
This
Can
Be
Excruciating.

Because no matter what you choose, there will be loss and grief.

 Jill feels this pull as a neurodivergent woman and speaks about masking, or 'acting normal' for others,"Sometimes we (neurodivergent people) wear a mask because it helps us understand what normal is, but in the process, we're ignoring our own needs, our personalities. It's very exhausting. I'm learning step by step how to stop. I'm tired of making other people comfortable. Making other people comfortable is one of the most exhausting things someone can do, and eventually, we lose ourselves and become ashamed of who we are. Eventually, we have to say, enough's enough."

Regret can weigh you down over past choices, all while shadow-coloring the future. A future choice can fill you with so much anxiety; all you need to add to make diamonds from the pressure you are putting on yourself is coal.

The way I handle this and the choices I've made is by using possibility threads.[8]

Each time you make a decision, the world shifts a little bit, and somewhere in a piece of the universe, the world and your story keep going down the other path, the one you didn't follow. Your 'life thread' splits, and another possibility thread is started. Your life and your current choices are all in the 'life thread' you are currently living.

I know this to be true because we are all threads in the giant tapestry of our world. Our threads interlace with others, adding bits of color and movement. I imagine kismet and fate weaving with Red Thread to bring people together and making moments of synchronicity. Sometimes we are woven tight with someone for a while, and then our threads fray or come apart. You often hear people say, don't look back. Keep moving forward. When making big decisions, I know it's hard not to look back and wonder, 'what if?'

In my case, Jer's decision to enlist in the Air Force had us moving around the globe for the last nine years. I don't regret our choice, but we have missed weddings, funerals, Christmases, and births. Friendships have also melted into the past because of it. This life we are leading right now represents one of the many possible threads created by our choices.

On days when I'm melancholic about not being present at an event, I imagine one of my possibility threads, specifically the one where Jer and I stayed in Iowa. I'm working at a camp somewhere as a program director, and Jer joined the Air Guard. In this thread, we adopted children and maybe even have chickens. I can see in the thread we're happy. We were able to go to everything and be with family more often. Simply knowing somewhere in an alternate universe that story plays out is enough for me.

Understanding the path we're on now is the only one I can make decisions about helps me live fully and show up well right where I am. I guilt-trip myself less for not being able to be everywhere all of the time and trust that what I can do is enough.[9]

There are possibility threads where Jer and I joined the Peace Corps and another where I have red hair, tattooed sleeves, and work at a hostel I fell in love with in South Africa.

A different thread has one where we risked it and had biological children, which splits off into even more possibilities.

There are also threads where I made a choice that didn't honor my values, with a job or friendship, and I feel sheer relief I made the best decision in my current life. The idea of knowing these threads exist is so when I wonder about those choices; I can 'check' in with that thread and see it's being 'lived' out. It's happening somewhere else, on an alternate timeline. This imagining allows me to relax, knowing that at this moment, the divine plan has me here for a reason: to learn something, help someone, and be a part of the community where I am. I'm on the right thread because I'm on *my* thread.

It can feel sticky when you see others on their threads, doing something that may look like one of your past possibility threads, but it's vital to allow other people's lives to be about their choices and values. Otherwise, we risk getting triggered and harming others while trying to defend our choices, much like the Facebook debacle.

 Mary-Grace does her best to remember to keep her eyes on her path, "I think everyone has their unique path, and I don't think those paths need to be the same. It's something I work hard on, how there's not a blanket way to be. Regardless of where you are from a faith standpoint, it's necessary to remember everyone is different. Regardless of what you believe, you deserve to be safe. You deserve an open door of possibilities. You deserve to have a connection with other people, and building tolerance and curiosity for other paths allows us to live and love well."

The important thing is not to be stuck in the past or on a possibility thread. This tool allows you to release dreams where the timing was wrong, or you made a hard choice, or feel regret.

It's not a matter of wishing things were different because we make the choices we make for a reason. Maybe our excuses were flimsy, but we have new chances today to do something differently. Minor two-degree shifts over time can have a dramatic impact. If you want to have children but can't have biological children, maybe fostering or adopting is right for you. Or, if you can't commit to that, you could help sponsor another family's adoption or host a foreign exchange student.

Check your possibility threads for dreams in your heart and see if there might be a way you can weave them into your future. You can also look at your current life thread to see where your values have shown up. What have you chosen time after time? When it came down to the moment to make a decision, what did you choose? Let that inform your future choices.

 For Taylor, she saw the choices she made previously weren't the healthiest of her life. "I wanted to be the person who showed up for everybody, and that meant I never showed up for myself. I kept my promise to my family or friends, but it was just at the expense of a slew of broken promises to myself. It felt like I could never progress on my own goals and growth because I had already given away all I had to other people.

Once I started to listen to my inner voice and treat her like she was my friend and not a weirdo who was trying to trick me all the time, I noticed a difference. It elevated the value I put into a promise, and I commit to way less now. Occasionally I feel guilty about it, but most of the time, I don't. I was canceling all the time, and breaking promises left and right. When you say yes to everything, something has to be let go. I'm done letting me be the first thing I abandon."

Another way to make decisions is to tune into your intuition.

 Author Lisa Lister talks about making decisions from a deeper place, "We place so many of our decisions in a thought system outside ourselves- and there are times when that's necessary-but when you focus on how it feels, you worry less about what you should be doing and you are led into behaviours that are coming from a more authentic place instead. You're led by your inner knowing. Your gut. Your fire. This is a practice. I repeat, this is a practice."[10]

Your life thread also continues by pulling in a future possibility thread. Have you ever stepped back and looked at what you could choose to do next? Go back to school, change jobs, start a new relationship, read a book, go to a new group, travel. Your future threads are endless. You can narrow them down by looking at your values and what you need next in your life, and this is how your current thread moves forward.

Weaving, choosing, moving. Loving, exploring, discovering.

Our life is a constant dance through choices, values, boundaries, and interactions with others doing the same dance. If we can remember this, how we're all trying to discern the best thread we can live, maybe we can give ourselves and each other a bit more grace.

I hope you remember your past possibility threads can be givers of grace when looking at your history. Remember, you have many possibility threads shimmering ahead of you. May your values guide and lead you.

QUESTIONS FOR FURTHER DISCOVERY:

What are the values you hold close to your heart right now? Are they different or similar to the ones you had growing up?

Do you value yourself? How does this show up in your life?

How do you prioritize your values when making decisions? If you don't, how would prioritizing your values change your decision-making?

BOOK RECOMMENDATIONS:

Falling Upward by Father Richard Rohr
Better than Before by Gretchen Rubin
Essentialism by Greg McKoewen

Value & Values Red Tent

Five minutes before the Tent Begins:

Leader: Lovelies, please put your phones on silent or off, grab your water, snacks, journal, and token and join me in the circle.

Opening:

Leader: Before we begin, I would like to state that this is a safe space. In order to make it so, there needs to be agreement around keeping what is said in circle, in the circle. I'm asking you all to agree to only speak of your own experiences, and only give advice when asked. We will be talking about deeply personal things in the Red Tent. A gentle reminder that we can disagree and still accept each other. Can I have a show of hands for everyone willing to keep this space confidential, for themselves and everyone here tonight?

Shakeout and Grounded Breathing:

Leader: Let us take a minute to stand up, shake out any worries, or frustration from your day. Twist your body, shake your booty, kick your legs, jump up and down. Audibly make sounds while relaxing your jaw. Stretch, or move in a way that feels supportive.

Please have a seat in this circle, and let's do some ground breathing. You can close your eyes, start to relax your shoulders. You can roll your neck from side to side, rest your hands on your stomach, knees, or the ground, whatever is most comfortable for you. Start breathing in from your belly. Take a deep breath. As you exhale, release anything that came before tonight that is on your mind.

Breathe in again, releasing anything to come in the future. Keep breathing, focusing on the sounds around you,

the breath of other women, and your heartbeat. As you release your breath, feel your body settling into this space. In this moment, here with us. You are safe. You are loved. We are glad you are here with us.

Call in:

Leader: We are gathered in our Red Tent, as women, as daughters, as mothers, as workers and dreamers. We come here to speak our heart's desires, our mind's thoughts, and share the song of our souls. We see with our eyes, hear with our ears, and will hum along in our hearts. May this space be open, sacred, and grounded for us here tonight. Let us hold hands as we travel deeper together, learning to better love ourselves, each other, and the world.

Gender Neutral Option:

We are gathered in our Red Tent Tent as humans, as explorers, as workers and dreamers. We come here to speak our heart's desires, our mind's thoughts, and share the song of our souls. We see with our eyes, hear with our ears, and will hum along in our hearts. May this space be open, sacred, and grounded for us here tonight. Let us hold hands as we travel deeper together, learning to better love ourselves, each other, and the world.

Song:

Leader: Close your eyes and think of what you want from this night and this week. It might be friendship, laughter, wisdom. We'll pass the bowl around one person at a time, and you'll say your blessing request, we'll sing the song with your word inside of it, and then after we sing over you, pass the bowl to the next woman. She'll share her blessing word, and we'll sing a blessing over her until we reach the end of the circle.

Call down a blessing x3, Call down, _____before you, _____behind you, _____Within you, and around you
Repeat for each person in the group, end with three call downs.

15: 1st Circle:

Leader: When speaking, please use the talking light, and when you finish, please say "I have spoken," so we know you have completed your thought. You can react with hand snaps, hand on your heart, and facial expressions. Please speak only of your own story, and don't give any advice unless asked.

For our first circle, what is your name, pronouns, and your intention for tonight? What comes up for you with the words value and values?

30: Quote and Response:

Leader: I'll share this quote and you can share how it makes you feel in a few words.

There is a voice inside of you, that whispers all day long. I feel that this is right for me. I know that this is wrong. No teacher, preacher, parent, friend or wise man can decide. What's right for you, just listen to the voice that speaks inside." —Shel Silverstein[11]

45: Activity 1: Value Mapping

Leader: Please grab your journal. We are going to map out of values both from the past and now. Remember we are bringing awareness to what we believe and not judging ourselves.

What were the top 5 values you had as a kid, or that you were told you should have?
Pause for them to write.

· · ·

What are your top five values right now? Without overthinking it, what comes up first for you? Examples: family, integrity, sustainability, faith, grace, achievement, responsibility, communication, money, time, etc.

Pause for a minute or two for them to write.

Once you have those written down, here are your next questions:

Give a minute or two between each question:

Where did you learn your values?

Does anything on this list surprise you?

Would you like your values to shift from here? Why or why not?

Where do you find your value? Where would you like to find your value?

When you forget your value, where do you go for support in remembering it?

1:00: 2nd Circle

If you would like to share from your journal, what were your values? Have they shifted? Were you surprised?

1:15: Womanhood story:

Leader: Womanhood stories are a core part of Red Tent, sharing our stories is a brave act. Sometimes they are joy filled, sad, frustrating, or a mix of all of it. The story may include periods, sex, birth, or any part of the woman and human experience. ___ has offered to share her story tonight. ____ the floor is yours.

See the appendix of the book for reaching out to your women to see who would like to share before the tent day.

· · ·

After her story:

Leader: Thank you ___ for sharing your story. Is there anything you need from us? Hug, encouragement, a listening ear during break?

*If they say yes, do what you can to fulfill that need if possible.

1:25: Soul Care Time:

Leader: Now is our soul care time. This is 20 minutes to stretch, nap, chat, get food, go to the restroom. We do ask that you don't use this time to be on your phone. I'll give us a five-minute heads up to tent, and a one minute come to circle heads up.

1:45: Activity Two: Values Meditation

Meditation is at the end of this script.

1:55: Journal

Please grab your journals, feel free to use markers or a pen. I'll share questions you can answer. You can follow these or free write on your own.

What was your island like? What was on your island? Was anything trying to get in? What was welcome on your island? What is not allowed? What is valuable on this island? How do you feel on your island? Are there any boundaries or other people there? Anything else you'd like to share.

2:05 3rd Circle:

You can share your experience from your meditation or takeaways.

• • •

2:20: Closer *Grab your red thread (yarn) and make sure scissors are within reach.*

Leader: Red thread represents our connection to the women around us and those who have come before us. You will take your red yarn and wrap it around your wrist. You can wrap as many times as you want, as you recite your matriarchal spiritual lineage. Your lineage are the women and people who have influenced and loved you.

They don't have to be biologically related, you can claim or not claim anyone you would like. You can say your name, mother of (any children), daughter of x, daughter of y, daughter of daughters, daughter of whatever resonates (Eve, Spirit, the moon, etc).You can also say descendent instead, or daughter of those who _____ instead of names.

When you have finished wrapping, pass the thread to the next person until it has gone all the way around the circle.

After the Red Thread has come back to you.

Leader: As we are connected, let us sing our song, we'll sing it three times, it goes flow, ebb, weavers, thread, weavers, thread, spiders, web. Sing it with me:

Song: We are the flow we are the ebb,
We are the weavers we are the thread,
We are the weavers we are the thread,
we are the spiders we are the web.
x3

Leader, pick up the scissors, and cut your thread, and as you explain the below, you can have the person to the left tie your thread.

Leader: When cutting the thread to tie bracelets, share your favorite moment and a takeaway. Have the lady to your left tie your yarn, twice in a square knot, and one slip knot, and this way, your thread will not come undone. After you have spoken, pass the scissors to the right, and the next person can go.

After the scissors make their way back to you and everyone has tied their thread, you can share the invitation below. Feel free to hold hands if you'd like.

Invitation to curiosity

   Leader: When you feel yourself wondering if something is aligned with your values, find a place where you can put your arms up in a similar way in what you did in your values meditation and go to your island, or imagine your island. From this place, ask yourself if the situation is aligned with your values. You might be surprised at the clarity you receive from doing this exercise. Thank you for being a part of tonight's Red Tent. You are all a treasure, and I'm glad you are here. Our Red Tent is now closed.

Values Meditation

Our meditation today is to explore your island of values. Remember whatever comes up for you is just what you need, and allow yourself permission to be and rest. This time is for you.

(Pause)

If at any time you need to move or adjust, know you won't be breaking your meditation but will be able to hop right back in where you need.

(Pause)

Get settled sitting down or leaning against a wall.

Let your eyes drift close and relax your body, letting your breath rise and fall like the tides of the ocean

(Pause)

In...and out.

In…and out.

(Pause)

Hold your arms out as if holding a giant barrel.

Let your shoulders relax and feel the space you are taking up with your arms out.

Imagine you are an island.

(Pause)

On this island, your values and your value are protected and can thrive here.

What do your values look like here? Is there lush vegetation? What happens on your island?

(Pause)

What is a day like here on your island?

(pause 1 to two minutes)

What does your island look like?

Who is here with you on the island?

What is most important on this island?

How is your island protected?

(Pause)

Is there anyone or anything trying to permeate your boundaries?

What will you do if they get through?

How will you deal with outside forces?

(Pause)

Take a few minutes to explore and be on your island.

(pause one to two minutes)

When you are ready bring your awareness to the tingling in your palms, and the sense of space you are taking up.

Know that at any time you can put your arms up to recall your island and sense if something is intruding or welcome in your life and space.

(Pause)

Tune into the steadiness of your breath, and your heart beating. You can put your hands down and take a deep breath in.

Feel into how grounded you feel right now.

After your next deep breath, open your eyes and come back to the circle.

GOOD GIRL, BAD GIRL, FULLY EMBODIED WOMAN

*G*rowing up, I thought being a Good Girl was my main goal in life. As I grew older, I saw other women rebelling against the box of Good Girl. Some women shied away from the idea of being labeled in any form. It felt like a dichotomy; you either choose, or people will choose for you. As I entered college and traveled with the military, I found that the world is less black and white than I initially thought. People are complex and dynamic, not always fitting into tiny, tidy labeled boxes. There is a wide range of human personalities, styles, and ways of living. Instead of recognizing we are multifaceted people, we tend to sort others, labeling ourselves and others into familiar tropes.

As I dove deeper into my work around menstrual cycles and Red Tents, I learned more about tropes, archetypes, and stereotypes. I had heard enough stories from women in Tent to know even the most laced-up woman had stories that would make you sob with empathy or shake with rage to feel like society was missing a piece of the puzzle in the way we label women. So when I read Lucy Pearce's *Moon Time* book, I was thrilled when she explained how we all go through different stages and have aspects of many different archetypes within us. Some archetypes felt familiar, like the Maiden, and the Mother, while others felt illicit and forbidden, like the Wild Woman. I remember wondering, "A Wild Woman can be a good thing?" Archetypes can open doors to understanding yourself better.

But what is an archetype?

> According to Joseph Henderson, a Jungian psychologist, an "Archetype defies simple definition. The word derives from a Greek compound of *Arche* and *Tupos*. *Arche* or' first principle' points to the creative source, which cannot be represented, or seen directly. *Tupos*, or 'impression,' refers to any one of the numerous manifestations of the first principle."[1]

This definition means archetypes are constantly morphing. Archetypes flex with our stories and lives as we all add our imagery and experience to what each type means. Archetypes are like facets of a jewel, but for a character or person. A Fool, a Player, a Crazy Woman, or a Witch all carry images and meaning to understand and explain stories. Each archetype holds a story even within just the label itself.

The question I find interesting is: what happens when archetypes and stereotypes overlap?

According to the Webster dictionary, a stereotype "is a widely held but fixed and oversimplified image or idea of a particular type of person or thing."[2] One of these I've noticed is the idea of the Good Girl and Bad Girl. We've seen it in redemption books and played out in movies when the Good Girl shuns her upbringing and becomes a bad girl. Within months of choosing this path, she wrecks her life and possibilities for a future. But have no fear, dear reader, because, by the end of the movie, she soars into her redemption arc. Usually, redemption is in the form of a boy, a trip that changed her life, or the rekindling of a long-lost parental relationship.

We've also seen this play out with the stereotype of the Goody-Two-Shoes. If you are the perfect girl, there are certain expectations of who you are and what you should be. Perhaps even being dismissed for being too nice.

Another example is *Grease*. Danny shuns Sandy as the good Girl during school, but when she and Danny are away from high school pressures, they are happy just being themselves. She winds up conforming to the *Bad Girl* archetype to be with Danny. How would the story have changed if Danny said instead, "No, Sandy, I was happy being myself this summer. Now I know who I am because I felt I was able to be my whole self with you and explore who I am."

The pressures of society telling us who we should be can weigh on us mentally and cause ripple effects in our relationships and how we think about ourselves.

LABELS WE USE ON OURSELVES

We need to be careful about the words we speak over ourselves. When we use Archetypes to identify and claim ourselves, it's asserting a one-sided mask. Although archetypes are multifaceted concepts, we are more than one archetype. For example, if you are in your waning moon stage, where your Archetype is the Wild Woman, it can be easy to be dismissive of yourself by saying, "Well, I'm just crazy and all over the place, because I'm in my Wild Woman stage." Sure, you might feel discombobulated because your hormones are swinging from the chandeliers, but you can choose how you want to process your stress—being labeled wild or crazy are not the only options you have at your disposal. You can choose to be kind and gentle to yourself so you don't lash out, or you can channel your restless energy into a project you need to finish.

In referencing the cycle archetypes and others, Mary-Grace reflects, "It's helpful to know I have a whole village of archetypes in my mind. I can call on the Mother or the Wild Woman; if I need to get still and get wise, there is the Crone. The range feels so inclusive, and I think a lot of times I was subliminally trying to put myself in a box in the way I was trying to describe myself, and now the box is open, and now I'm allowing myself to feel all of it."

When you repeat to yourself, "I'm stupid. What am I thinking?" Or "I'm just a hot mess." Or "I'm the bad girl, so who cares?" you are taking choice away from yourself. If you are locking yourself into any one archetype, you are spellbinding yourself into a fraction of who you are, creating a perfect storm for a self-fulfilling prophecy.

We overcompensate when we withdraw from our wholeness.

Dr. Hillary McBride, an embodiment therapist, says in her book, *Mothers, Daughters, and Body Image*, "What if...the things we are doing as women to earn our "enoughness" in this culture or to feel valuable are empty, actually leading us further away from ourselves and from what it means to be whole? If that is the case, then we need something more — a new narrative, a different story with which to align ourselves, and a healthier way of knowing our worth. If that's the case, I don't want to be what culture thinks it means to be a 'good woman, or girl, if being good in our culture means having to disappear in our bodies, minds, and thoughts."[3]

When we repeatedly silence or shame ourselves for

aspects outside of the Good Girl's society-approved version, we are slowly beating ourselves to death. Silencing yourself might look like not sticking up for yourself in a meeting, agreeing with someone else to avoid an argument, or saying yes to a request because you don't feel like you can say no. Shame eats away at you when you think you can't trust yourself and need to put others first. It becomes a death by a thousand cuts.[4]

By seeing ourselves only in one way, it creates a rut in our thinking which builds up over time like a plaque. This thought-plaque can distort our thinking about ourselves and how we believe the world perceives us.

Stylist Hilary Rushford Collyer[5] shares an idea about the way we see our bodies, and I think it applies to our inner selves as well. It's called the 150% rule. We hyper-focus on one thing and think, "My thighs are so big!" or "Oh, my shoulders are broad." The truth is, your thighs are completely normal, and your shoulders aren't any different than the person next to you. No one else would comment on what you've highlighted. We can hyper-focus on things other people have told us in the past. Believing we're such a good girl, or we're always a joker. These stories sink in, and we create fences around our behavior on what is or isn't allowed.

We divide ourselves when we categorize our various aspects and emotions.

 In *Burning Woman*, Lucy Pearce writes, "Nice girls don't feel angry. We are taught that early on. We should focus on the positive. Send love and light. And so we push it down, distract ourselves, and learn to turn the anger in on ourselves, to pick ourselves apart. And gradually we become fragmented in order to survive, cutting off from our bad body parts, our big feelings, our traumatic memories, the horrific news stories."[6]

Sometimes we don't share our full thoughts because it can feel terrifying when we say the whole truth of reality. A fully embodied woman is aware of the good and bad, the shadow and the light. By saying, "I'm just a *Good Girl*. I have to stay happy all the time," we are cutting ourselves off from experiencing and processing the whole breadth of living.

We bury the parts of ourselves we despise instead of asking our emotions what they are trying to tell us. We let labels get in the way of our learning. Instead of seeing anger and asking what boundary was crossed or asking fear why it is scared, we cast them into the depths of our hearts, letting them slowly eat away at us instead of letting understanding and compassion wash over them.

We need fewer women focused on fitting into the nice-good ideal and more women focused on allowing themselves to be a safe place for them to be whole.

Striving to be perfect instead of listening to our Inner Voice can make us second guess every decision. Thoughts can race due to worrying about others approval, or about conflicting opinions from those you love.

You might be thinking, "Yeah, but they think I'm out of line." Possibly. You may also be projecting, and they don't think of you at all. Be careful of putting words in other people's mouths. We don't have to deny ourselves at the door because of what we think other people are thinking. *This type of mind-reading is not healthy and has a wide margin of error.*

Let us bring our whole selves as we walk into each room. As my best friend Kelsey says, "Don't negotiate with yourself." Not negotiating with yourself means trusting your Inner Voice and Knowing and showing up as your whole self, regardless of other people's opinions.

GOOD GIRL FOR WHO?

"Good for who?" is a question we need to start asking ourselves. A *Good Girl* can mean being good and doing the 'right thing. It can also be a refusal to rock the boat even when the ship is sinking. What does good even mean? Sometimes good is used as a weapon, a shifting definition to keep you in line and on your toes. So what happens when the idea of good traps us in the opinion of who we SHOULD be. What should we do then?

 Author Lucy Pearce shares how the expectations of what a *Good Girl* is, pressures us into taking up less space: "We have been taught that we are too much: too loud, too needy, too emotional, that we take up too much space for what we are worth. And so we are silently shamed into smallness."[7]

A friend told me 'shoulds' feel heavy because they don't resonate. After all, it's what you *should* do. Should is what society has deemed as logical or essential.

An example being the should of "You should go to college, get married, and then have children." Sometimes what society tells us what we should do is precisely what we want! Other times, the shoulds make us cringe or feel isolated if we can't make it happen. The frustration of shoulds often leads to wondering if there's a different path we can take. People told me I was a bad wife for not having children. Others shamed my friend as a bad Christian for speaking up against an injustice happening in her neighborhood. Don't let the shoulds that feel weighty crush your soul, just so you aren't labeled a bad person.

Questions you can ask yourself are:

What do I truly desire here?
What are my wants or needs?

There may be more to the story that others don't always see. Wants/needs are not a copout to ignore human decency. But asking these questions is a way to dig under the surface and see what is going on. *What is the yearning in your heart?*

If you want to explore a new path or change direction after giving a prior commitment, there is permission here to trust your Intuition, even if others don't understand.

BAD GIRL

Brooke, one of our Red Tent women, experiences the *Good Girl, Bad Girl* archetypes differently. She became the bad Girl to feel safe. Being the angry goth chick was safer than putting herself out there. Others judged and assumed she did drugs simply because she wore a lot of black and was stand-offish.

Those seen as bad girls can potentially be society's definition of a Good Girl minus the physical aspects. Vice versa for the Good Girl as she explained, "I got away with so many things because I knew how to pander to certain adults." Sometimes, there is also an in-between: a Good-Bad girl or a Bad-Good Girl.

Brooke was a good-bad girl to defend herself from being made fun of to her face. The bad-good Girl showed up when her parents would fight, so she "studied" after school, which was cover for sneaking to a boy's house to feel security and acceptance.

When women in history have been too much, they get labeled hysterical and put in asylums, drugged, or end up drinking because they are continually gaslit by the people around them. We can write off bad girls, but what if bad girls got handed a bad reputation they don't always deserve?

Bad Girl might be labeled bad, but what if it embodies more freedom? Less people-pleasing? What if someone chooses to live in a different way than yours, but it feeds their soul? What if what we think is wrong is (sometimes) someone deciding to listen to their Knowing, over what society tells them, even if they get ostracised?

We need to become aware of the whole realm of archetypes at our disposal. We can say, "Yes, I'm strong, and this doesn't make me wrong or less feminine." Our society sold us an either-or bill of goods, but it's more yes/and. Think of it as a wheel that is around us, and we are in the center. *Fully embodied means you have access to your entire range of emotions.*

 Tent Keeper Michaela shares her reflections on archetypes: "I love the archetype work. Through Red Tent meditations, I've met a variety of archetypes. There's a component similar to online personality tests: 'How does your Maiden speak? 'What does your Wild Woman wear?' I love the idea of using allegory to explore the subconscious. It feels somewhere between a personality test and creating an avatar, but it's all coming out of your subconscious.

Pulling from archetypes is about taking opportunities to explore different components of yourself. The Mother archetype is fascinating because it's associated with ovulation, but ovulation is when my PMDD (Premenstrual Dysphoric Disorder) flares up, so I struggled with that particular archetype. Instead of feeling nurturing, I feel angry and like breaking things. I wondered, 'how do I reconcile feeling rage when the Mother archetype is about nurturing?' This opposition allowed me to look at what it means to me and wonder how to explore through this.

My Mother Archetype is feral, a bit crazed, with wild hair and mud on her face. My first thought was, 'What am I supposed to do with this?' I realized my Mother archetype is a protector; she's not necessarily the one at the hearth. My Crone is the domestic goddess; she nurtures everyone, but my Mother is the defender, the boundary keeper who screams her anger when others (or I) ignore my boundaries. She yells, "Our territory is being abused, and it's not okay!"

She will fight to the death for what is mine and protect it. There's a part of myself that wondered, "Where do I separate myself from my illness?" That's a struggle for anyone who has any illness where it impacts your brain chemistry. "Who am I without the disease?

It was a big breakthrough for me to realize this was a different Mother-esque energy, and I realized she doesn't yell when I listen to her. If you listen to her in the first place, she doesn't get angry. Using archetypal imagery helps me unpack things about my illness, childhood, and about surviving a narcissistic first marriage.

I struggled with many things, and I made peace with the rage part of me. I could understand it better and don't need to be so angry because now I know how to listen. I've seen a lot of healing in myself and my reactions because of my work with archetypes helping me understand who the whole of me is."

When we shut off a part of ourselves like jealousy or

rage because they are inconvenient, we ignore what they reveal. Emotions aren't trying to control us. They are trying to uncover deeper truths about ourselves, our wounds, and the world. When acted upon, jealousy can ruin friendships; but when you notice it flaring, you can ask yourself, "Why am I jealous?" or, if it's a matter of someone relaxing while you are hard at work, you could ask, "Would I like to rest as well?" Flip the script by looking at the root of the desire.

Heal your life instead of being envious and poisoning a relationship. Anger is a marker of boundary-crossing, and rage means you've ignored it for too long. It could be a broken system or a friend that has pushed you too far. Be honest before it gets to the point of destruction so you can make a plan before a friendship, job, or life lies in ruins. Being alive is a matter of continuous learning and realizing that you are more than just a *Good Girl* or a *Bad Girl*.

You are a Fully Embodied Woman.

QUESTIONS FOR FURTHER DISCOVERY:

What stereotypes have you believed about yourself? Have you pigeonholed yourself into one of these categories?

After hearing about these two archetypes, what about you falls under a Bad Girl or Good Girl? Can you find the components of both?

What is the next step for you to peel back layers of stereotypes and archetypes you or others have placed on you?

BOOK RECOMMENDATIONS:

Here All Dwell Free: Stories to Heal the Wounded Feminine, by Gertrud Mueller Nelson
The Road Back to You: An Enneagram Journey to Self-Discovery by Ian Morgan Cron
Cultivate: A Grace-Filled Guide to Growing an Intentional Life by Lara Casey

Good Girl, Bad Girl,
Fully Embodied Woman Red Tent

Five minutes before the Tent Begins:

Leader: Lovelies, please put your phones on silent or off, grab your water, snacks, journal, and token and join me in the circle.

Opening:

Leader: Before we begin, I would like to state that this is a safe space. In order to make it so, there needs to be agreement around keeping what is said in circle, in the circle. I'm asking you all to agree to only speak of your own experiences, and only give advice when asked. We will be talking about deeply personal things in the Red Tent. A gentle reminder that we can disagree and still accept each other. Can I have a show of hands for everyone willing to keep this space confidential, for themselves and everyone here tonight?

Shakeout and Grounded Breathing:

Leader: Let us take a minute to stand up, shake out any worries, or frustration from your day. Twist your body, shake your booty, kick your legs, jump up and down. Audibly make sounds while relaxing your jaw. Stretch, or move in a way that feels supportive.

Please have a seat in this circle, and let's do some ground breathing. You can close your eyes, start to relax your shoulders. You can roll your neck from side to side, rest your hands on your stomach, knees, or the ground, whatever is most comfortable for you. Start breathing in from your belly. Take a deep breath. As you exhale, release anything that came before tonight that is on your mind.

Breathe in again, releasing anything to come in the

future. Keep breathing, focusing on the sounds around you, the breath of other women, and your heartbeat. As you release your breath, feel your body settling into this space. In this moment, here with us. You are safe. You are loved. We are glad you are here with us.

Call in:

Leader: We are gathered in our Red Tent, as women, as daughters, as mothers, as workers and dreamers. We come here to speak our heart's desires, our mind's thoughts, and share the song of our souls. We see with our eyes, hear with our ears, and will hum along in our hearts. May this space be open, sacred, and grounded for us here tonight. Let us hold hands as we travel deeper together, learning to better love ourselves, each other, and the world.

Gender Neutral Option:

We are gathered in our Red Tent Tent as humans, as explorers, as workers and dreamers. We come here to speak our heart's desires, our mind's thoughts, and share the song of our souls. We see with our eyes, hear with our ears, and will hum along in our hearts. May this space be open, sacred, and grounded for us here tonight. Let us hold hands as we travel deeper together, learning to better love ourselves, each other, and the world.

Song:

Leader: Close your eyes and think of what you want from this night and this week. It might be friendship, laughter, wisdom. We'll pass the bowl around one person at a time, and you'll say your blessing request, we'll sing the song with your word inside of it, and then after we sing over you, pass the bowl to the next woman. She'll share her

blessing word, and we'll sing a blessing over her until we reach the end of the circle.

Call down a blessing x3, Call down, ____before you, ____behind you, ____Within you, and around you

Repeat for each person in the group, end with three call downs.

15: 1st Circle:

Leader: When speaking, please use the talking light, and when you finish, please say "I have spoken," so we know you have completed your thought. You can react with hand snaps, hand on your heart, and facial expressions. Please speak only of your own story, and don't give any advice unless asked.

For our first circle, what is your name, your pronouns, what is your intention for tonight, and what does being a fully embodied woman mean to you?

30: Quote and Response:

Leader: I'll share the quote below, and then you can share how it resonates or a few words on how it makes you feel.

"Don't let the expectations and opinions of other people affect your decisions. It's your life, not theirs. Do what matters most to you; do what makes you feel alive and happy. Don't let the expectations and ideas of others limit who you are. If you let others tell you who you are, you are living their reality — not yours. There is more to life than pleasing people. There is much more to life than following others' prescribed path. There is so much more to life than what you experience right now. You need to decide who you are for yourself. Become a whole being. Adventure."

— Roy T. Bennett[8]

· · ·

45: Activity 1: Selfish Questions

Leader: Sometimes we feel guilty or bad even when we don't need to. In this activity we'll peel back a layer of expectation so you can uncover where you'd like to rest more.

Grab a pen and paper please and answer these questions.

Leader, go slowly, take about a minute or two between each question.

If you had one hour to do something selfish what would you do?

Why does this feel selfish? Is that true?

Whose voice is that telling you it's selfish? Where did you learn this?

How do you actually feel about it?

How has it helped you? How has it held you back?

Does this belief of it being selfish help me now?

What is the new belief I could replace it with?

1:00: 2nd Circle

What came up for you in the Selfish Questions activity?

1:15: Womanhood story:

Leader: Womanhood stories are a core part of Red Tent, sharing our stories is a brave act. Sometimes they are joy filled, sad, frustrating, or a mix of all of it. The story may include periods, sex, birth, or any part of the woman and human experience. ____ has offered to share her story tonight. ____ the floor is yours.

See the appendix of the book for reaching out to your women to see who would like to share before the tent day.

. . .

After her story:
Leader: Thank you ___ for sharing your story. Is there anything you need from us? Hug, encouragement, a listening ear during break?
   **If they say yes, do what you can to fulfill that need if possible.*

1:25: Soul Care Time:
Leader: Now is our soul care time. This is 20 minutes to stretch, nap, chat, get food, go to the restroom. We do ask that you don't use this time to be on your phone. I'll give us a five-minute heads up to tent, and a one minute come to circle heads up.

1:45: Activity Two: Alignment Charting[9]
Grab your journal and your preferred coloring goodies. Draw two big circles, with you on the inside of each. In your first circle, draw what is currently true in your life of your values, and what is welcome in your space. Put it in the circle. Put whatever you don't allow in your space on the outside of the circle. (Examples of things that could be in or out, family, joy, laughter, guilt, feeling rushed, shame, rest)
   What is not allowed? Where do you start and stop? What is in your field of responsibility.
   Everything that feels too close, or too far. Draw it on or around your circle.
   Give a few minutes for everyone to draw their first circle and items inside.

Your second circle is what would feel more aligned. Are there things you want to move to the outside of your circle? What would that look like? If rest or support were on the outside of your frist circle, how could you bring those in?

Give a few minutes for everyone to draw their second circle and items inside.

Looking at these two circles, what needs to shift or change to bring things more into how you would like them to be? What changes would feel more aligned and true to you?

1:55: Circle
Share what came up for you in the Alignment Charting activity.

2:10 Closer *Grab your red thread (yarn) and make sure scissors are within reach.*

Leader: Red thread represents our connection to the women around us and those who have come before us. You will take your red yarn and wrap it around your wrist. You can wrap as many times as you want, as you recite your matriarchal spiritual lineage. Your lineage are the women and people who have influenced and loved you.

They don't have to be biologically related, you can claim or not claim anyone you would like. You can say your name, mother of (any children), daughter of x, daughter of y, daughter of daughters, daughter of whatever resonates (Eve, Spirit, the moon, etc). You can also say descendent instead, or daughter of those who ____ instead of names.

When you have finished wrapping, pass the thread to the next person until it has gone all the way around the circle.

You can start the process and do your lineage and wrap and then pass it to the person on your right.

After the Red Thread has come back to you.
Leader: As we are connected, let us sing our song, we'll

sing it three times, it goes flow, ebb, weavers, thread, weavers, thread, spiders, web. Sing it with me:
Song: We are the flow we are the ebb,
We are the weavers we are the thread,
We are the weavers we are the thread,
we are the spiders we are the web.
x3

Leader, pick up the scissors, and cut your thread, and as you explain the below, you can have the person to the left tie your thread.

Leader: When cutting the thread to tie bracelets, share your favorite moment and a takeaway. Have the lady to your left tie your yarn, twice in a square knot, and one slip knot, and this way, your thread will not come undone. After you have spoken, pass the scissors to the right, and the next person can go.

After the scissors make their way back to you and everyone has tied their thread, you can share the invitation below. Feel free to hold hands if you'd like.

Invitation to curiosity
Leader: This month, tune into the expectations around you and how you are reacting to them. Use this to set the tone for how much space you need, and how to ask for it. Thank you for being a part of tonight's Red Tent. You are all a treasure, and I'm glad you are here. Our Red Tent is now closed.

WILD

I firmly believe when women gather, magic happens. It happens dancing around a fire in the forest together. It occurs on cross-country road trips with girlfriends. It even happens at middle school sleepovers when you share your secrets, candy, and makeup until two in the morning.

Magic happens in moments of bonding.

I read *Burning Woman* by Lucy Pearce a year before attending the College of Wizardry LARP, and she had done a burning woman ceremony. This ceremony was like the hushed stories you hear of women dancing skyclad (naked) in the woods. Her book starts with calling the awareness to the judgments and assumptions around women gathering. Specifically how when women gather together, people think of scary witches and discount the life-giving aspects being in the circle could have for them. There is a power of self-ownership and vulnerability in circles and Red Tents, which can feel equal parts inviting and terrifying.

Although dancing in the woods around a fire was

something I sincerely wanted to do, I was nervous. Her book circulated our Red Tent library, and other women started dreaming about the idea as well. Exhilarated whispers abounded: "This would be a remarkable evening!" or "What if we did this?" We talked among ourselves about what our dream fire dancing night would look like, but I would always respond in jest, "Someday, we'll dance naked around a fire, but not today."

I was scared of being seen; *not my body, but my soul.*

Dancing naked in the woods felt like a step towards something wild. I yearned for more honesty in my every day about what I truly wanted. I wanted to have a more magical life and more moments of what dancing felt like to me. I was scared to desire these things for fear of them not being what I imagined in my mind and for what wanting those things would mean about me. I was also terrified of what others outside of Tent would think of me if I said this desire outloud.

Our Tent women knew all of this and so were persistent in wanting this magical forest dance and reminded me that now was as good a time as ever. We shared our concerns and ideas, "Would this be too wild—and is that a bad thing?" "What if a car comes by?" "What about bugs?" "Who is bringing toilet paper?" Each question made the upcoming dance more and more tangible. Electric excitement raced through my body as we planned more details of the evening, feeling a bit astounded it was going to happen.

We wanted to feel free, luxurious, and decadent. A few of us bought yards of velvet fabric to create robes we could wear while dancing under the moonlight. Each woman sent me songs that made her feel alive and resonant in her bones. Everything from *Queendom* by Aurora and Justin

Timberlake's *Can't Stop the Feeling!* to *King Ruby* from Ider. We rented tents, and I made special batches of my homemade sangria. I told each woman to wear clothes that would make her feel like a forest queen and easy to dance in. It felt like the theme of the night was permission to be your brightest, wholly embodied self and not apologize for being yourself. We set the date and looked ahead with giddy anticipation.[1]

A few months later, two days after my May birthday, twelve of us drove out to a secluded farm for our evening of dancing around the fire.

It felt like we were all princesses and each other's handmaidens all at once. Decadence surrounded us as we donned our flower crowns and dresses. We used paint pens and glitter to decorate our bodies and braided each other's hair.

 Elissa remembers, "It was a true embrace of "everybody's body is perfect." Every body is holy and sacred and deserves reverence and praise. It just felt like we were celebrating. We were celebrating each other. We were celebrating our friendship and the sacredness of the bonds we had forged in Tent."

As the sun began to set and the musical selection soaked into the night air, we gathered around the fire. Each woman shared her intentions for why she was there and who she was claiming herself to be. Our glitter and glee sparkled against the light of the fire. Some women wrote themselves a letter, and others shared a poem as a blessing over us.

As our words came to a close, we let the music begin to lead us. We started dancing to Florence + The Machine, then slowly peeled off layers as the music went on. As a past choreographer, I will never pass up an opportunity to craft a musical moment into real everyday life. As a group, we created a dance to *This is Me* from *The Greatest Showman*, and tears ran down our faces as we shouted into the night sky the reclamation of those lyrics, refusing to bow to shame and guilt any longer. As our last song *Dance of the Druids* from *Outlander* came on, we picked up our candles and twirled to a dance I had taught earlier in the evening. The candles and the moonlight illuminated our bodies and joy.

As the final notes played, we looked at each other in awe. We were radiant.

Each woman was glowing with pure joy and the thrill of it all. There was a moment we could feel us all seeing each other and knowing we were also being seen, and we knew it was okay. The sense of knowing we were exactly where we were supposed to be sunk into our bones. As we nestled in the amazement of actually doing what we had dreamed of doing for a year, we wrapped scarves, blankets, and warm clothes back around our bodies.

 Elissa smiles when she recalls, "It was this absolute high of we said we were going to do it, and we did it. Nobody held back or was afraid. In the actual moment when it happened, I remember us feeling like the personification of womanhood, friendship, trust, and vulnerability. I literally don't remember looking at anyone else as we were dancing around the fire bare. It wasn't about that, you know? Our evening involved no shame. It felt like we were a bunch of celestial beings together. It was sacred, beautiful, and wonderful. I felt honored to have participated in it. We were all just glowy and happy."

From performing in burlesque in college, I knew the value in reclaiming your body and sexuality as your own through dance, but I felt the dancing we just finished on a deeper cellular and soul level. The woods' sounds were the new background music as we went around the circle sharing our thoughts and experience we just had. We stayed up late laughing, talking, and dreaming about the future until sleep bid us in, and we crawled into our sleeping bags under the sky.

That evening is still imprinted my soul. I felt limitless and in tune with the earth and the women around me. I remember thinking, "If this is possible, what else is?" To this day, dancing naked in the woods is one of my favorite bravest things I've ever done. I wouldn't trade my magical evening in the woods for the world, and I'm glad I didn't let my worries and what I 'should' do get in the way.

You might be wondering, "How does one plan dancing bare in the woods?"

Great question! Careful planning went into cultivating a safe space for us to have this beautiful, enchanting evening.[2] We asked questions like "What songs do we want to play?" and "Do we want to burn anything in the fire?" I made sure to include like-minded women from Tent who had mentioned dancing in the past, and in our past conversations, said they would be comfortable dancing in this environment. All we needed were tents, food, fire, and ourselves. Sangria, biodegradable glitter and snacks were helpful too.

 Hillary Mcbride shares how moments like these can help us tap into feeling powerful mentally. "Our mind and our body, together, intricately interwoven, and together are all parts of who we are. This is why when we don't like our bodies, we feel bad about our whole selves. Or when we feel really powerful in our bodies, we feel really powerful in ourselves. If our identity is just as much our bodies as it is our minds and thoughts, then we can use our bodies to help us experience power in a way that is just as important to the self as having thoughts and ideas or words that make us feel powerful."[3]

Fire dancing was an evening of reclamation and saying, "Yes! THIS IS ME. This is my temple. Here I am!"

When you tap into an altering event like this and have others witness you, it can create a perma-shift in how you view yourself. Even if you don't have a fire pit or friends to dance in the woods with, you can hold what I like to call a "Fire Evening."

A "Fire Evening" is where each woman brings a "Fire Share," which I refer to as a verbal offering people bring to the fire. Shares might look like a song, a poem, something personally written, or a powerful quote. You don't have to be undressed; you can wear clothes that make you feel abundant, free, or dazzling! Enjoy your time together! If you would like to dance in the woods to reclaim your skin and own it to feel fully alive, then create an evening like our gathering where you can do so safely."

If the outdoors feels uninviting to you, you can do this in your backyard or living room. Deep heart-led sharing and soul dancing don't lose their resonance if you choose to be in a place you feel more safe in.

Sometimes, we get a crazy idea, and we need to run with it. We need to try new things and see what happens. It can be scary, and doubts love to creep their way in with their "What if's?" and "Are you sure?" questions. When you feel the tug towards something, trust it's happening for a reason, and know it's worth exploring what's underneath.

You might be surprised by what you discover.

OUR WILD NATURE

I believe that a God who made Liopleurodons, which are essentially giant dinosaur crocodiles who could swallow you in one gulp, colored a bit outside the lines and liked a little wild in the world. I think we get so afraid of the wild because everyone else's opinions of what is okay, perfect, and good.

Wild is the natural order of things.

A forest is wild until it is paved over; animals are wild until they are domesticated; kids run barefoot until they have to put on shoes.[4] What if wild is our natural state? We as humans have modernized and tamed the wild through the centuries, *and although some things are needed—roads, medicine, schools...ice cream*—I still wonder, "Have we tamed ourselves along the way?"

When I think about it, I think the OG Garden of Eden looked more like a wild, thriving forest ecosystem than the lawn-of-the-month gardens we see in most modern depictions.[5]

Being aware of the wildness around us while others do their best to scrub it away can help weave wild into our lives by being present instead of living in the future or past.

 Michaela shares, "Wilderness is something existing in its natural state. It's not necessarily a hunting lion; it can be the deer drinking water at the stream. Both are equally representative of the wild. The natural state also means leaning into the way things are. If things are quiet, kind of like right now, when I'm in Italy in the middle of the COVID pandemic, it's helpful to stay home, be still, and I'm leaning into it. It's the natural state of things, like the quiet stream with the birds singing in the trees. Starlight and snow on mountain tops and glaciers with their incredibly slow but persistent movement, all of this is a part of the wild. Trusting everything will happen in its own time is what the wild has come to embody for me. The wild is the sense of connectedness of the way things are, and being with them as they are."

Wild might mean something entirely different for you, and that's okay.

But what DOES it mean to you?
What COULD it mean for you?

Have you been afraid to develop your definition of 'wild' in fear of what could come up? How would your perspective change if the idea of wild is the wind in your hair, the moment when you trust your gut, when you dance with abandon, or take a leap of faith.

What would it mean for you if wild is when you fully laugh or feel every fiber of your being resonating with joy as you close out a day surrounded by those you love. Wild isn't necessarily drunken debauchery— *soul* wild is being aligned with your mind, body, and Spirit right where you are.

When we are fully present is often when we feel most vulnerable, because we aren't controlling the situation or planning ahead which can feel unpredictable. Vulnerability can feel like being in the wildness and uncharted territory, but is also the path to presence and wholeness.

WILD CHANGES

Wild doesn't always feel like a good thing. Part of friendship is walking through the wild aspects of each other's lives. Sometimes the tumultuous changes of life can take us by surprise at how they change us. Children, mental and physical health, deployments, moves, career shifts, death, and relationships can irrevocably change our lives in a not-so-fun way.

Obbie brings up the wilderness of motherhood, "There have been negative times I've felt wild and not in a great way. To me, that's destructive wild, where everything is spiraling, and nothing is going your way. Everything feels like it's crashing around you, and you lose yourself in ways where you can't pick yourself back up. I lost my sense of self after having my daughter Ellie. I felt like nothing but a feeding machine and mom. There's a wildness of losing yourself. Tent and the women in it were guides as I reclaimed myself and is the thing Tent helped me with the most."

When the wildness of life throws you off-center, it's essential to know where you can find dry land. The first is knowing where your wild is. Is it inside your mind, your life, or in a situation? When you know where your wild is, you can find stable ground. It could look like various things—a therapist, a Tent, a friendship, a relationship, or your faith.

Tending yourself while going through the wild is essential. It could be taking medicine or eating in a way that fuels your body. When the whirlwind is going, discover what grounds you so you can find moments of peace and rest in your day. It's crucial when a wild change comes into your life to give yourself space to adjust. Even if the world is spinning on as if nothing happened, you may need to pause and take time to process the life shifts.

When Jer goes on deployments, the first week is a hot mess express, and then I vary between Being-On-Top-Of-Everything-House-Is-Spotless to I've-Barely-Slept-And-A-Tornado-Ran-Through-This-House on and off till he comes back. Even though I know that deployments happen, it still is a thing that knocks military spouses for a loop. It's like living in a tornado alley—you know tornadoes will come, and you are prepared for them coming, but every time they happen, it still knocks you for a loop because you didn't know how differently this particular tornado would hit. Sometimes you get your whole porch ripped off, and sometimes you have to pick underwear up off the front lawn.

There is good wild and bad wild. But they're all part of the same wild—just different facets. Sometimes, the wild tears up the domesticated aspects of our lives, and to be honest—sometimes we need it as we get caught up in our routines and forget to look up and around at our life. A forest fire can be utterly devastating, but it paves the way for new growth. If we are going to talk about destructive wild, we can explore the idea of accepting it into our spaces and seeing it. Even the disruptive wild has lessons to teach us.

Wild change is a part of life, but navigating it alone doesn't have to be. If you are going through a tumultuous change, what do you need for support? How can you give yourself grace? Maybe this looks like dropping a few commitments or telling friends you need help, accountability, or encouragement this week.

WILD CHILD

Growing up in Iowa, wild was a bad thing. Our corn is in rows, and our families are in pews. Iowa nice is the name of the game. Wild was too much. Being in excess of emotions, excitement, or obsessed with a hobby is looked at with side-eye. My Dad was a wild child coming out of a divorced home with ADHD energy for days and a knack for finding trouble, both on and off bikes. In the '70s, there was no middle ground for helping kids navigate being neurodivergent except for being told, "Don't be stupid," and admonished to "Get it together."

The turning point academically was when his stepmom, Annie, took three months of her lunch hours and trained on how to mentor students with different learning styles. She taught my Dad one on one for almost a year to develop study habits and held him accountable to every class and every test by visiting with teachers weekly. My Dad went from a student that had little or no reading retention to a college graduate, and now, he jokingly says, has 'total recall.'

As a person with Dyslexia, he found ways to study in school and earned his degree in college, but he never lost his need for a bit of 'extraness' in his life. Between motorbike racing, BMX, and mountain biking, he's always trying a new way to ride smarter and jump better, even as an adult. He'll jump 15 to 20 feet jumps and reach speeds up to 30 mph on the BMX race track. He even created a bike track in the backyard a few years ago. Because *why not?* My Dad holds onto his wild dreams with both hands, and it is something that I always admired, even while I saw that it was difficult for him not to listen to the naysayers.

People always told him to tone it down, but he refused to and stayed committed to keeping his goals alive. He calls those who ask him to calm down "dream stealers." Dream stealers are the ones who prod, "When are you growing up?" and "That's a kid's sport."

In reality, people of all ages ride bikes, and my Dad is not the oldest out on the tracks by a long shot. My Dad is doing things he loves, despite those he loves not seeing or understanding how much joy these things bring him.

He does understand, though, that if you are an adrenaline junkie, you will eventually get hurt. My Dad has been injured for months at a time, breaking collarbones, cracking ribs, and tearing tendons from falls or crashes on the track. As hard as he goes on the track, he is equally as ferocious about mending his body. After an injury, it can take a couple of weeks to get comfortable with his skills again, and even after all these years, there's fear whispering, "Be careful; you might get hurt again."

The thing is, you might get hurt doing anything. For

Dad, that risk is a price he's willing to pay to live a wild life of joy. *Full Send*, his riding nickname, is written on his bike, meaning, all in, full out, every time.

> Ayesha was also a wild child and now embraces being a Wild Woman, "Everyone called me a wild child because I didn't fit in with society's expectations of me. Growing up in S. Carolina as a woman of color who wanted to be anything other than a barefoot, pregnant housewife, I was never accepted. There was not a single thing I could do to be accepted. Girls needed to wear dresses and lacy socks and dress shoes and sit nicely, and I would be naked barefoot running around in the backyard looking for dinosaur bones. I didn't fit the expectations of society, and that was considered wild. Did I feel wild? No, I felt like I was listening to my heart.
>
> Now wild almost has the same note to it. Being wild is being free. I can have some magical forest time, kick off my shoes, and dance around a fire. That may seem wild because it's not something everybody may approve of, think of doing, or believe is the norm, but it brings me joy. Wildness makes me feel connected with the earth, free and me. Now when people say, 'Oh, you're too wild!' I ask, 'Am I, or am I just not your expectation?'"

Reclaiming your wildness doesn't mean you'll always be safe, but the return on investment is living a fully embodied life by doing what you love.

If you aren't sure what this looks like for yourself, you can ask yourself some questions:

What are some ways I'm scared to show up or take risks?

*When I regret not taking leaps of faith in my past, what
were they about?*
*What are the themes in my life right now where I feel drawn
to be wilder?*

Sometimes we make it harder for ourselves by thinking
we have to prove that we are allowed or deserve to take a
wild risk.

Laying our value on whether or not we feel 'brave
enough to take a risk is nonsense. Do you know what's not
nonsense, though? You weighing the risk, tuning into your
Inner Voice with curiosity, seeking wisdom, and deciding
your path with both eyes open.

WILD RISKS

Taking a risk can feel vulnerable, wild, and scary.

I wonder if some of the things we think are wild are
labeled like that because we would love to do those things
but believe they are out of reach for ourselves. Those "wild"
things are great for other people, but... not *us*, right? Some
of my favorite memoirs and stories have adventures that
are a bit wild, and I wonder if I'd be willing to take those
same risks. It's easy to say, "Oh, I would do this too!" but
would we? Would we have the guts to say yes to
adventure?

It's easy to say yes when we have already experienced an
event we are used to seeing the outcome of, but what about
when you have an opportunity for something exciting right
in front of you and don't know which path to take? What
about living our wildness in our lives?

A question I started asking myself is, "When I'm 80,
what am I going to regret?"

I'm going to regret not following where Spirit leads and
living the most embodied and truest life I can. As simple as
this sounds, when I first realized this, it surprised me

because it's the most complicated and easiest thing all at the same time.

At the start of each year, I see life coaches and Instagram influencers worldwide asking what the 80-year-old version of ourselves loved about her life, enjoyed doing, and then encourages everyone to plan accordingly.

I love this idea, and I also love the flip side: asking about regrets.

It's easy to say yes to dreams of family, love, and a dream job, but what would 80 year old me say? Maybe, "Goodness, I could have done x, y, or z, but I never got around to it. I wish I would have spoken up, but I stayed quiet, and I regret it." Now I try to push myself, trust my nudge, and take the risks that call me. There's a bit of "Screw it, let's try and see" kind of energy attached in taking this approach. I do my best not to regret a risk I feel called to anymore.

I know some people who refuse to believe in having regrets, but I think reflection on what could have been better or done differently can serve us well if we are willing to learn and grow from it.

Most of the time, our reasons for doing things are because of a vision or goal. Saying, "I know I'll regret not trying this," feels a little harder to explain because it's less tangible. "Why" is often more compelling than "Why not?"

For me, "Why not?" feels a little dangerous, and I can hold myself from going after these wild risks out of fear of what others might say. When we contain ourselves out of fear of what other people will say, we're dismissing ourselves and our souls for someone else. All that excitement of possibilities and the disappointment from shoving it down and not exploring it has to go somewhere. It turns into us resenting the people we dimmed our light for and resenting ourselves for not chasing the possibility.

Friend, other people aren't even thinking about us as much as we believe they are. They are busy weighing their own "Why" and "Why not" questions for their lives.

For my Dad, the risk is sometimes pain or rejection from others who don't get it. He thinks, "Oh, this might hurt, but damn, it's worth it."

While shrinking is excellent for mortgages and credit card debt, it's not for your soul.

Take a moment and listen to your Knowing. You may feel called to do something that is right for you, and sometimes this next right step can be laced with apprehension. Apprehension and understanding of the right step to take can both be there at the same time. Recognize your thoughts when you ask yourself,

"What will people think?"
"Will they approve?"
"Am I capable of this?"

See if you can't give yourself an inch of space by saying,

"_____ would be proud of me for trying this."
"Others might not understand, and that's okay."
"I can try this new thing to the best of my ability and see what happens."

Don't let "I wish I would have" be on your lips at 80.

WILD LIVING

In the becoming and unfurling, I have realized I don't want to carve off a piece of myself for the comfort of other people any longer. Maybe you are also done with specific ways you've lived, spoken to yourself, or dimmed yourself. I wonder if it doesn't take some of us showing up as our whole wild-hearted selves to make it safe for other people to do the same.

In the book *Untamed*, Glennon Doyle talks about

disappointing others over disappointing ourselves, and the first time I read we could do that, it hit me like a baseball bat to the face. It shocked me because I've disappointed myself often for the pleasure of others over the years. I'd like to have people be pleased when they are in my life, but people having that pleasure should not require my self-induced denigration or resentment.

When you lean into your wild, others may react with disappointment, questions, and fear, but you are still allowed to choose

I see this with the LGBTQIA+ community, and people recognizing themselves in those who are out of the closet, and realizing they can let their insides show on their outsides as well.

 Jill agrees, "I've noticed the more I've owned who I am, as a neurodivergent Pansexual woman, the more I've become myself. The more I've expressed myself, and who I am, and what my needs are, others have come to me or confided and came out to me with their sexuality. I've become a safe space. I'm proud of it. The more of us that do that, the safer the world is going to be. I want everyone to know they are loved. They are valuable. Their identity is valid, and who they love is valid."

More and more communities are banding together to tend to one another, care for one another, and be a landing space to lament, share ideas, and be inspired. It's not always safe to speak up or bring your whole self to the table in our day-to-day world. So when you do speak up, make some elbow room for the people behind you who got caught up in the nets of oppression. If enough people work together to create a thriving world where equality is rooted in reality, it would indeed be a wild and beautiful world.

Wildness breaks the barriers of 'should' and 'this is how it's always been.' Instead, saying, "Are we living in union with the Earth, and are we living in ways that honor the dignity of each human being?"

Wildness feels like a breath of fresh air, kindness, and a gentleness of not rushing to react but responding. Wildness is remembering who we are and what could be when we allow all of ourselves to be present: feelings, hopes, fears, and all.

QUESTIONS FOR FURTHER DISCOVERY

How do you embrace or apologize for your wild?

What makes you feel wild? What feels like the destructive wild or natural wild for you?

When was the last time you felt wild?

BOOK RECOMMENDATIONS

Untamed by Glennon Doyle-Melton
Burning Woman by Lucy Pearce
Women Who Run with the Wolves by Clarissa Pinkola Estés

Wild Red Tent

Five minutes before the Tent Begins:

Leader: Lovelies, please put your phones on silent or off, grab your water, snacks, journal, and token and join me in the circle.

Opening:

Leader: Before we begin, I would like to state that this is a safe space. In order to make it so, there needs to be agreement around keeping what is said in circle, in the circle. I'm asking you all to agree to only speak of your own experiences, and only give advice when asked. We will be talking about deeply personal things in the Red Tent. A gentle reminder that we can disagree and still accept each other. Can I have a show of hands for everyone willing to keep this space confidential, for themselves and everyone here tonight?

Shakeout and Grounded Breathing:

Leader: Let us take a minute to stand up, shake out any worries, or frustration from your day. Twist your body, shake your booty, kick your legs, jump up and down. Audibly make sounds while relaxing your jaw. Stretch, or move in a way that feels supportive.

Please have a seat in this circle, and let's do some ground breathing. You can close your eyes, start to relax your shoulders. You can roll your neck from side to side, rest your hands on your stomach, knees, or the ground, whatever is most comfortable for you. Start breathing in from your belly. Take a deep breath. As you exhale, release anything that came before tonight that is on your mind.

Breathe in again, releasing anything to come in the

future. Keep breathing, focusing on the sounds around you, the breath of other women, and your heartbeat. As you release your breath, feel your body settling into this space. In this moment, here with us. You are safe. You are loved. We are glad you are here with us.

Call in:

Leader: We are gathered in our Red Tent, as women, as daughters, as mothers, as workers and dreamers. We come here to speak our heart's desires, our mind's thoughts, and share the song of our souls. We see with our eyes, hear with our ears, and will hum along in our hearts. May this space be open, sacred, and grounded for us here tonight. Let us hold hands as we travel deeper together, learning to better love ourselves, each other, and the world.

Gender Neutral Option:

We are gathered in our Red Tent Tent as humans, as explorers, as workers and dreamers. We come here to speak our heart's desires, our mind's thoughts, and share the song of our souls. We see with our eyes, hear with our ears, and will hum along in our hearts. May this space be open, sacred, and grounded for us here tonight. Let us hold hands as we travel deeper together, learning to better love ourselves, each other, and the world.

Song: Call Down a Blessing

Leader: Close your eyes and think of what you want from this night and this week. It might be friendship, laughter, wisdom. We'll pass the bowl around one person at a time, and you'll say your blessing request, we'll sing the song with your word inside of it, and then after we sing over you, pass the bowl to the next woman. She'll share her blessing word, and we'll sing a blessing over her until we reach the end of the circle.

Call down a blessing x3, Call down, ____before you, ____behind you, ____Within you, and around you
Repeat for each person in the group, end with three call downs.

15: 1st Circle:

Leader: When speaking, please use the talking light, and when you finish, please say "I have spoken," so we know you have completed your thought. You can react with hand snaps, hand on your heart, and facial expressions. Please speak only of your own story, and don't give any advice unless asked.

For our first circle, what is your name, pronouns, your intention for tonight, and what does wild feel like to you?

30: Quote and Response: *Depending on the size of your group you can have a few people share, or have each person share for a minute about their response.*

Leader: I'll share this quote below, and then you can share a few words about how it resonates for you.

"The Feminine is your wild instinctive self, your core longing, your deepest life force. It is that which feels most true to you as a woman: uncultivated and raw. The Feminine is that which makes you alive and makes you burn. The Feminine is your passion: your expression of love, sexuality, creativity, relationship, beauty, devotion…through your female body and mind. The Feminine is the felt sense of acting in the world, based primarily in the body, rather than through the mind." -Lucy Pearce, *Burning Woman*, pg. 17

• • •

45: Activity 1: Wild Woman Meditation
Meditation Script is after this Red Tent Script.

1:00: Journal
Leader: Please grab your journal and pen. You can answer the following questions or free write about your experience.

What did your path look like? What did your Soul Door look like? What did your Wild Soul Self look like? What question did you ask, what was her response? How did she move? What did she give you? What were you wearing? Journal anything else that stuck out to you.

1:10: 2nd Circle
Share what you would like from your meditation.

1:25: Soul Care Time:
Leader: Now is our soul care time. This is 20 minutes to stretch, nap, chat, get food, go to the restroom. We do ask that you don't use this time to be on your phone. I'll give us a five-minute heads up to tent, and a one minute come to circle heads up.

1:30: Activity Two: Write a letter from your wild woman to yourself
Leader: Write a letter from your wild woman to yourself on how you can show up this month, or this week, you can also write it from her perspective in regards to something happening in your life. This may look like a drawing or a letter.

. . .

1:45: 3rd Circle:
Share your letter, or any thoughts about your experience writing your letter.

2: Womanhood story:
Leader: Womanhood stories are a core part of Red Tent, sharing our stories is a brave act. Sometimes they are joy filled, sad, frustrating, or a mix of all of it. The story may include periods, sex, birth, or any part of the woman and human experience. ___ has offered to share her story tonight. ____ the floor is yours.
See the appendix of the book for reaching out to your women to see who would like to share before the tent day.

After her story:
Leader: Thank you ___ for sharing your story. Is there anything you need from us? Hug, encouragement, a listening ear during break?
If they say yes, do what you can to fulfill that need if possible.

2:10: Closer *Grab your red thread (yarn) and make sure scissors are within reach.*
Leader: Red thread represents our connection to the women around us and those who have come before us. You will take your red yarn and wrap it around your wrist. You can wrap as many times as you want, as you recite your matriarchal spiritual lineage. Your lineage are the women and people who have influenced and loved you.
They don't have to be biologically related, you can claim or not claim anyone you would like. You can say your name, mother of (any children), daughter of x, daughter of y, daughter of daughters, daughter of whatever resonates

(Eve, Spirit, the moon, etc).You can also say descendent instead, or daughter of those who ____ instead of names.

When you have finished wrapping, pass the thread to the next person until it has gone all the way around the circle.

You can start the process and do your lineage and wrap and then pass it to the person on your right.

After the Red Thread has come back to you.

Leader: As we are connected, let us sing our song, we'll sing it three times, it goes flow, ebb, weavers, thread, weavers, thread, spiders, web. Sing it with me:

Song: We are the flow we are the ebb,
We are the weavers we are the thread,
We are the weavers we are the thread,
we are the spiders we are the web.
x3

Leader, pick up the scissors, and cut your thread, and as you explain the below, you can have the person to the left tie your thread.

Leader: When cutting the thread to tie bracelets, share your favorite moment and a takeaway. Have the lady to your left tie your yarn, twice in a square knot, and one slip knot, and this way, your thread will not come undone. After you have spoken, pass the scissors to the right, and the next person can go.

After the scissors make their way back to you and everyone has tied their thread, you can share the invitation below. Feel free to hold hands if you'd like.

· · ·

Invitation to curiosity

Leader: Tune in for the moments when you feel wild this month. You can tune into your Wild Soul Self for approval. Thank you for being a part of tonight's Red Tent. You are all a treasure, and I'm glad you are here. Our Red Tent is now closed.

Wild Soul Self Meditation

This is a meditation for you to meet your Wild Soul Self. Remember whatever you see, whether it's visuals, colors, or simply grounding is what you needed today, and trust you'll receive whatever you needed from this meditation.

Find a place to rest and be comfortable. Check in with your body on how she would like to sit, or lay.

You can rest your hands on your legs, your heart, or on your stomach.

Let your body sink into the ground, or the chair, like you're melting into yourself.

Any thoughts that come in, acknowledge them and let them pass.

Breathe in from your belly, and audibly exhale, letting go of any fears, or notions of what's to come.

(Pause)

With each breath, let yourself sink deeper into your seat, into the ground. You are safe, you are held. Sinking deeper, and deeper. Relaxing your muscles and letting it be.

Let your body root down in rest.

Envision a path before you. Begin to walk down it.

(Pause)

What does this path look like? The path soon starts going downwards, into a winding staircase. Walk down them.

Your hand may glide on the railing as you go down, what does it feel like?

What are your steps made of? Stone? Wood?

Keep going down, pass your heart door and keep walking.

(Pause)

In front of you is a door. Your Soul Door.

Take a moment to look at it. You can touch it. What colors are on it?

What is it made of? See if there is anything written on it or above, there may or may not be.

Take a moment to explore the textures and design of your door.

Take a breath and you have a knowing that you understand how to open the door, there may or may not be a handle. Know on the other side is the place where your dreams are crafted and you can rest and be rejuvenated. When you are ready, open the door and walk through.

Take a moment to explore the area around you. What do you see? Is it forest? A cafe, your grandparent's living room? A backyard garden?

(Pause)

Are there any sounds in your space? Birds, or people?

You notice to your right that there is a small path, and something in you nudges you to go down it.

(Pause)

This path takes you to a clearing, and in this clearing is your Wild Soul Self.

Take a moment to take your Wild Soul Self in, they may be a person, an animal, or something else entirely. There is no right or wrong answer.

What does your Soul Self look like? How do they move?

Your Wild Soul Self may or may not greet you. Do they say anything? Your Soul Self is your possibilities, your wild intuition, the nudge when you know something isn't right. You may greet them as well, take a moment to get acquainted.....

(pause)

Tell them about your intentions, and fears. Do they give you advice?

Tell you anything? You may hear in words, images, or just a Knowing you feel.

Know your Soul Self is a facet of you, they may seem

scary or different, or not what you expected, but there is something for you to learn from them

Your Soul Self has an item for you to remember them by, and to recall when you forget who are. Hold out your hand to receive it.

What is it? A piece of jewelry? A key, or a stone? Do you recognize it? What does this item mean to you?

Spend a few minutes with your Wild Soul Self, whether you are dancing, resting, or walking together.

(Pause one to two minutes)

When you are ready, say your goodbyes.

(Pause)

Before you walk back to your door take a look at what you are wearing. How do you feel in this space? Is there anything from this space in the way you feel you want to bring back to your everyday world?

(Pause)

Walk back to your door, taking in this space around you. You can breathe in the moment here if you'd like in your nature space, remember that you can come back anytime you'd like.

When ready, walk through your door and back up your spiral path.

Up up, past your soul door. Keep walking.

Pass your heart door and keep walking.

(Pause)

Go all the way to the top where light starts to shine through, and come up to fresh air on your path you started on.

Start walking back to you, to this room, and the sound of your heart in your chest.

Lay for a moment taking in the sounds, the smells, how your body feels.

When you feel complete, stretch, wiggle, yawn, and find your way back to the room and open your eyes.

ANGER

I am not a fan of anger. To be honest: it freaks me out because anger tells the truth.

Anger shows us where things are out of alignment when a boundary has been crossed or reveals memories that haven't been processed and are coming out at the seams. Anger feels loud. It is the color red—vibrant and hard to control. Yet, we try to control it.

We refuse to let it breathe or get air at all in our lives. Anger gets side-eyed because of how it expresses most often, but anger isn't inherently a bad feeling. Emotions are signposts of what we are feeling. The problem is: emotions do not die when we repress them.

They change form.

When we do not process our anger, it turns into resentment and bitterness. Both of which are rough on relationships and your inner life. Sealed anger, when simmering on low heat, can quickly turn into rage when ignited. Igniting could be someone asking you the same question for the tenth time that day. Or a series of events lined up like dominos, and when they all fall in succession, it's just too much. When rage comes out, it is like a volcanic eruption; it goes everywhere and gets on everything. Rage is not an emotion —it is a reaction to not listening to your anger in the first place.

All emotions are helpful, and we can use them as guides for understanding what's happening in our lives. If we don't ask our anger what it's trying to show us when it first reveals itself, we begin poisoning ourselves from the inside out. We eventually become Te Kā from *Moana*, burning everything in an attempt to protect ourselves, even if it hurts us and those we love in the process.

This chapter isn't about why anger is wrong. This chapter is about how we've vilified anger and how we can remember that anger is an emotional cohort in our journey trying to get our attention when things are off.

Acceptability politics have wrapped themselves around anger. Boys learn they cannot be sad, but they are allowed to be angry. Often trained oppositely, girls can feel sad but should not get mad. For my friend Cat, anger was just 'not something you do or have,' so she wasn't given any tools to see her anger as a child. It wasn't until she was an adult in a relationship and her partner told her anger was okay that she even realized she had any and started acknowledging it. Luckily, gender norms are changing, and all genders are beginning to embrace their emotions and chart a new path towards wholeness and reclamation. However, when a swath of humanity believes certain emotions are only for part of the population, a rift forms. Emotions will find paths to follow to express themselves when they are not acknowledged, regardless of gender.

"Be a good girl." "Smile and be nice." Many of us have heard these phrases whispered to us before interacting with others. Feminists are often labeled as angry as an insult, but women worldwide are reclaiming all of their emotions and acknowledge this anger saying, "Yes, I'm angry because of this injustice." Anger is the alarm bell telling us there is smoke and fire. If you ignore the fire alarm and say, "it's no big deal; it's probably just smoke," you could very well be missing the signal you needed to get out or fix the situation before it turns into a five-alarm fire.

When submission and silent agreement are said to be the only acceptable forms of recourse if you disagree, it's no wonder the easiest way to dismiss reactions is by labeling them unnecessary and over reactive. Righteous anger can fuel change and be a rallying cry towards what needs to shift or change in our society. When anger is used as a tool, it can be a force for good and wholeness. Even Jesus felt anger and flipped some tables.

RECOGNIZING CORE EMOTIONS

To even talk about anger means we need to have a certain level of emotional awareness. Our emotions are like water: sometimes it's a deep ocean of joy, a bubbling brook of contentment, or other times it's a tide pool of fear dragging you over the rocks. Various things impact our emotions, current life events, the past, hormones, relationships, and even societal trends at large.

When you remember your emotions are signposts to something more, you can dig under the surface because there is always a layer beneath the emotion. For instance, if you feel angry and hurt, go a layer deeper. Do you feel betrayed? Manipulated? Rejected? Knowing this deeper emotion allows you to pinpoint where the anger is coming from. Perhaps your anger comes from a deeper Heart Wound, a world event, a memory, or an overwhelming day.

Sometimes emotions are like a merry-go-round: spinning you in circles, making you want to vomit from feeling trapped and dizzy. When you label your feelings, you're getting off the merry-go-round and reorienting yourself. You can only get directions to where you want to go by finding out where you are.

Here's an example of the layer peeling process from when I burned out last year in 2020.

Top Feeling: I feel anger.

What's underneath? I feel betrayed and exhausted.

Why? Underneath the anger is the betrayal by past-me over-committing and not doing things present me could use at the moment. I also feel exhausted at the idea of doing more and growing my business.

Is there anything I can do to fix the past from happening? No.

What are the feelings underneath trying to tell me? They say, "I don't want to burn out again. I let myself down, and I don't want to screw up the future."*

If I was to repress the anger and not get curious and ask what is underneath, betrayal and abandonment might turn into fear, leading me to decide not to set goals or try new things. I might not allow myself to rest because I haven't 'earned it yet' while also not hiring the help I need to fix the problem. You can see how this one emotion can sprawl out and start causing toxic behavior pretty quickly.

Here's the catch:

If I address my underlying emotions and acknowledge past-me-made choices that put current-me in a pickle, I have to feel it.

And let's be honest.

Feeling emotions sucks sometimes.

It just does.

But emotions want to be felt—all of them. *I know. Lame sauce, and yet, it's how we are.*

You might be worried the feeling will suck you under, but if you genuinely feel it and see what's under it, you can understand what you need to do next.[1]

Here are some questions you can ask to peel the layers:

What is the situation?
What do I need?
Is there a way to calm down my system to get perspective on what is happening?

I've also found journaling from the perspective of anger tells me the truth of what is going on. When it's on the page, I can see where I'm hurt and what I need to move forward instead of swirling everything around angrily in my head.

SHOULD STORIES

Once we have clarified our core emotions, we can identify our *Should Stories*. Byron Katie leads "The Work," a series of four questions to help you drill down to the core of what is bothering you. She says emotional clarity comes down to acknowledging reality as it stands in this moment and what you can know as absolute truth. Which, according to her, is nothing, so we might as well be present in reality as it stands in the moment.

When we use Should Stories: we say, "I should have known better," or "they should not have done that." These Stories keep us from processing our anger and emotions by allowing us to wield our anger outwardly instead of feeling it. But the more we harbor radioactive anger at others, the more we feel it, too, even if we think we don't. When we can take the *Should Story* away about what should have happened, we can identify the root of this emotion. We can say, "I'm furious at myself for getting myself into this situation."

Well, now you know the truth of the matter: You are angry. You understand what is underneath your anger.

And you are in this situation.

So what are you going to do now?

When you see reality as it stands and understand why you are angry, you can choose your path. You can ask questions to figure out what happened and diminish the possibility of it happening in the future.

Some questions I like to ask are:

Did I define the boundary?
What lines of communication got crossed?
Did I ask for help?
Did I give myself the time or support I needed to accomplish this?

It's hard to decide to be manipulative or guilt-trip yourself even longer when you are in the place of acceptance, saying, "Okay, here I am. What's next? What is out of alignment here? What boundary do I need to set, or conversation I need to have?" As strange as it sounds, listening to and digging through the Should Story behind my anger has been game-changing.

Sometimes we are just angry at ourselves. When we feel our angst for so long, it can feel embedded in our skin. Forgiveness is one way to work through anger, and it's just like boundaries. It's not always about the other person; it's about ourselves. It allows us to be released. Forgiving doesn't always mean reconciliation or forgive and forget. It can be, "I forgive you, and here's my new boundary." Other times it is moving on and saying, "This was on me. Here's what I'll do in the future to navigate this." Talking it out and addressing the underlying fears can take away the fierce aggressiveness of anger.

> Ayesha realized how anger was an undercurrent in her relationship with her Dad and used anger as a guide to figuring out what needed to shift. "My relationship with my Dad was nonexistent as a child. He was a Debbie Downer. He would walk into the house, and the house would shift entirely in the feeling and the atmosphere and ambiance. When he and my mom split up, he did not want me to have anything to do with her, he took on trying to be a parent, and it did not go well. I realized blood is not enough to call family, family.
>
> Tent taught me what anger feels like. I remember thinking, 'Oh, this is what anger is! I can't misuse it.' Using my anger wisely, I created a new relationship with my Dad with boundaries to guide us to a healthier place. I feel like it's helping my Dad realize, 'Oh, hold on, she's an adult woman who is making her own decisions and standing up for herself and the things she deserves. I can't treat her the same way I used to.' So that helped in difficult situations. I finally know what I deserve. I don't listen to what anyone else says my boundaries 'should' be, anymore."

PROCESS YOUR ANGER

Identifying your Should Story and your core feelings doesn't mean your body automatically calms down. Your adrenaline and body might be running on high alert, especially if you are in a stressful situation. Our body is like a pressure cooker, so how do you want to let off steam? Yelling can help make you feel heard, but it makes the situation worse if directed towards someone. You can run it out, stretch, dance it out, nap, craft, or go on a long walk. There are even businesses where you can safely destroy things, and rage out by smashing old broken cars and plates.

When I'm feeling like a live wire and like I could lash out, I take myself to a clearing near my house and lay in the woods for a little bit. Sometimes I'm there for ten minutes, and sometimes two hours. It helps me regroup my thoughts and get perspective before I say or do something I'll regret.

When her kids are on edge, a friend told me she either puts them in the dirt outside or in some water, whether a shower or a hot bath, and it works like a charm. I think this holds for all humans. I usually say if you are feeling off, "Jesus, sleep, food, bath, or touch will usually do the trick." So far, it hasn't led me wrong.

Your 'emotional forest clearing' might look different. Maybe it's a hot bath, stress cleaning, or finishing a yard project. Letting your body switch gears allows it to calm down, so you aren't feeling like a loaded gun.

Sometimes though, a run or a nap doesn't cut it. If we have been repressing our emotions for a while, they metastasize in our bodies. More and more, people understand the impact our energy, mind, and stress has on our bodies. We feel the tension in our necks and get stomach ulcers. Our body, mind, soul are all connected. If you do not process it—whether through finishing the stress response cycle, talking to someone, or journaling it—the emotion simmers and festers.

 Lindsay has been working to process and listen to what the anger is telling her, "My relationship to anger hasn't been a bad one, but when I get livid angry, I cry instead of raging. My anger comes out silent and brooding. After being in the Red Tent a couple of months ago, my Dad said a brutal offhand comment to me. I've never been that angry and upset before at him. I held my tongue and listened instead of lashing out, and it was weird. It was like I could step outside of the situation. I told myself to wait before responding. I knew it didn't mean I was taking it and allowing it, but I could look above and see that my pausing didn't mean any of the things he said were true. I didn't overreact. I said "Okay" and walked back to my home.

Even though I felt anger and cried, I did my own thing the rest of the evening. Usually, I'd beat myself up for not fighting back or retorting. The next day after work, I was still processing and heard a knock at the back door. He was in tears and apologized for being out of line. I didn't have to do anything or retaliate. It felt like me taking a different route in anger was enough and spoke for itself. I just had to lean in and be present."

The odd thing about simmering emotions is, when it comes time to heal, we are so used to having these deep emotions that we can be defensive about letting go. It's almost like our simmering emotions are the one ring from *Lord of the Rings*.[2]

In *LOTR*, there is a creature named Gollum who keeps trying to get the powerful ring, even though it's already rotted his body and heart. (Spoiler: he eventually dies trying to get it.)

Let us not be Gollum with our simmering, repressed emotions.

It's easy to feel self-righteous about our anger. Self-righteousness allows us to use anger as a weapon against others. We become better than others in our heads if we can say, "SEE, you did X! I have proof to be angry!" But secretly, we believe if we let it go, we will be used again or let the injustice happen again.

We can also use anger to build walls between ourselves and other people. This wall can become a too-thick barrier other people can't cross, and that's no way to live either. If it eats you alive, the anger is doing nothing but being destructive towards yourself.

Instead, direct the anger into action and change-making.

Anger is great at noticing and naming injustice as well. We can use our anger as fuel to push us to create the change we want in the world. We can use our anger to see where people made mistakes and state new boundaries.

Let's use the destructive power of anger to tear down broken systems to build ones where all humans can thrive, including ourselves!

GENERATIONAL ANGER

I have a beautifully blended extended family, which means I had three sets of Grandparents, which I thought was the best growing up. Many of my childhood memories involve being at a grandparent's house, whether eating fudge in Michigan, running around in the snow after being in a hot tub in Iowa, or having a grill out and playing card games at the kitchen table. Anger can be sneaky because it can coexist side by side with beautiful memories through sharp words and loud, harsh reactions.

My biological grandfathers were both amazing men and fantastic storytellers. My Grandpa Ray was a generous man and a mean card player. My Grandpa Tim always had space at the table for you and threw great gatherings with drinks always in the fridge, but neither had the tools to process their anger, so they turned to alcohol to help them cope, and to this day, it breaks my heart.

All of my grandmothers loved their husbands to the best

244 | RED THREAD

of their ability and taught me what it meant to stay peaceful, resourceful and how to handle pressure-filled situations.[3]

My Grandma Grace, who got a divorce with four young ones in tow, taught me when to say enough was enough and that everyone deserves a love where they feel safe when she married my Grandpa Steve. My Grandma Annie creates an atmosphere you feel joy in, holds peace with both hands, and creates beautiful art. My Grandma Julie was a woman of prayer and raised her kids with compassion and resourcefulness.

Generational trauma passes down via alcoholism, anger, silence, or other coping mechanisms, including abuse. People get angry and lash out because they don't have the language to express the layers beneath the anger or feel like they can be vulnerable and honest. Our older generations weren't given space to process their emotions. The society our grandparents grew up in told them to "suck it up and figure it out" and "man up."

Society didn't embrace vulnerability, it was scoffed at, and it impacts families, including mine still to this day. The amount of conversation around mental health and emotions has changed since my grandparents were growing up. We have so many more tools at our disposal for emotional processing. Although some may say mental health awareness is everyone being overly sensitive, I think it is beyond time we allowed ourselves to de-armor and be honest about our hurts and feelings.

Because they both experienced the destructive power of words said in anger when they grew up, my parents did their best not to speak out of fury. When my Dad was angry, he would get quiet and go for a bike ride, but my Mom carried angry reactions with her for longer, and it was a bigger battle for her to overcome.

Mom shared that she and Dad had to create an anger plan to curb her reactions before crossing a line. Dad would put up a hand or ask for space, or Mom would notice she was feeling rage, and they would take ten minutes to an hour to cool off and then come back together to solve the situation. Through the years, her reactions have been less and less, she says, thanks to prayer, counseling, a good church home. She also found solace in support groups for those who struggle with anger after growing up in an abusive home.

I'm a carbon copy of my mom emotionally, and both of us are pretty sensitive,[4] so I have to watch my reactions, as my face is a narc and shows everything I'm thinking. Seeing how anger worked in my family line, I suppressed anger for a lot of my life so I wouldn't be reactionary. Looking back, I can see it would come out via snarky quips, yelling, breakdowns of feeling overwhelmed, and I have often used alcohol as a coping tool instead of listening to what anger was trying to tell me.[5]

I think 2020 was the first time I think I truly tapped into anger and felt absolute rage. Funnily enough, the rage came out when reading a political Facebook post a family member made, and the resulting insults that were slung my way when I responded.

My Should Story was "be quiet to make my family happy, bite my tongue, nod my head, and agree." Beneath the feelings of rage and anger were betrayal, distrust, feeling unseen and belittled, and frustration with myself for not advocating more fiercely for my own beliefs and the recognition of the humanity of my friends.

I kept shoving all these emotions down until they all exploded with the one political Facebook post. It only takes one straw to break the camel's back. Anger is waiting for you to address it.

It only takes one small thing to blow the cap off and expose the truth of how you feel.

Fury demands to be heard and witnessed.

. . .

After that situation, I had some honest conversations with my family. I drew new boundary lines about what Jer and I were comfortable talking about online with family and started being more open about where Jer and I stood. Doing so helped me feel like I was speaking up and not just smiling and nodding not to cause trouble.

It is sometimes more important to prioritize safety instead of sharing the truth piling up inside. If you can, get support and speak up; if it's not safe to do so, I encourage you to find a place you feel you can, whether that's an online forum, group, or mentor. That way, your anger isn't roiling only inside you, but you feel heard and seen by others. Realizing you aren't the only one who is going through a situation can be a balm for your soul.

Anger can be a whirlwind to feel fully. With the way society treats anger, it can seem like the best offense is a good defense. In reality, our anger is more like the strategist on the side of the field, to show us where the gaps are, guiding us to find what is right and good in our lives.

> *What would a shift in the way you approach anger in your communication look like for you?*
> *Is it possible for you to take pauses or not respond until you are ready with the words or boundaries you want to set and say?*
> *Where have there been boundary crossings, misspoken words, or injustice in your life?*

Take some time to tune in and see where you are holding your anger and what it's trying to tell you. Remember, your emotions are signposts, and they can't control you. But if you repress them, they will leak out one way or another.

Let's gently unpack and see what one step closer to wholeness and kindness towards ourselves and those around us can look like by using our anger as a map instead of a weapon.

QUESTIONS FOR FURTHER DISCOVERY

How do you process your anger?

Is there anger you feel now? What's underneath it? What is the story you are creating around it? Once you've identified your *Should Story*, what is your next step?

How has anger been treated in your life? Your family? Your friendships?

BOOK RECOMMENDATIONS

How to do the Work by Dr. Nicole LePara
The Dance of Anger by Dr. Harriet Lerner
The Work of Byron Katie by Byron Katie

Anger Red Tent

Five minutes before the Tent Begins:

Leader: Lovelies, please put your phones on silent or off, grab your water, snacks, journal, and token and join me in the circle.

Opening:

Leader: Before we begin, I would like to state that this is a safe space. In order to make it so, there needs to be agreement around keeping what is said in circle, in the circle. I'm asking you all to agree to only speak of your own experiences, and only give advice when asked. We will be talking about deeply personal things in the Red Tent. A gentle reminder that we can disagree and still accept each other. Can I have a show of hands for everyone willing to keep this space confidential, for themselves and everyone here tonight?

Shakeout and Grounded Breathing:

Leader: Let us take a minute to stand up, shake out any worries, or frustration from your day. Twist your body, shake your booty, kick your legs, jump up and down. Audibly make sounds while relaxing your jaw. Stretch, or move in a way that feels supportive.

Please have a seat in this circle, and let's do some ground breathing. You can close your eyes, start to relax your shoulders. You can roll your neck from side to side, rest your hands on your stomach, knees, or the ground, whatever is most comfortable for you. Start breathing in from your belly. Take a deep breath. As you exhale, release anything that came before tonight that is on your mind.

Breathe in again, releasing anything to come in the future. Keep breathing, focusing on the sounds around you,

the breath of other women, and your heartbeat. As you release your breath, feel your body settling into this space. In this moment, here with us. You are safe. You are loved. We are glad you are here with us.

Call in:

Leader: We are gathered in our Red Tent, as women, as daughters, as mothers, as workers and dreamers. We come here to speak our heart's desires, our mind's thoughts, and share the song of our souls. We see with our eyes, hear with our ears, and will hum along in our hearts. May this space be open, sacred, and grounded for us here tonight. Let us hold hands as we travel deeper together, learning to better love ourselves, each other, and the world.

Gender Neutral Option:

We are gathered in our Red Tent Tent as humans, as explorers, as workers and dreamers. We come here to speak our heart's desires, our mind's thoughts, and share the song of our souls. We see with our eyes, hear with our ears, and will hum along in our hearts. May this space be open, sacred, and grounded for us here tonight. Let us hold hands as we travel deeper together, learning to better love ourselves, each other, and the world.

Song: Call Down a Blessing

Leader: Close your eyes and think of what you want from this night and this week. It might be friendship, laughter, wisdom. We'll pass the bowl around one person at a time, and you'll say your blessing request, we'll sing the song with your word inside of it, and then after we sing over you, pass the bowl to the next woman. She'll share her

blessing word, and we'll sing a blessing over her until we reach the end of the circle.

Call down a blessing x3, Call down, ____before you, ____behind you, ____Within you, and around you
Repeat for each person in the group, end with three call downs.

15: 1st Circle:

Leader: When speaking, please use the talking light, and when you finish, please say "I have spoken," so we know you have completed your thought. You can react with hand snaps, hand on your heart, and facial expressions. Please speak only of your own story, and don't give any advice unless asked.

For our first circle, what is your name, pronouns, intention for tonight, and what has your experience of anger been like?

30: Quote and Response:

Leader: I'll share the quote and then you can share how it resonates with you.

"Where there is anger, there is always pain underneath."-Ekhart Tolle

45: Activity 1: Peeling Should Layers

Leader: Part of the reason anger comes up is because it is a symptom of hurt or fear. This hurt or fear when not addressed, then expresses itself as anger. Anger can also show where a boundary line and shows where something is broken, or a situation is not okay.

When we think a situation should be different or get wrapped up in *why* it 'should' be different, or how we should feel, we can let our anger eat at us. We can stigmatize anger, and shame ourselves for feeling it, when there may be a valid reason anger is present. Emotions are sign points to how you feel about situations. We can use our anger to direct us into action.

This question sequence will help us dig under the top layer of emotion, and figure out what is going on beneath it, and how you can take the next right step to resolve it. Please grab your journals, and write down and finish these sentence starters.

Pause between each statement for people to write their answers.

I feel x
   I feel x because/about y
   I believe y should be _____
   Is the previous statement true? (Could be yes could be no)
   If Y is reality right now what does that mean? What is not sustainable? What do you need? How can you get it? What needs to change or shift?
   If you don't make this shift or change what will happen?
   What do you need to make this shift happen?
   What support do you need to make the shift? (Accountability, a boundary conversation, therapy, money, etc.)

1:00: 2nd Circle
   Leader: Share your takeaways from the 'peeling shoulds' exercise.

1:15: Womanhood story:
   Leader: Womanhood stories are a core part of Red Tent, sharing our stories is a brave act. Sometimes they are joy filled, sad, frustrating, or a mix of all of it. The story may include periods, sex, birth, or any part of the woman and

human experience. ___ has offered to share her story tonight. ____ the floor is yours.

See the appendix of the book for reaching out to your women to see who would like to share before the tent day.

After her story:

Leader: Thank you ___ for sharing your story. Is there anything you need from us? Hug, encouragement, a listening ear during break?

If they say yes, do what you can to fulfill that need if possible.

1:25: Soul Care Time:

Leader: Now is our soul care time. This is 20 minutes to stretch, nap, chat, get food, go to the restroom. We do ask that you don't use this time to be on your phone. I'll give us a five-minute heads up to tent, and a one minute come to circle heads up.

1:45: Activity Two: Releasing Anger

Leader: Sometimes there is so much pent up emotion around the anger we can't see what we are actually angry about. During each person's time to vent the rest of us will hold grace sponges for her.

A grace sponge is a Jason Momoa sized sponge that is soaked with love and grace so that when things come at you, you can distance yourself and say okay, are they meaning to hurt me, or are they acting out of a place of hurt? Am I reacting because of this person, or because I had a rough day, or because this is a heart wound for me? So many times we react harshly without taking a minute to look at what's really going on. So imagine yourself holding a sponge of grace to not absorb any of the anger that is being released.

Depending on your format, you can do this in pairs and three minutes each, or if virtually, give each woman one to two minutes on the clock to let it all out. After each person goes have her shake it off, or brush herself off to let go of any stagnant energy.

2: Circle

What was holding space for someone else to let it all out feel like?

2:15: Closer *Grab your red thread (yarn) and make sure scissors are within reach.*

Leader: Red thread represents our connection to the women around us and those who have come before us. You will take your red yarn and wrap it around your wrist. You can wrap as many times as you want, as you recite your matriarchal spiritual lineage. Your lineage are the women and people who have influenced and loved you.

They don't have to be biologically related, you can claim or not claim anyone you would like. You can say your name, mother of (any children), daughter of x, daughter of y, daughter of daughters, daughter of whatever resonates (Eve, Spirit, the moon, etc). You can also say descendent instead, or daughter of those who ____ instead of names.

When you have finished wrapping, pass the thread to the next person until it has gone all the way around the circle.

You can start the process and do your lineage and wrap and then pass it to the person on your right.

After the Red Thread has come back to you.

Leader: As we are connected, let us sing our song, we'll sing it three times, it goes flow, ebb, weavers, thread, weavers, thread, spiders, web. Sing it with me:

Song: We are the flow we are the ebb,
We are the weavers we are the thread,
We are the weavers we are the thread,
we are the spiders we are the web.
x3

Leader, pick up the scissors, and cut your thread, and as you explain the below, you can have the person to the left tie your thread.

Leader: When cutting the thread to tie bracelets, share your favorite moment and a takeaway. Have the lady to your left tie your yarn, twice in a square knot, and one slip knot, and this way, your thread will not come undone. After you have spoken, pass the scissors to the right, and the next person can go.

After the scissors make their way back to you and everyone has tied their thread, you can share the invitation below. Feel free to hold hands if you'd like.

Invitation to curiosity

Leader: Whenever anger comes up for you this month, think about if this is something you need to release in a healthy way, or something that indicates a change needs to be made.

Thank you for being a part of tonight's Red Tent. You are all a treasure, and I'm glad you are here. Our Red Tent is now closed.

BOUNDARIES

'Boundaries' may feel like a loaded word. If you have boundaries, are you being a bitch, or being assured of yourself and what you deserve? Are you pushing other people away or claiming your choice-making sovereignty?

Sometimes boundaries aren't as clear-cut as those questions make them sound. I once saw a post saying, "Screw everyone else. Do what makes you happy."

Sorry to inform you, but that's not a reasonable boundary either.

Boundaries should be sustainable guidelines for interacting with the world and the people around you. They should allow you to avoid burnout and to thrive where you are.

Boundaries are not:

- Manipulative tools.
- A type of aggressive punishment.
- A way to isolate yourself from the world.

Think of boundaries as a picket fence with a gate. You are letting people know where your responsibilities, thoughts, and energy end and theirs begin. To set boundaries, we need to have the words to let others know how we feel and what we need.

There are symptoms you can pay attention to so you know when you need to set a boundary.

> Nedra Glover Tawwab a therapist and author of *Set Boundaries, Find Peace* writes, "The most significant symptom is *discomfort*, which manifests itself as anger, resentment, frustration and burnout. When we feel any of these, we likely need to set a boundary. We tolerate unhealthy boundaries because we don't understand our feelings, and we fail to notice the discomfort. We see that something is "off," but we're unaware of what is causing the discomfort."[1]

A boundary you set for others could be to not make fun of you or not to assume you'll do a task you were never assigned at work. You can set boundaries with a friend who is always late or a family member who makes inappropriate comments. Boundaries can range from words, time, touch, energy, and even space. They can be between you and others, you and yourself, and even you and God. While it is important to not close yourself off from the world with impenetrable boundaries, you also need to make sure you don't set too weak boundaries. If you find yourself always pleasing people or not saying no, you may need to strengthen your boundaries.

> DeLandrea sets a boundary around her identity and how she shows up, "A boundary I have is I'm not going to hide who I am — my blackness or my pride in being black and everything that comes with that. For the longest time growing up in Oklahoma, I had to be ashamed of being Black. So a big boundary for me is I won't tolerate having to shrink my blackness or make it not be a part of me because it's always there. I try to educate, and sometimes I have to remove myself from a situation because I don't like to say things out of anger."

When you start enforcing boundaries, the words can feel stuck in your throat. It is normal to have trouble finding the right words to use or may feel uncomfortable and scary. Remember, close relationships build on truth, kindness, belonging, and speaking your boundaries. Communicating what you need allows your relationships to thrive.

Think about it in terms of making a Christmas or birthday list. You let the person know what you'd love. Does it always happen? No. But the odds of them knowing what you would appreciate skyrocket.

Choosing vulnerability, and looking to understand the intention and heart of yourself and others in the present moment, can mitigate destruction and lessen regret later.

> In her book *As Is*, Erin Brown talks about how people need time to adjust when you shift, "You might experience some strange behavior or resistance to your newly blossoming attitude toward yourself and others; know that your inner circle may change. Some of them will

adjust and simply need time to do so. Some may leave you for a time and come back healthier (many of mine have). Just acknowledge that any change in YOU requires new behavior from others and lovingly allow them the space to adjust."[2]

Lovingly allowing others space to adjust means acknowledging there will be differences in how you interact. Sometimes adjustments are more challenging than you might expect. Let's explore how we can adapt our boundaries and relationships with grace and using clear words.

MIND READING

One of my favorite questions to ask people is, "What would be your dream superpower?"[3] People respond most with the ability to fly, followed by teleporting, general wizard magic, or breathing underwater. Mind reading gets brought up often as well. Still, many of us already live our lives as though those around us can read our minds, which can undermine our relationships.

I know I have a terrible habit of assuming those around me are mind readers—no need to tell them information or my expectations because they already know—*Except they don't*. When plans fall through, or feelings are hurt, it's easy to blame others. Assumptions of blame are more accessible than taking time to dig beneath the surface of where the miscommunication has happened.

What if we approached our partners with requests for what we need instead of hoping they choose the proper reaction to have based on our emotional venting? Telling them what you want will be the most direct way to ensure the best outcome and resolve your inner turmoil. Otherwise, their only option is to guess about whether you want to be left alone, hugged, encouraged, reminded about your goals, given accountability, or advice. These can either fan the flame or put out the fire depending on the wind's direction.

Jer and I would get frustrated in these conversations and started asking for what support we were looking for upfront. An example being, "Hey Jer, this isn't related to you. I need to vent about this situation. I would love insight on how I responded, or if I need to follow back around with something else." He then knows exactly what I'm looking for and how he can best support me.

Another example when I'm not in the mood for advice is, "I don't want any advice. I realize it is solvable, but my feelings are hurt, so can you hold me while I cry and tell me the world won't end because they said this?" Asking for what you need helps others in the best way possible, so they don't have to take stabs in the dark.

Asking for what you need doesn't just apply to partners, though; this applies to all humans. Just remember, while it is okay to ask for this, we must create space for other people to be human and react. Asking, "It would be supportive if you could …" gives people a map to meet you where you are and to know how to make the best connection. Maybe someone cannot provide advice or gets angry in response to sorting through a complicated conversation, do what you can and know you are doing your best. If someone says no or can't meet you heart-to-heart, acknowledge and respect their no. You can explore meeting your needs in another way. Using this language can help defuse a situation before it gets messy.

YOU ARE ALLOWED TO SAY "NO."

It was a beautiful day on the North Shore in Hawaii, and I was all set to deliver the performance of my life for a little girl's birthday party. The parents had requested I swim in and meet the birthday girl and her friends on the beach, and I was happy to do this as I had done it before; it's a magical experience for the kids. That day, however, I felt a nudge in the back of my mind, a whisper to not go into the water because the waves were a tad stronger than I was comfortable with.

As a mermaid, there are few things better than being in the ocean. You can stretch your fins fully and extend your muscles as you sway back and forth. Getting out to the deep of the ocean from the beach is another story. The tide can quickly grab your fin and turn you around, the surface area of your tail making it harder to swim as your fin suctions to the sand as the water recedes. It took me a few minutes of effort and the conquering of a few rough waves to swim out into deeper water where I could tread comfortably.

After a few minutes of treading water, the girls walked onshore. I did some fin flips from afar to say hello, smacking my fluke into the water to make a big splash. As I gathered my breath to swim back in, I told myself, "You can make it. This is no big deal."

I made it safely to the other side, but it was harder than the first time. Have you ever seen a seal scooting through wet sand? That's how I looked. Two dads came to help pick me up to bring me to dry sand to do the birthday party.

We sang songs, played games, and the girls were beaming from ear to ear. Halfway through the party, one of the girls asked if we could go in the water. The shallows are the best for small children, but the shallows are the absolute worst place for a mermaid with the water behaving the way it was. I didn't want to cause a stink by being a mermaid who didn't want to get into the water, so I said, "Sure!" and off we went.

We played, and I gave rides as much as I was able to. At the end of the party, the parents had told me they wanted me to swim back out to the ocean so the girls could leave. By this time, I was exhausted and wrestled with the idea of telling them "no." I shrugged it off, thinking, "What's one more time?" said goodbye to the girls, and dove under the waves.

I timed my dive wrong.

I dove into the middle of a wave, and the current grabbed my fiberglass monofin and twisted me like a wet towel. Shooting pain ran up my back, the salt stinging my eyes as tears ran down my face. I gasped for air as I breached the water with my wig falling off. I clutched my crown with frantic determination as I swam to deeper water. As I passed the shallows, I got my tail off in record time, occasionally smiling and waving at the girls as they left the beach.

As they cleared the ridge, I let myself feel the pain. The water held me as I floated on my back as if apologizing for the misunderstanding of twisting me like seaweed earlier. My back was seizing, and I needed to get on land. I gingerly made my way back.

The burning sand on my feet was a painful reminder that I should have stayed on land. I should have said "No."

I did my best to make their dreams of what a mermaid should be a reality. But instead, I put myself in a risky situation and paid the price for it. I gingerly wrapped my tail, the saltwater from the tears in my eyes mixing with the salt of the sea, and walked back to my car. I put my key in and cried the whole way home. At home, I curled tightly into an Epsom salt bath, berating myself for not being brave enough to say no.

As a people pleaser, I never want to let anyone down, but I had let myself down by trying to be the perfect mermaid. When I called another mermaid to commiserate, she was shocked I hadn't said no. I didn't realize I was allowed to set my boundaries and say "no."

EXPRESSING THE WORD 'NO.'

I have felt bad in the past saying no. I believed if you could make a "yes" happen, I should to the best of my ability. Not anymore. If I need to say no because of risk, morals, values, sanity, health, or over-commitment, I explain myself and say no.

Something I've learned is the more we say no, the more we can say yes. Saying no to say yes may seem oxymoronic, but the default for many people is to say "yes."

If you say a hundred "yesses," that means you're only giving 1% to everything. Are you trying to give more than 1% to all of your commitments? Overcommitting maxes you out, and you know what follows? Burn out.

You think, "Oh, it's fine. Get back up. Keep moving, act as nothing happened." You brush it off, but it's not okay, and the "yesses" you wish were "nos" will catch up with you eventually.

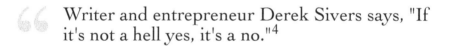

Writer and entrepreneur Derek Sivers says, "If it's not a hell yes, it's a no."[4]

Sometimes we don't want to do something, but we have to say yes, *hello dishes, and piled up laundry.* I'm not saying we become pampered princesses and never do the chores or a work assignment again because we only want to do things we love. What we CAN do is look at what is within our delegating realm to work around an issue. My favorite workaround is my fabulous accountant and my Roomba. Sometimes workarounds are deciding Sundays are for week planning and cleaning; other times, they ask, "What am I willing to pay for this to be off my plate?" Home chefs, trading sitter nights with friends, virtual assistants, and car mechanics are all types of workarounds.

Sometimes, we have to do things that aren't always fun. For these, look at the reason you are doing them. Are you taking care of your home because it's a sanctuary? How much of a 'hell yes' is that? Then tending your home and cleaning it probably falls under your umbrella of 'hell yes.' Do you want to help your local organization thrive? If that's a 'yes,' does that look like serving on the Board or volunteering one day a week?

Considering your options can make that 'yes' a 'hell yes.' Are you excited about the paperwork of running a business? No, but it's probably worth it to keep your company running. Maybe you have a new job you are super happy about, but you don't like one specific task, Okay. Maybe on Wednesdays, you can play your favorite song and take care of it.

Liz Gilbert calls this the 'shit sandwich': The choice and job you choose always comes with a shit sandwich; you just have to determine if it's worth the good and the bad.[5] If not, find something different, and see if you are willing to eat that sandwich instead. A personal example is that Jer is in the military, so we move every two to three years. For some, moving isn't worth being enlisted, but we thrive off the adventure and the newness. Being the new kid on the block every three years and far from home is a sandwich we are willing to eat.

We're all making choices, so if something is constantly grating, we either need to remove ourselves from the situation or figure out how to move ahead. We can often wrap ourselves up in 'shoulds' and 'shouldn't. We say, "It shouldn't be this hard," or "I should do this, but I hate it," These shoulds contract around us and choke us. Remove the Should Story. What is reality as it stands? Do you have to change your kid's diaper? Then you have to change the diaper. Does the presentation or paper have to get made? Yes? Then what do you need to get it done? If we have to do it anyway, we can choose our attitude and how we move about it, perhaps including a workaround, but that's on us and speaking up for what we are willing or unwilling to do.

There are systems of oppression in place that make life harder for some than others. It's easy to grow resentment when you compare lives or dismiss lived experiences. When you can take advantage of help or assist in creating a world where others thrive more fully, then do so. Be a part of weaving a better world for all of us, including yourself.

PLATES

You may have seen plate spinners and are amazed, like me, at how much balance and control they have at any given point. They may be spinning actual ceramic plates, but we are spinning multiple hypothetical plates every day. These plates are made up of our commitments and choices. Plates are things we've already agreed we'd do. Our family is a plate; our faith might be a plate; our work could be a massive plate; a volunteer opportunity or carpool for the kids' soccer practice are other plates. Part of saying yes is looking at how many you are currently balancing in the air.

Take a moment to write in the corner of this page, or your journal, what plates you have spinning right now. Some plates might be more extensive than others, and some may be temporary plates. All of this is okay. Some people can spin eight plates, but maybe you are a four-plate person. What is your max number of plates? I can tell my max plate number by looking at how many plates I was spinning (meaning what I had going on in my life) when I burned out last.

Sometimes we need help to spin more plates. If you are a military spouse, like me, life can add plates against your will. For example, when a spouse goes on a six-month-long deployment overseas, getting help spinning extra plates can look like a meal delivery service, having parents come help, or hiring someone to clean your floors every three months. That's okay—we are human, we can only do so much.

If you only need to shift a plate for a little bit of time, you can say, "I'm sorry, I need another day," or "I need another week." If you can be honest about what you need, it will help you figure out the next right step.

Don't let watching others spin their plates start a comparison game in your mind.

Remember, we are all made differently, and sometimes others have help you can't see. It's okay to put plates away to keep others spinning and pick those plates back up when you can. Some plates are plastic and durable, and others are fine china. Making the call to turn down a commitment, ask for a raise, or quit an organization can be rough. But if you realize you are consistently dropping plates, you've got to give yourself a break. Otherwise, you may be the next thing to fall.

The language you can use when setting down a commitment is,

"I need to prioritize x in this season, so I need to put in my two weeks notice about y,"

"I will finish the project this month, and then I will be stepping away."

"It's been wonderful being a part of this, but I can no longer give my commitment."

People may very well push back or react, but stay calm and firm. If it's possible to give a heads up when putting a plate down, that can make the transition easier. Just because others don't believe you can say no doesn't mean you have identical requirements.

When was the last time you said no? Was it to yourself or someone else? How do you feel about the word no? Sorting through your personal layers of meaning on the word no can help you say it clearly and purposefully when you need to.

HAVING THE HARD CONVERSATION

When you realize something has to give, a Knowing sets into your body. You know what needs to happen, but how? Where to even start? Most of the time, it begins with honest conversations. One tip would be using a level-setting strategy when you need to talk through a challenging discussion.

I can't remember where I found this from, but essentially you tell the other person the intensity of the conversation you want to have. There are levels 1 through 5. Level 1 is an easy everyday conversation. Level 3 is, "Hey, I want to be serious; please don't laugh at me. I'm vulnerable here." Level 5 is death, divorce, and devastating destruction. As exaggerated as level 5 may sound, levels aren't a joking matter. They're a way of washing away any pretense and getting down to brass tacks so you can have clear expectations between both parties. Beginning the conversation aware of how serious the other person feels allows for a safer space to be vulnerable.

I had a level 4 conversation with my husband about going on a family trip in the middle of a pandemic. Level 4 was also the conversation level we had about having surgery to have my tubes removed. Completely different subjects, but the level I chose portrayed to him how serious I felt about each.

Sometimes, when we have hard conversations, we've been preparing for them in our brains for a while. We come in prepared, but the other person may not know what is coming and is surprised. The conversation can veer off track, leaving hurt and confusion in its wake. Using levels with someone you trust reminds you that it's not you against them; it's you and the other person facing a problem —together.

We all know the dreaded "we need to chat" words can lead straight to a what-happened-what's-wrong mindset, and it can queue them to spin up a story in their head about what could be wrong. The other person starts their replay game and goes into defense mode. They put barriers up instinctively when you just wanted to chat about what you want to do for dinner or about a double date next week. Their adrenaline starts pumping through their system, waiting for the shoe to drop, which is not great for the mood.

Having healthy boundaries creates an atmosphere for your relationship can grow. Being on the defensive can make it hard to set boundaries when you feel like they will act wounded the second you establish them. Setting the stage for the conversations and the tone you want helps reduce defensiveness.

Here's an example, Abby says to Kaylee, "Hey love, I want to talk about what it would mean if I accept a job offer and we have to move out of state. I want to have a Level four convo about it. Do you have time now, or can we put this in the calendar for later today?" If Kaylee is in the middle of something, she might switch gears quickly, but maybe she's in the middle of work and doesn't have the brain space. So, if she responds with, "Hey, I'm swamped till 5, let's talk tonight," both Kaylee and Abby know what's coming up and can organize their thoughts accordingly. Kaylee also understands where Abby is at with the level of sincerity she would like the conversation to have.

If the person you want to talk with tends to make jokes when they are uncomfortable, and it shuts you down to where you feel you can't share, this is the time to say, "Please don't joke about this, I want to have a level 3 convo about a friend situation at work, can we chat now or later?"

You don't have to do this for all conversations or with all people. Levels 1 and 2 are rarely mentioned in my house because most of our chats are at that level, so we only use levels for 3+. You can have lighthearted, joking conversations and all that jazz. Not all conversations have to be serious. Still, if you don't have solid communication, you can't be surprised when people resort back to their coping mechanisms of laughter, sarcasm, blaming, or brushing you off whenever you decide to spring something on them.

Even when you do have these skills, miscommunication will still happen. Unfortunately, friendships can and will still end. We're always learning and growing, but we can shorten our response times between screw-ups and apologies when we grow and communicate better.

When we don't feel heard or are not comfortable enough to have difficult conversations with those we love, it creates a disparity that's hard to bridge. Levels are one brick we can use to build the road back to one another and towards a collaborative future and be more present in the messy middle.

If you cannot have an honest conversation about your heart with a non-responsive person, you can state your boundaries and explain what happens if they are not respected. For example, "I will leave the room if you call me names." "I will no longer loan you money. If you ask, we will end our conversation and start again when we can talk about something different."

There can be fear about what will happen after you ask for what you need.

 Therapist Nedra Glover Tawaab shares, "The fear is, "Things will be awkward between us after this." well, declaring a fear makes it so. If you state that you'll behave awkwardly during your next encounter, you *will*. What if you continued the relationship normally instead? State your boundary, and proceed with typical business. You can't control how your request is received, but you can choose to behave in a healthy way afterward. Maintaining a level of normalcy will help keep future encounters healthy. Do your part. Model the behavior you'd like to see in the relationship."[6]

All of these are tools for you to navigate, listening to your knowing and following through. Letting the people around you know your shifts can help ease your burden. Boundaries don't always have to be difficult, but they need to be strong enough to give you the space you need to feel happy in your life and to help you create better relationships.

Look at boundaries as a way of living your life from a place of integrity—no more mind-reading or jumping to conclusions and less spiraling based on false assumptions.

Walls keep people out, while boundaries show them how to interact with you in a sustainable life-giving way. You are allowed to ask for what you need, listen to your Knowing, and set boundaries that enable you to flourish and love well sustainably.

QUESTIONS FOR FURTHER DISCOVERY

How many plates are you balancing right now?

What plates do you need to set down or shift?

What hard conversation do you need to have?

What has been your experience in saying "No"?

BOOK RECOMMENDATIONS

Boundaries by Dr. John Mcloud & Dr. Townsend
*The Subtle Art of Not Giving a F*ck* by Mark Manson
Set Boundaries, Find Peace by Nedra Glover Tawwab

Boundaries Red Tent

Five minutes before the Tent Begins:
Leader: Lovelies, please put your phones on silent or off, grab your water, snacks, journal, and token and join me in the circle.

Opening:

Leader: Before we begin, I would like to state that this is a safe space. In order to make it so, there needs to be agreement around keeping what is said in circle, in the circle. I'm asking you all to agree to only speak of your own experiences, and only give advice when asked. We will be talking about deeply personal things in the Red Tent. A gentle reminder that we can disagree and still accept each other. Can I have a show of hands for everyone willing to keep this space confidential, for themselves and everyone here tonight?

Shakeout and Grounded Breathing:

Leader: Let us take a minute to stand up, shake out any worries, or frustration from your day. Twist your body, shake your booty, kick your legs, jump up and down. Audibly make sounds while relaxing your jaw. Stretch, or move in a way that feels supportive.

Please have a seat in this circle, and let's do some ground breathing. You can close your eyes, start to relax your shoulders. You can roll your neck from side to side, rest your hands on your stomach, knees, or the ground, whatever is most comfortable for you. Start breathing in from your belly. Take a deep breath. As you exhale, release anything that came before tonight that is on your mind.

Breathe in again, releasing anything to come in the future. Keep breathing, focusing on the sounds around you,

the breath of other women, and your heartbeat. As you release your breath, feel your body settling into this space. In this moment, here with us. You are safe. You are loved. We are glad you are here with us.

Call in:

Leader: We are gathered in our Red Tent, as women, as daughters, as mothers, as workers and dreamers. We come here to speak our heart's desires, our mind's thoughts, and share the song of our souls. We see with our eyes, hear with our ears, and will hum along in our hearts. May this space be open, sacred, and grounded for us here tonight. Let us hold hands as we travel deeper together, learning to better love ourselves, each other, and the world.

Gender Neutral Option:

We are gathered in our Red Tent Tent as humans, as explorers, as workers and dreamers. We come here to speak our heart's desires, our mind's thoughts, and share the song of our souls. We see with our eyes, hear with our ears, and will hum along in our hearts. May this space be open, sacred, and grounded for us here tonight. Let us hold hands as we travel deeper together, learning to better love ourselves, each other, and the world.

Song: Call Down a Blessing

Leader: Close your eyes and think of what you want from this night and this week. It might be friendship, laughter, wisdom. We'll pass the bowl around one person at a time, and you'll say your blessing request, we'll sing the song with your word inside of it, and then after we sing over you, pass the bowl to the next woman. She'll share her

blessing word, and we'll sing a blessing over her until we reach the end of the circle.

Call down a blessing x3, Call down, ____before you, ____behind you, ____Within you, and around you
Repeat for each person in the group, end with three call downs.

15: 1st Circle:

Leader: When speaking, please use the talking light, and when you finish, please say "I have spoken," so we know you have completed your thought. You can react with hand snaps, hand on your heart, and facial expressions. Please speak only of your own story, and don't give any advice unless asked.

For our first circle, what is your name, pronouns, your intention for tonight, and what do boundaries mean to you?

30: Quote and Response: *Depending on the size of the group you can have a few people share, or have everyone share their thoughts.*

Leader:I'll share the poem, and after you can share what resonates with you.

"Compassionate people ask for what they need. They say no when they need to, and when they say yes, they mean it. They're compassionate because their boundaries keep them out of resentment."— Brené Brown from her book *Rising Strong*

45: Activity 1: Drawing our Boundaries

Leader: We can identify boundaries by thinking about them like you would a house. Not everyone is welcome in your bedroom, or even in your home. So too in our lives we have fences and boundaries for different people and how much access or information they have to us.

What does that look like in a practical way?

Take a piece of paper and imagine you are at the center of your house. What feels safe and good inside the walls of your house? Kindness, encouragement? Some commitments you have? What is in your lawn? Maybe a job, or acquaintances?

Are there any guidelines for entering your 'boundary house'? Who is on the street or outside of the fence? Perhaps it's social media, or certain people who drain you right now.

What makes you feel safe inside the house? What are the different boundaries you need as people go through the different stages? To be people of integrity? Share similar values? What is needed as support in your house? Do you need space just for you as well? What does that look like?

After 5 minutes of drawing

What are your realizations and takeaways from your boundary house?

What are 1-3 things you struggle to put boundaries around? What would feel good or supportive to put into place after looking at your drawing?

55: 2nd Circle:

Share what you would like from your house boundary drawing.

1:10: Womanhood story:

Leader: Womanhood stories are a core part of Red Tent, sharing our stories is a brave act. Sometimes they are joy filled, sad, frustrating, or a mix of all of it. The story may include periods, sex, birth, or any part of the woman and human experience. ___ has offered to share her story tonight. ____ the floor is yours.

See the appendix of the book for reaching out to your women to see who would like to share before the tent day.

After her story:

Leader: Thank you ___ for sharing your story. Is there anything you need from us? Hug, encouragement, a listening ear during break?

If they say yes, do what you can to fulfill that need if possible.

1:20: Soul Care Time:

Leader: Now is our soul care time. This is 20 minutes to stretch, nap, chat, get food, go to the restroom. We do ask that you don't use this time to be on your phone. I'll give us a five-minute heads up to tent, and a one minute come to circle heads up.

1:40: Activity Two: Saying No

Saying no can be a hard thing to learn, and harder to say, but it's important we are able to say it confidently. We will say it in a group together, starting with a whisper, and each time get louder and louder until we shout it.

Commence saying no together in a circle, each time getting louder and louder.

Okay, this time, we're going to go individually around the circle, and you'll say no three times. Each time from your stomach, use your diaphragm. Stand tall, keep your head up, and confidently state or yell no in a way that makes you feel strong.

Go around the circle once, with each person going. It's okay to encourage someone to stand taller, or to breathe from their stomach. Sometimes there are tears during this activity, but it can be a powerful one.

. . .

1:50: Third Circle

How was saying no? How did you feel?

9: Closer *Grab your red thread (yarn) and make sure scissors are within reach.*

Leader: Red thread represents our connection to the women around us and those who have come before us. You will take your red yarn and wrap it around your wrist. You can wrap as many times as you want, as you recite your matriarchal spiritual lineage. Your lineage are the women and people who have influenced and loved you.

They don't have to be biologically related, you can claim or not claim anyone you would like. You can say your name, mother of (any children), daughter of x, daughter of y, daughter of daughters, daughter of whatever resonates (Eve, Spirit, the moon, etc). You can also say descendent instead, or daughter of those who _____ instead of names.

When you have finished wrapping, pass the thread to the next person until it has gone all the way around the circle.

You can start the process and do your lineage and wrap and then pass it to the person on your right.

After the Red Thread has come back to you.

Leader: As we are connected, let us sing our song, we'll sing it three times, it goes flow, ebb, weavers, thread, weavers, thread, spiders, web. Sing it with me:

Song: We are the flow we are the ebb,
We are the weavers we are the thread,
We are the weavers we are the thread,
we are the spiders we are the web.
x3

.   .   .

Leader, pick up the scissors, and cut your thread, and as you explain the below, you can have the person to the left tie your thread.

Leader: When cutting the thread to tie bracelets, share your favorite moment and a takeaway. Have the lady to your left tie your yarn, twice in a square knot, and one slip knot, and this way, your thread will not come undone. After you have spoken, pass the scissors to the right, and the next person can go.

After the scissors make their way back to you and everyone has tied their thread, you can share the invitation below. Feel free to hold hands if you'd like.

Invitation to curiosity

Leader: This month when something feels itchy or off, tune into what needs to shift, and what you might need to say no to.

Thank you for being a part of tonight's Red Tent. You are all a treasure, and I'm glad you are here. Our Red Tent is now closed.

SANCTUARY

*W*hen asked what the word *sanctuary* means to them, some of my Tent women responded,

"A lapping ocean at your feet as the sun slowly sets."

"A table full of friends and family laughing and talking about life."

"Fishing, even if I don't catch anything, because it's so peaceful in the water."

"A church with an altar or holy space to approach God and seek wisdom."

According to Oxford, "Sanctuary is a place of refuge or safety."[1]

For me, Sanctuary is a place to dip back into the rhythms of the universe, the slow, steady heartbeat of the seasons, tides, and our breath. To listen and be held by God and truly let my guard down to rest. Sanctuary feels like hot chocolate, the thrill of glee from seeing the leaves turn, or a deep hug that makes me melt.

Unfortunately, our modern-day society treats rest and slowness like explicit four-letter words, and natural sanctuaries for animals are harvested for oil, wood, or any number of limited resources. The rule of law is faster, more efficient, and *now*. We are shoving in more food, more pills, more TV, more overtime.

More *everything*.

The constant drive to be faster and have more means we aren't slow enough to hear what is wrong. If we do feel off, we ignore it and hop right back on the speeding train of busyness.

The world expects us to succeed at doing all of the things and never complain — the good-ole bootstrap mentality. It feels a little bit like putting feet on both the gas and brake at the same time. Hitting the gas and brake pedals of our lives simultaneously is more than a metaphor for how we live, and it shows.

Nervous breakdowns, stress, and depression are on the rise in America and around the world.[2] Businesses and advertisements ignore this and tell us to do and buy more, so we keep going. Society constantly changes what contentment should feel like, so we don't know when to say enough.

What would it look like to know when to push the gas pedal or the brake pedal without worrying if you are pressing the right pedal?

Sometimes it's okay to push the wrong one, and we can push through, like when I thought I had fractured my heel after cartwheeling into a locker and ended up wearing a boot. Still in the boot, I wanted to join our final performance in the high school show choir, so I ripped off the boot and pushed through. It turns out I had just bruised my heel, so I, thankfully, didn't permanently damage myself.

However, most of the time, it turns out badly, like the time in college when I decided to do a dance show with injured knees for someone who had to drop out of the show last minute. I filled in during the final week of rehearsals for Sissy's Sircus (a local burlesque troupe) and collapsed sobbing backstage in between sets with two knee braces on. The only way I made it through was using Tylenol and a few shots of vodka before the show because my body hurt so badly. My body was begging me to slow down and rest, but I refused to listen.

I thought the show was worth the price of my battered body.

For me, it was worth it at the time, *but where do we draw the line?*

When we are exhausted and don't know how to carry on?
    When we have our 5th, 10th, 100th breakdown?
    When do we allow ourselves to figure it out and speak the boundaries we need out loud?

We'd sooner put a band-aid on an overwhelmed, bleeding-out society than pause and ask, "Is this how it should be?" "Is this the life we want to live?"

Are we filling out to the edges of our life because we think more is more, or are we fully living into the moments we have?

Even with these question invitations, it can feel insane to believe you are allowed to pause and rest. Sometimes we need to force ourselves to chill out. We may have to create reminders and timers to put rest into our schedule. That's what this chapter is about: how we can weave sanctuary into our body, mind, spirit, and community.

Sanctuary, to me, feels like an invitation towards wholeness, to explore your soul and life with new perspectives that allow you rest and nourishment. By doing this, we can be walking sanctuaries as we interact with those around us, becoming beacons of grace and peace.

WHY WE NEED SANCTUARY

> "When it comes to machines, continuous uptime is a good thing. For human beings, not so much. We need downtime. A lot of downtime. When we deny ourselves our need for it—and many of us do—we eventually crash. For human beings, downtime is not a bug but a feature."

When I read this quote in *Thrive* by Arianna Huffington, I realized how many unrealistic expectations we have of our bodies. Although routines can make us feel like it's the same thing every day, our bodies do not run on clockwork. We use 'quick fixes' and 'shortcuts' to bypass the news our body sends us, but this does us no real favors. You can feel when your gut tells you something is off or when you tense your shoulders from stress.

When we avoid acknowledging and dealing with stress, it metastasizes in our hearts, muscles, and lives.

> In *Burnout*, Doctors Emily and Amelia Nagoski say when your body feels scared or threatened, "it activates a generic 'stress response,' a cascade of neurological and hormonal activity that

initiates physiological changes to help you survive."

The stress response can look like heavy breathing, sweats, fast heartbeat, tense muscles, heightened senses, and a narrower thought catalog because your brain and body are focused on escaping the problem. In our modern-day society, we can get stressed because of doom scrolling on Facebook, a sticky friendship situation, or the next business step.

All of these stressors layer themselves in our bodies. Although our bodies are aching for support, we usually muffle the nudge for help with distractions like food, busyness, or outright ambivalence. Often our thoughts are, "It's not as bad as other people have it, so why should I complain at all?"[3]

The problem here is not that it could be worse. It's that your body is ringing the alarm, and it doesn't take platitudes as payment of understanding.

Overwhelmed is overwhelmed.

I have a colorful military spouse friend I adore named Ari. She has multiple kids, works in the church as an army spouse, home-schooler, and full-time artist. The things she can juggle all at once astound me. When I burned out last year, I kept repeating to myself, "But I'm not doing as much as she is, so I shouldn't complain. I'm not doing a lot.[4] There's no reason I should feel burned out!" You know what, Dear Reader? My body did not care if Ari was doing more than me and seemed okay. My soul was still blaring the critical alarm that I was burned out and needed to slow down.[5]

During 2020, I took my wholly in-person business with

two tents a month, a few henna gigs, and mermaid parties online within a month. By June of 2020, I was leading ten tents a month to serve the women in my community, and my edges started to fray, and I could feel burnout coming around the corner.

When I knew I was burning out, I decided to create a sanctuary month for myself in December to recover before hopping back into the bustle of life. It was time off from business after a year full of pivots. I wanted to pause and take stock of where I was going, discover what I needed, and just breathe. Sanctuary time for me is time to get in touch with God, my goals, clean up a bit, and give myself some breathing room. During December, I worked on this book and a few other things, but I also watched a new show, laid in the forest, went on many walks, sat by the fire, and hung out with a few friends for a social distanced picnic.

When I realized I needed a second sanctuary month after December, I freaked and burst into tears. I thought, "People will be so disappointed. There's no way I can keep going slow!" I realized what I wanted more than anything was even more slowness.

I used to think people who went slow were absurd because there were things to do, people to see, and tasks to accomplish! As an enneagram 7, and social butterfly, slow wasn't in my vocabulary. Now that I've been moving slower, I realize that I love this pace. It gives me the freedom to think and breathe and to check in with what my body needs.

Recovering from burnout is a frustrating process, and it can be a long one.

Burning out is a wake-up call to something not being sustainable in your life. I got to the point where it was worth being honest with myself on what I needed, but I fought myself the whole way to the realization. When we say our actual needs out loud, it makes them real.

It means we acknowledge we aren't okay.

We learn from a young age the most important things to do are productive things. It's important to remember, 'productive' is a subjective term as well. We can be productive for work, our home, our soul, even sleeping is productive regeneration time. What if you flipped the script and thought of the things you do to feed your soul as productive for you to thrive? We let kids play but remove it from our lives as adults. Our bodies yearn for play and feel safe from the go go go.

Our bodies need downtime.

Humans need rest and restoration time. We aren't made to run on full steam endlessly.

CREATING SANCTUARY IN YOUR BODY

 Taylor lived the burnout cycle on loop until she tuned in with her hormonal cycle, "Being more in tune with my cycle helps because I'm a lot more conscious of when I'm trying to schedule plans. I look at the calendar and think, 'Nope, next week I'm going to be in bed.' Because I'm turning in to my own needs first and checking my cyclical energy, I'm saying no more. That was the first thing I heard in Tent, 'No.' is a full sentence.'

I'm used to saying no and then share every reason why that's there and then say it's okay if you push it. Now I say, 'this is my boundary.' Checking in with myself upfront has narrowed the amount of time I've needed to recover because before it was burnout, and now it's more cyclical with rest instead."

Rest comes more easily when our body isn't feeling overwhelmed and stressed out. Finding ways to make our bodies feel safe is one of the first steps towards rest and sanctuary. One of the easiest ways to feel safe is moving our body, whether exercising, walking around the block, or a three-minute dance party for one.

Being in the water, or sitting in nature, or meditating is also refreshing for those who movement is less accessible. Getting your heart rate up helps release tension and stress from your body. For me, I love lifting heavyweights in the gym and dancing. Orgasms are also great stress relievers. Not only does the build-up and release help reduce tension, but the release of Oxytocin (the cuddle hormone) supports your good feelings.[6] Meditating, naps, journaling, and playing with pets are also great grounding activities.[7]

Another way to help our bodies feel stable is by getting the sleep we need. Everyone is different, so maybe the rest you need is six hours, but someone else's is nine. Most of us are around the eight-hour level, except for those rare birds like my friend Lina the Mermaid. She can run on 3 hours of sleep consistently and be just fine. She is one of the 1% of the population that can do that and survive long term.[8]

The odds of you being 100% functional with three hours of consistent sleep are slim to none. So don't go getting any ideas.

. . .

When we get 4-6 hours a night, it slowly wears on our reaction times and thinking abilities, exhausting us even more and causing frustration. Having a whole night's rest can do wonders for stress. If you have trouble sleeping, try blackout curtains, thunder sounds, prepping your space before bed, incense, calm lighting, or even reading a book before bed instead of using your phone. Arianna Huffington's book *The Sleep Revolution* goes in-depth to help you find deep rest while you sleep.

I struggle with putting my phone down at the end of the night, so I do my best to put it in the kitchen with my alarm on full volume. *I do not always succeed in this task.* Placing my phone in the kitchen prevents me from night scrolling. Adults set up bedtime routines for kids, but we think we don't need to do it for ourselves as we get older.

YES, WE DO, LOVELY.

Instead of begrudging our nighttime selves for not cleaning the dishes or staying up too late, when we take stock of the day ahead of us, we can set ourselves up to feel better in the morning by doing little tasks the night before. These tasks can be as simple as washing your face, setting out workout clothes, or double-checking to ensure the alarm for the morning.

Although they aren't clocks, our bodies thrive on rhythms and can get into a groove. (Hello, 6 am wide awake on a Saturday, when you have the free time to sleep in, but your body isn't having it).

I'm not saying spontaneity is a bad thing, but maybe save the spontaneity for what you'll have for dinner and not what time you'll go to bed. Think of a toddler changing bedtimes each night between 6 pm-2 am. We can imagine how they'd be reacting throughout the week, right? So why do we think that, as adults, we are any different?

Something that has helped me get to bed on time (around 9:30 on a good day) is recognizing that I can't teleport to bed at 9:30 and fall directly asleep. My bedtime routine starts around 7:30 pm when my phone turns grey and lets me know to start winding down. I'm usually chatting with someone, and this gives me a heads up to pause and figure out what needs to be wrapped up or do things like taking the dogs on their last walk. By 8:30, I'm in the bathroom brushing my teeth, flossing, maybe taking a hot shower, and changing into pajamas. By 9, I've grabbed a book and am curled up in bed so I can read and chat with Jer for 30 minutes.

At 9:30, lights are out (sometimes 10, *and sometimes even later when I lose track of time or am hanging out at a friend's house*), and my alarm in the kitchen is set for 5:30 am. Jer wakes up about 5, so arranging a bedtime helps us get 8 hours of sleep without feeling rushed into bed. Sometimes we stay up late, but it's an active choice. I notice a massive difference in how I respond and interact with others when I stay up late and don't get the sleep I need.[9]

What could be your routine? What time do you want to go to bed?

Maybe you're a night owl, and your 'sleep prep time' starts at 9 pm. If you can feel yourself being crabby, ask yourself what you need, and as ridiculous as you may feel, trust that your body is probably telling you exactly what needs to happen. Sometimes we're thrown off track by our hormonal cycle or our body becoming ill. *If your body has severe reactions to stress or feels like something is wrong, talk to a doctor.* We need to allow our bodies to recharge and rest. The more we do this, the better ability we will have to cope and regulate our emotions.

Giving ourselves rest when we need it applies to both sleep and the everyday.

> Red Tent leader DeAnna L'am is a supporter of knowing when you need time to breathe and weaves it into her cycle. "I realized we as women had not honored our blood because we didn't know how to set boundaries. We need time off when we bleed. We need to be in our cocoon and our quiet zone and replenishing. Without boundaries, we give, give, give and do, do, do, especially if women have children or work full-time or both and never stop. So that's where boundaries begin. When I started healing myself, I began taking the first day of my blood off. I was clear with my partner that I needed to close the door and be self-contained and do nothing, and he was supportive of that.
>
> Taking that pause was something my mother never did, and I hadn't seen another woman do. The support of my husband came last because I had to give myself permission first. When I was clear, he was able to support it without a problem. I wasn't asking for permission; I was speaking my needs. It then developed into my work, and I incorporated that rest into what I teach because we can not give when we are depleted. To fill up, we need to set boundaries."

Let's remember to charge ALL of our batteries, not just the electronic devices but also our human batteries.

CREATING SANCTUARY IN YOUR LIFE

I would break down every three months like clockwork in high school because I felt overwhelmed with everything.

I mean, yes, hello hormones and high school teenage drama as well.

I was in show choir, dance team, color guard, school, youth group, theatre, and taking an AP class. I remember being spread out on the floor of my living room at 10 pm crying into my math book, realizing I had another hour of homework to go, after getting home at seven from theatre practice, and knowing I had dance practice at 6 am.

Did I love my life and all of my activities?

100%

But looking back, I honestly don't know how I did it.

I can feel how tired high-school-me was and how confused I was in those moments because I thought my job was to be happy and do it all. My parents told me I could drop something, but everything felt too important, and I refused to drop anything. Nothing was 'bad' or worthy of getting cut. Everything was a priority, *and when everything is a priority, nothing is.*[10] Burnout has been a theme ever since — going non-stop and then crashing hard. I would take a day or a weekend to recover and then hop right back into the fray.

It wasn't sustainable.

Becoming a military spouse taught me to start being honest about what I could handle. I started pairing back on my commitments. Saying "No" felt equal parts terrifying and freeing. Setting boundaries has been a constant journey for me and became even more of a focus in 2020.

As I was burning out, I heard about social media breaks; I thought it seemed laughable. Now they are a weekly part of my life, and I call them my Sanctuary Days. I realized Sanctuary Days was something my body needed. I work on the weekends, so social media-free weekends felt impossible, but Sunday and Monday, I had no tents, so those became my new 'weekend' rest days. I would step back and focus on myself and what needed tending. My Sanctuary Days now feel like taking a bra off at the end of the week.

Sometimes I keep Instagram on my phone as a beautiful inspiration. Other times I have to hop on Facebook to send a message to a friend who is coming over that afternoon or work on writing for a little bit. There are other weekends where I do my best not to touch my laptop or my phone. Sanctuary Days shouldn't feel like you are 'cut off from the world or starving yourself; it should feel like freeing yourself from the expectations of others and yourself.

Sanctuary Days are different for each person, so try not to use what you *should* do as another form of self-flagellation for how you aren't doing enough. THAT SAID, it is essential to have recovery time as a human.

You might be reading this thinking, "Eh, I don't need any sanctuary in my life." But friend, wouldn't it be nice to have time just for yourself to breathe and reset? It doesn't have to be a whole weekend or even a whole day, but I bet there is a small shift you can make to tend your soul in a liberating way.

What would feel liberating at the end of the day or week?
What could this look like for you?
Is there a way you can weave in sanctuary time?

Maybe you start small and work your way up.

Sanctuary time reflects on what needs to come more into alignment and be honest with yourself even if you aren't honest with anyone else about how you are feeling.

There's an overarching theme with women that they can't have time to themselves because it's selfish. The idea of filling your cup only so you can pour it out for others is something I learned early. But friend, this is how you burn out.

Even twenty minutes to yourself can be a lifesaver between kids and commitments. Sometimes sanctuary might look like a retreat away or sitting in the car half a block away for ten minutes after your partner gets home from work. If Jesus, son of God, needed time in a closet to breathe and took long walks by himself to take time away from people, so can you. It's hard when people need you, and people will always need you. You know the adage of "You can't pour from an empty cup," and it's true.

Regardless, many of us still find ourselves scraping the bottom of the barrel, not for ourselves but the people around us.

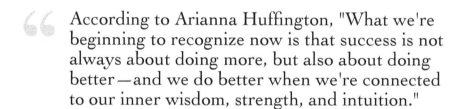

According to Arianna Huffington, "What we're beginning to recognize now is that success is not always about doing more, but also about doing better—and we do better when we're connected to our inner wisdom, strength, and intuition."

We are better humans to ourselves and others when we have time to rest and recharge.

CREATING SANCTUARY IN YOUR HOME

"The Human world, it's a mess!" I love this line from the Disney movie, *The Little Mermaid*, and I laugh because the sentiment resonates more than it should.

The world is bustling with ideas, and humans are bumping against one another, spilling their trauma, pain, joy, and frustrations onto one another. It's messy, exhilarating, and sometimes flat-out exhausting.

We need a peaceful place where we can be our whole selves and not feel like we have to shrink-wrap ourselves to be more enjoyable for the pleasure of others. If this calm atmosphere is in our home, it can be a haven for others as well. When I was growing up, our house always had people in it, whether guests, family gatherings, or neighbors. My parents put up a ping-pong table and had a fridge overflowing with snacks. My friends could come over, enjoy, and have a safe place to hang out. Everyone was welcome.[11]

So what does sanctuary in your home look like for you? Where can you create a place in your home that is rest filling? Maybe it's your living room with soft blankets or a closet where you install a small sacred space. Perhaps you find sanctuary in a different physical place, like the woods, a church, or a grandmother's house.

You deserve rest, goodness, and peace where you live, my friend. Don't deprive yourself of creating rest right where you are. If possible, let your home, or a part of your home, be where you feel safe from the outside world.

 Ayesha, a marine biologist, and mermaid, has taken her love of the sea into her home. "I decorated my room like a mermaid cove. Walking into my mermaid grotto is where I feel the calmest and most at home. I can be free and make my own decisions in this place. I find sanctuary in the water. It's where I belong. Everything else goes away; the chaos of the world can't reach me there. It's magical. This sense of safety is why I created a place in my home that makes me feel like when I'm in the ocean."

CREATING SANCTUARY IN YOUR FRIENDSHIPS

Friendships are safe places to land when you are stressed and tired. Creating a relationship where you can trust one another depends on being honest. One of the things we emphasize in Red Tent is asking for what you need. I 100% recognize this is hard to do because sometimes, when we have asked for what we've needed, we've been denied. Being denied in the past can make us think it will always be that way, but it doesn't have to be. When we make our needs known, we allow others to meet us where we are.

As a human, you have needs. You are allowed to have needs and voice them. Often, needs are swept under the table and labeled a nuisance, but everyone has needs lovely. You, me, and even yes, that one person on your mind. All of us.

In sharing where you are, it can be helpful to see if the other person can help that day. One way I ask this is by using the concept of 'spoons.' Spoons are a reference point for those who struggle with chronic illness. Created by Christine Miserandino, spoon theory explains how each task you do each day takes a spoon, but you only have a limited amount, so you need to choose wisely. Sometimes you might not have any spoons for other people left over after a day. Being aware your spoons are running out can help you not feel overtaxed or used.

Asking a friend, "Hey do you have spoons to help me process XYZ, or to listen to me vent" gives them the space to say, "Yes, but later today" or "No, but we can have a zoom date later this week." When we create a safe environment to say no to our friends, it creates a sanctuary space and allows both in the relationship to be honest with their needs and boundaries.

We can do this in our friendships and Red Tents. Let's create places of vulnerability and sanctuary for women to come together and be honest with themselves and each other. Not the performing we sometimes do in the outside world, but as women, vulnerably saying, "Here's me, will you take me as I am?" and walking together in that growth.

Sometimes we might not have the spoons to hold space for other people, but we can intentionally use our words wisely and respond accordingly.

We don't have to react or be all over the place with the

hustle and bustle. We can bring sanctuary with us into our friendships and lives in the outside world.

CREATING SANCTUARY IN YOUR BELIEFS

When the world feels crazy and overwhelming, I imagine myself curling up in the lap of God and just being held. Faith or belief in something more can be a refuge amidst the whirlwind to catch our breath before facing the dragons of taxes, carpools, meals, and piled-up dishes. Unfortunately, faith can be a loaded term for many people. With various beliefs in our world and conflicting opinions, the idea of faith can easily be contentious.

Faith can also be a beautiful thing, one which gives us hope and joy in the midst of living in a world where sometimes things don't always go to plan. For our use here, I'd love for you to see faith as trusting you are supported by more than just yourself and that you are uniquely connected to the universe and those around you and not here by mistake. You can even imagine how the Red Thread of fate brought this book to you at this moment. Divine timing? Kismet? A little magic of synchronicity of feeling stuck and needing inspiration?[12]

Faith can be a counterweight to toxic lies and heart wounds. Sadly, sometimes we receive heart wounds from a house of faith or religion. The lies we've believed about who we are can echo even after leaving a relationship or toxic environment.

Part of the problem we as humans have is we try to surmount each other with the best way to believe or do or live, and at it's worst, faith brings people to murder or ostracise those who disagree with them.[13]

At their core, most faiths tell us the way to show up in the world is to love your neighbor as you love yourself. Deciding to love others as yourself is a big deal when you think about it. It means to tend to those you love and those you don't. It means to believe in kindness and generosity and invites us to be a part of peacemaking, not just peacekeeping.

Open-heartedness is at the core of finding sanctuary in your faith. Regardless of what you believe, spirituality is about being a part of an immense tapestry where we take care of one another. Jewish, Christian, Wiccan, Muslim, Pagan, Buddhist, and many others all trust we are inextricably connected. If this much is true, then it means you are here for a purpose and a reason and your job is to show up and bring your spark, your joy, and your ideas to the table.

> Nadia Bolz-Weber reminds me that this belonging to ourselves is vital because "Holiness happens when we are integrated as physical, spiritual, sexual, emotional, and political beings."

I believe this is why the Divine created us: to love God and one another to the best of our ability while fully embodied.

There are sacred moments in life we pause in: sunsets, babies being adorable, death beds, and the first time you hold somebody's hand and feel the electricity between the two of you. These sacred moments are faith rippling through to remind you; it's all connected. We're all here.

Together.

And you?

You're supposed to be here too, and I'm asking you to tend to your soul and life with the kindness you might only reserve for others.

Rest should not be reserved only for yearly vacations and your Netflix time on your comfy couch.

Find sanctuary, friend, weave it into your life so that when you get to the end of the line, you can look back and say, "Look at the goodness. Look at the joy. I truly lived."

QUESTIONS FOR FURTHER DISCOVERY

When was the last time you felt like you were in a sanctuary? Perhaps it was in church, in the woods, with friends?

Where can you create days or moments of sanctuary in your life?

What does being a walking sanctuary mean to you? How can you be a sanctuary for yourself?

BOOK RECOMMENDATIONS

Braiding Sweetgrass by Robin Wall Kimmerer
Searching for Sunday by Rachel Held Evans
Love Does by Bob Goff
An Altar in the World by Barbara Brown Taylor

Sanctuary Red Tent

Five minutes before the Tent Begins:

Leader: Lovelies, please put your phones on silent or off, grab your water, snacks, journal, and token and join me in the circle.

Opening:

Leader: Before we begin, I would like to state that this is a safe space. In order to make it so, there needs to be agreement around keeping what is said in circle, in the circle. I'm asking you all to agree to only speak of your own experiences, and only give advice when asked. We will be talking about deeply personal things in the Red Tent. A gentle reminder that we can disagree and still accept each other. Can I have a show of hands for everyone willing to keep this space confidential, for themselves and everyone here tonight?

Shakeout and Grounded Breathing:

Leader: Let us take a minute to stand up, shake out any worries, or frustration from your day. Twist your body, shake your booty, kick your legs, jump up and down. Audibly make sounds while relaxing your jaw. Stretch, or move in a way that feels supportive.

Please have a seat in this circle, and let's do some ground breathing. You can close your eyes, start to relax your shoulders. You can roll your neck from side to side, rest your hands on your stomach, knees, or the ground, whatever is most comfortable for you. Start breathing in from your belly. Take a deep breath. As you exhale, release anything that came before tonight that is on your mind.

Breathe in again, releasing anything to come in the future. Keep breathing, focusing on the sounds around you,

the breath of other women, and your heartbeat. As you release your breath, feel your body settling into this space. In this moment, here with us. You are safe. You are loved. We are glad you are here with us.

Call in:
Leader: We are gathered in our Red Tent, as women, as daughters, as mothers, as workers and dreamers. We come here to speak our heart's desires, our mind's thoughts, and share the song of our souls. We see with our eyes, hear with our ears, and will hum along in our hearts. May this space be open, sacred, and grounded for us here tonight. Let us hold hands as we travel deeper together, learning to better love ourselves, each other, and the world.

Gender Neutral Option:
We are gathered in our Red Tent Tent as humans, as explorers, as workers and dreamers. We come here to speak our heart's desires, our mind's thoughts, and share the song of our souls. We see with our eyes, hear with our ears, and will hum along in our hearts. May this space be open, sacred, and grounded for us here tonight. Let us hold hands as we travel deeper together, learning to better love ourselves, each other, and the world.

Song:
Leader: Close your eyes and think of what you want from this night and this week. It might be friendship, laughter, wisdom. We'll pass the bowl around one person at a time, and you'll say your blessing request, we'll sing the song with your word inside of it, and then after we sing over you, pass the bowl to the next woman. She'll share her

blessing word, and we'll sing a blessing over her until we reach the end of the circle.

Call down a blessing x3, Call down, ____before you, ____behind you, ____Within you, and around you
Repeat for each person in the group, end with three call downs.

15: 1st Circle:

Leader: When speaking, please use the talking light, and when you finish, please say "I have spoken," so we know you have completed your thought. You can react with hand snaps, hand on your heart, and facial expressions. Please speak only of your own story, and don't give any advice unless asked.

For our first circle, what is your name, pronouns, your intention for tonight, and what comes up for you with the idea of sanctuary?

30: Quote and Response:

Leader: I'll share this quote, and after you can share what resonates with you from it with a few words.

The word Sanctuary rose originally from the latin Sanctus, directly translating to the simple word holy. Another definition is that a sanctuary is "the inmost recess or holiest part of a temple." Since your body is your temple, indeed the temple of your soul, where lies the inmost recess, the holiest part? Could it be that you are in your entirety a sanctuary, that you contain the sacred, the holy in every one of your cells? Could it be truth that the mere fact of that breath that just now filled your lungs qualifies you as a miracle? We are all being breathed and we are each of us held inside of a mystery so vast, so wildly outside of our present understanding that the only sane thing to do is to surrender and celebrate! Of course, as we all have free will, what you decide to do with this breathing in and out life thing is ultimately up to you! -Author unknown

45: Activity 1: Sanctuary Meditation
Meditation script is after this Red Tent script.

1:00: Journal
What was your path like? What did your door look like? What did your sacred space look like? Did you meet anyone there? You or spirit? Did it have any smells, or feelings or remind you of any place?

1:10: Circle 2:
Share what you would like from your meditation.

1:25: Soul Care Time:
Leader: Now is our soul care time. This is 20 minutes to stretch, nap, chat, get food, go to the restroom. We do ask that you don't use this time to be on your phone. I'll give us a five-minute heads up to tent, and a one minute come to circle heads up.

1:45: Activity Two: Soul Art of your Temple of Life
Leader: Grab your journal and coloring items. Imagine your life as a sanctuary or temple. Draw an expression of what the Temple or Sanctuary of your life looks like.

What are the pillars that hold you up? Friends, therapy, dancing?
(Pause)
What are your windows made of? What can you rest

on? Soft beds, a partner, a hot bath? What is the door that you walk through the world with?

(Pause)

How can you create sanctuary in your world? Do you need to create sacred time in your Temple foundation? Does having people over bring color to the walls? Because sanctuary can come in many different forms, what are the different possibilities for you to enjoy?

(Pause)

What or who provides a quality of sanctuary for you now? Have you experienced a sense of sanctuary anywhere in your life?

(Pause)

If not, what will it look like when you create a quality of sanctuary for yourself as you are right now?

2: Circle

Share what you would like from your Soul Art.

2:15: Womanhood story:

Leader: Womanhood stories are a core part of Red Tent, sharing our stories is a brave act. Sometimes they are joy filled, sad, frustrating, or a mix of all of it. The story may include periods, sex, birth, or any part of the woman and human experience. ____ has offered to share her story tonight. _____ the floor is yours.

See the appendix of the book for reaching out to your women to see who would like to share before the tent day.

After her story:

Leader: Thank you ___ for sharing your story. Is there anything you need from us? Hug, encouragement, a listening ear during break?

If they say yes, do what you can to fulfill that need if possible.

2:25: Closer *Grab your red thread (yarn) and make sure scissors are within reach.*

Leader: Red thread represents our connection to the women around us and those who have come before us. You will take your red yarn and wrap it around your wrist. You can wrap as many times as you want, as you recite your matriarchal spiritual lineage. Your lineage are the women and people who have influenced and loved you.

They don't have to be biologically related, you can claim or not claim anyone you would like. You can say your name, mother of (any children), daughter of x, daughter of y, daughter of daughters, daughter of whatever resonates (Eve, Spirit, the moon, etc). You can also say descendent instead, or daughter of those who _____ instead of names.

When you have finished wrapping, pass the thread to the next person until it has gone all the way around the circle.

You can start the process and do your lineage and wrap and then pass it to the person on your right.

After the Red Thread has come back to you.

Leader: As we are connected, let us sing our song, we'll sing it three times, it goes flow, ebb, weavers, thread, weavers, thread, spiders, web. Sing it with me:

Song: We are the flow we are the ebb,
We are the weavers we are the thread,
We are the weavers we are the thread,
we are the spiders we are the web.
x3

Leader, pick up the scissors, and cut your thread, and as you explain the below, you can have the person to the left tie your thread.

. . .

Leader: When cutting the thread to tie bracelets, share your favorite moment and a takeaway. Have the lady to your left tie your yarn, twice in a square knot, and one slip knot, and this way, your thread will not come undone. After you have spoken, pass the scissors to the right, and the next person can go.

After the scissors make their way back to you and everyone has tied their thread, you can share the invitation below. Feel free to hold hands if you'd like.

Invitation to curiosity

Leader: Today, wherever you go, whatever you see, whomever you encounter, ask yourself, "How can I be open to the possibility of sanctuary here?" If something feels opposite of sanctuary, see where you can create some sanctuary right where you are at. Thank you for being a part of tonight's Red Tent. You are all a treasure, and I'm glad you are here. Our Red Tent is now closed.

Sanctuary Meditation

This is a meditation to explore the inner sanctuary of your soul. You may see images, or colors, or simply feel relaxed. Whatever you see is what is here for you today and trust that you will get what you need from this meditation regardless of what you see.

Close your eyes and lean on a nearby wall, sit in a chair or lay down, however you feel most comfortable.

You can find a comfy blanket to wrap around you, and allow yourself to settle in.

(Pause)

Take three deep breaths, with audible exhales, releasing any tension of your body.

Let your body root down in rest, imagining you are held safely and warmly.

(Pause)

Imagine a path in front of you, and start going towards it.

Walk along this path, and notice, what is your path made of? Dirt, road, rocks, sand?

Your path slowly starts spiraling down like a staircase.

Keep walking, you are safe, and curious on what is ahead.

(Pause)

What do your stairs feel like?

Is there a wall? What is it made of?

You pass your heart door, and keep walking down.

Soon you come to another door, this is your soul door.

What does it look like?

Is it carved, painted?

What's the shape of it? What is it made of? Take a minute to explore the intricacies of your door. It may not look like any door you've seen before.

(Pause)

On the other side of the door is your soul scape. Where your dreams and the inner sanctuary of your soul is.

How do you open your door? As you open the door, walk through.

(Pause)

Notice what's around you; this is the place where your dreams are made, your ideas, desires, and even goals you haven't even thought of coming to the surface.

Finished or completed dreams may be nearby.

Take a moment to see how everything works.

(pause for one to two minutes)

You see a space off to the side that catches your eye. Start moving towards it. As you do, the space becomes clearer, this is your innermost sanctuary of your soul. A place for you to rest, breathe, and listen.

What does it look like? A temple? A church? A room? A field?

If it's a place you can enter, walk in and explore.

There may or may not be others there, if you need time alone, you will find it.

You can tune into your heart, what's on your mind, or talk to God or Spirit, or someone else here. I'll give you a few minutes to rest and explore your space.

(pause one to two minutes)

Take a deep breath in. This sanctuary is for you to be restored in.

Is there anything you would like to do in this space? Maybe light a candle? You can dance, drink tea, light a fire, stretch, or pray. If you want you can leave an offering as well.

(pause one to two minutes)

When you are ready, walk back into your Soul Scape, and meander back to your soul door.

Take another pause here before you go through your

door. If everything gets too loud in your mind or in the world, come here for a few minutes and rest.

(Pause)

Move through or open your door and begin back up on your spiral path.

Go up past your heart door, as you start to feel light on your face, whether this is sunlight, moonlight, or starlight.

As you walk to the top of your path, is anything different?

How do you feel?

(Pause)

Gently bring awareness back into your body, wiggle your toes, your fingers, and on your own time, come back to the room by opening your eyes.

VULNERABILITY

*I*f you know about Enneagrams, you know people can feel attached to their number. Enneagram is a personality test, but it goes deeper into why you are the way you are. I am an Enneagram 7. 7's are labeled The Enthusiasts or The Adventurer. Sevens love being around people and feed off of other's energy and ideas. Part of how 7 energy showed up for me is if I received less than stellar feedback, I believed I wasn't good enough, and something was wrong with me. I attached my self-worth to how much others enjoyed my presence and ideas.

The opinions of others when taken to heart wind their way into our minds and bodies, and they begin to feel like core truths. We remember them not as "Just their opinion" but "This is who I am."

Our inner critic has a hay day with these lies, keeping us stuck in stagnant cycles, turning the lies into festering Heart Wounds. Heart Wounds are places where we are vulnerable to any insults, attacks, or offenses. For me, this meant searching for others' approval was more than just to feel good. It turned into a Heart Wound that told me if I didn't have their (parents, friends, husband, *really anyone honestly*) approval, I wasn't worthy of anything good. Heart wounds twist desires and keep us bound in unhealthy ways without realizing how believing these lies impact us.

Sometimes our heart wounds take a long time to heal. One of mine is a deep-rooted fear of being rejected. When I was in high school, I fell head over heels in love with the most outgoing man I've ever met named Grant. He was charming to everyone, so I wasn't the only one with a crush. He was generous with his attention, and when he looked at you, it was like nothing else mattered. We became friends, interacted through theatre, and we became close.

Very close.

I had previously read *I Kissed Dating Goodbye* by Joshua Harris about not dating and only courting with the intent to marry, and as a child of the 90's purity movement, this seemed like a wise choice.[1] Because of that book, I wasn't Facebook-official dating, but I still would hang out and act like it was a possibility. He went to my school, and besides the label of girlfriend, we were together. I imagined I was his girlfriend he couldn't mention, even though my friends knew. I had decided after high school I would date again, which was only half a year away, but soon it all came crashing down.

Senior year I was jolted awake by my phone ringing at two A.M. He called to tell me it was over because God had told him to move on. My world promptly shattered, and I cried for weeks about it. I felt betrayed and hurt and stupid. Thoughts circled my mind of, "How could I think anyone would want to be with me?" and "Who would be willing to wait for me?" After high school, I dated new guys, but these thoughts never left. I was like a deer, reacting at any hint someone was pulling away or that they'd leave suddenly.

You can imagine, this was not the healthiest mindset, and the clingy overcompensating was not a good look on me.

• • •

308 | RED THREAD

I found out later he told people we were never together, which is technically accurate but hurt nonetheless. I ran what-if scenarios in my head and beat myself up for every little comment I made. I, unfortunately, let it cloud many of my relationships, and you better believe I was angry at that don't-date book too.

My pain and fear morphed into becoming a Heart Wound of, "No one wants you, you'll never be enough." Although it's not true, my Heart Wound still sometimes makes me afraid that Jer, my husband, will wake up and toss me aside as my non-ex-ex did. In these moments, I have to pause and remember this is a different story, a different man, and I can make other choices. I can let light in by speaking my fear out loud and remember I'm not seventeen anymore.

Heart wounds don't just make us react but sometimes impact why we act. For example, I tend to strive for love and approval because I'm scared of not being enough. When I notice I'm seeking from a place of scarcity, I know I'm leading from my Heart Wound, fearing I won't be enough as I am. There's a difference between going after a goal because you are motivated and going after a goal to prove your Heart Wound wrong.

Jer is an amazing husband, and he calls me out on my nonsense when I let fear lead. I can be my whole self with him, and he sees me in a humbling and soothing way.

When we acknowledge our Heart Wounds, we can be vulnerable and let those we love see the parts we are most scared of showing. The grace we receive when we're seen and still wanted is an absolute gift. Although it can feel scary, this gift of vulnerability is why I believe we lean towards those who welcome our whole selves to the table: heart wounds and all.[2]

I thought when I got older I wouldn't struggle with being scared to show my whole self, but author Madeleine

L'Engle reminds us this idea isn't real, "When we were children, we used to think that when we were grown-up, we would no longer be vulnerable. But to grow up is to accept vulnerability... To be alive is to be vulnerable."[3]

The sooner we recognize that being in any kind of authentic relationship requires vulnerability, we can be honest about what we need to show up with integrity. To see past Heart Wounds, we have to look them in the eye, step into the surrounding fear, and be vulnerable enough with ourselves to speak truth to its core.

I've worked harder to be more diligent about recognizing and trying not to react when I feel my Heart Wounds reacting in the past six years. Everyone has at least a few, and some are larger than others. Maybe you believe you can never do anything right or think you are not fun to be around. When we aren't aware of our Heart Wounds, we leave ourselves vulnerable to lashing out at those around us instead of responding with grace. When we are at war with ourselves and others because of wounds, it automatically sets us at odds.

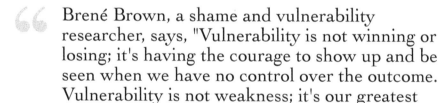

> Brené Brown, a shame and vulnerability researcher, says, "Vulnerability is not winning or losing; it's having the courage to show up and be seen when we have no control over the outcome. Vulnerability is not weakness; it's our greatest measure of courage."[4]

Courage doesn't always feel bold and brave. The moment between choosing to be vulnerable and sharing can be terrifying.

Thoughts can race in this in-between space and freeze us where we stand:

. . .

"Will they still love me?"
"Will this change how they see me?"
"What will they think of me?"

We have to *deliberately* choose to risk it when we are vulnerable with others. (I wish it were easier too). When we can step back from trying to have the upper hand in the relationship, we can change how we approach feelings and one another. Here are some ways I have learned to navigate challenging conversations and being vulnerable.

NAVIGATING THE WOUNDS OF OUR PAST

Notice the way your body reacts and tightens the next time you feel the need to defend yourself. You may be acting in response to a Heart Wound. Heart Wound reactions are defensive and sharp. Take time to process what is happening before replying, as our first words when wounded can be ones we regret later. At the base of a Heart Wound is a lie.

We did Theophostic, a prayer-based therapy at church growing up, which addresses the lie you believe in the past and asks God to heal the still sore Wound with the truth. Maybe you didn't do well on a project or test. But you are not dumb, you just didn't do well this time, *and* you aren't a mistake. Perhaps you didn't belong with a specific group, but maybe you haven't met your people yet, *and* you are worthy of love and goodness.

When you remember the big picture, it can relieve tension from past events and see that your past self was doing the best they could with what they had at the time. Lies gain weight when you forget opposing truths. Maybe you lied over here, but you told the truth this other time. Perhaps you were unprepared for a meeting, but you aren't always unprepared—last week, you got your work done early. Let all the facts enter the story you are creating around the lie, so you can help see the truth about who you are. We are creative beings with imagination, heart, and drive. If we can remember this, it changes the game.

When you recall the past and see your younger self, you have a perspective you didn't before. When we do this work of peeling back old stories and lies, you may feel shifts in your mind and body. Our bodies remember the stress we felt when people commented or we were embarrassed, even though we may not always recall the event as adults. Whether it's becoming tense in the presence of someone angry or feeling frozen when someone disagrees with you, it's all rooted in your body trying to protect you. Excess energy from an old situation can turn into ulcers, tension, tight muscles, and more.

Somatic Experiencing (SE) is body-mind trauma therapy and helps our bodies learn how to process memories. I have been going for over a year now. It is helpful even if we feel we don't have 'Big-T Trauma.' 'Little-t trauma' are events and moments we couldn't process at the time fully; this can be awkward situations, comments someone made, or a feeling of unworthiness from a memory. To have someone else hold space for us to explore lies, we hold close as truths, and to see new ways to process these old stories is a gift you won't regret giving yourself. Talk therapy is also beneficial for looking back and speaking the truth to your wounded younger self.

It is not your job to carry the open wounds of your past. It is your job to help your younger self-heal as much as possible. Doing this helps you love yourself and others well. There are times we feel shattered or cracked.

You are not worthless.

· · ·

Trust me when I say: You are *not* a lost cause.

Maybe you are just moving slower than usual. Going to therapy or doing soul work is not a sign of weakness. It's a willingness to say, "I don't want to carry this anymore by myself." Admitting as much, my friend is the start of a path to healing.

GRACE SPONGES

A tool shared with me by a mentor is a Grace Sponge for when you will have a tough conversation. A grace sponge is an imaginary human-sized sponge filled to the brim with grace. You use it when you enter a tense atmosphere to catch the offenses and hurtful words. This sponge gives a degree of separation to have patience and not take what others say instantly to heart.

It is not easy or a fix-all.

It's a simple visual tool reminding you to breathe, think, and respond instead of reacting immediately. The phrase "sticks and stones will break my bones, but words will never hurt me" isn't true, but it's helpful to imagine sharp words smacking into a Grace Sponge the size of Andre, the Giant, instead of directly piercing your heart.

Having a Grace Sponge also allows you to ask deeper questions. When we aren't rushing to the defense, we can ask, "Why are they saying this?" "What's under the hurt or words they are saying?" Sometimes seeing where someone is coming from can give us more information to diffuse a tense situation and be aware of what needs to happen next — whether it's boundaries, help, space, or mutual understanding.

LOOK AT WHAT YOUR RESPONSIBILITY IS

I mean, it's never our fault...right?

Unfortunately, sometimes it is. After an occasion when

you feel hurt or know you reacted out of integrity, ask yourself, "What can I do better next time?" Sometimes you need to wait after a hot bath and a mimosa to answer this question without snark — not that I'm speaking from personal experience.[5] At a minimum, it gives us a new perspective on what we can do in the future.

Even if it turns out you have no horse in the race, you can learn something from the conflict. Perhaps, you need healthier boundaries or remember to check in with your friends about plans and not assume everyone has the information they need. *This type of mind reading would be so helpful. Alas, we are not there yet.*

One example of recognizing my responsibility was after I led my first retreat. I thought cooking on the fire would take only 30 minutes (it took two hours), and then because I don't drink coffee, I didn't bring any. I made all these plans for what I wanted people to learn, and because food went over, I made everyone stay up till 2 am doing activities to fit into my vision of what they'd learn at the retreat.[6] The response forms made it very clear the activities were great, but the rushing and required attendance of said activities were not.

Lesson learned: Don't rush hungry women because exhausted women need downtime to breathe. Who knew? Not me.

REACTING VS. RESPONDING

Our first reaction can sometimes be, "Well, if I am this, you are too!" Flipping the accusations in this way is not helpful and can be pretty harmful. If someone is coming to us with a problem, they have probably thought about it for a while. Another possibility is if someone says something off the cuff, they might be remarking about something unrelated to you entirely. My house is not usually Martha-Stewart-level clean, and so when I had cleaned for two hours before a friend came, and the first words she said walking through the door were, "Oh good, someone else's house also looks messy, I'm not the only one." I didn't take it as a statement of relief, that they could relax on their end, but as a shame bullet straight to the heart.

If you react out of hurt and lash out at them, they may be confused, hurt in return, and even angry. You will only escalate a situation that wasn't malicious in the first place. If you have feelings of frustration towards a person, reacting from a Heart Wound's pain is not the time to bring it up. Schedule another time to discuss when you have processed and know you need to talk.[7]

We are hard-wired as animals to either fight, flight, or freeze.[8] Moving outside of this momentum almost requires pausing the moment and stepping outside of yourself. By remembering your Heart Wounds, you can say, "Yes, this is what I'm thinking, but what am I feeling right now? How do I want to interact within this moment? How do I want to be?" We usually examine our reactions after tense moments and say, "Oh, I shouldn't have said that!"

These moments are where we need to pause and ask ourselves what we need to feel safe. I've even paused and asked my body, "Hey, you are panicking hardcore right now. What do you need?" We can do this by excusing ourselves from the room or asking for 10 minutes to get our thoughts together to respond. If you have someone who shuts down with conflict and you are more confrontational, there will be a larger and larger divide if neither uses their words, even if it started over something minor.

TO LET IT GO, OR BRING IT UP.

When you know your Heart Wound is hit, the best thing is to go home and journal it out. We do not need to hash out every instance where we are hurt or frustrated by someone with that specific person.

If I feel like a relationship will not be the same if I don't address it after a week of introspection, I try to set a time to meet up and have a chat. I like to let the person know what I'd like to chat about ahead of time because I don't particularly appreciate feeling ambushed, and others do not either.

I often ask my husband to be a sounding board for these situations. *I am a verbal processor, which has pros and cons.*

The problem comes when the offending conversation plays back like a scratched cd in my mind, with me becoming more innocent with each playback. Jer's standard response after my storytelling is, "Did they/you *actually* say that?" I often respond with a very tart, "Yes, they did!" He then asks again, "Did they/you say those exact words?"' Then the truth comes out, "...Well...no. They meant them, though! They *definitely* gave me a look!" Sometimes having a third party can diffuse tension and help shed light on the next steps.

Anger can be fresh on the surface when your heart feels wounded. Remember your Grace Sponge and breathe. If mended well, you can have a deeper connection with your friend because you untangled the situation together. If you isolate and ice out every friend that hurts you or says something that puts you off, you will have no friends left.

Remember, they are human.

And lovely...remember you are too.

STAY FOR THE AFTERMATH.

In Germany, my house was in a state of disarray. I had a friend who cleaned houses, and I just wanted a clean slate. I had Melissa come over to clean for about 3 hours, and my floors and bathroom looked brand new. It was such a relief. I sang her praise to everyone.

A few weeks later, we were at a Christmas party together. Everyone gathered for an evening of food and deliciousness. While we were talking, she joked about how my shower was purple because of my hair dye. I barely remember what she said. She laughed, and everyone else laughed. I died inside while outwardly chuckling.

One of my heart wounds is the lie, "I'm a mess." In her one sentence, I felt like everyone saw the truth of my messiness, and my heart shrank. I went home and cried. I journaled, I prayed. I was distraught. *A bit overly so, to be honest.* I played it over and over in my head, as we often do. After a week of consideration, I decided to chat with her the next time I saw her. After all, in the Red Tent, we use our words and ask for what we need.

Maybe you know where this is going.

It was the New Year's Eve party, which is a terrible time to chat with anyone, but I thought it would be easy enough because I knew it would be in the back of my head every time I saw her. I thought I was being honest and doing the right thing.

I told her about my Heart Wound and how I felt like it was at my expense when she made a joke, and I was embarrassed. She apologized and explained how most houses have dirt and grime, and mine had glitter and purple hair dye. As we chatted, I thought everything was good, and wow, was that weight off my shoulders!

Five minutes later, Elissa grabbed me and asked why Melissa was sobbing in the bathroom. I was bewildered. Why was she crying? I was the one who had been offended. I had solved this like an adult.

I forgot when we solve things; it is between two people.

I had essentially announced to Melissa in a quick little moment that I had been offended, forgave her, requested she not make cleaning jokes about me again, and said we should move on. I then hugged her and walked away—leaving her shell shocked because she had had no clue that she had said anything harmful in the first place.

She was one of those sweet people who wants everyone

to get along and not inconvenience anyone. So when I had come to address her, I hit her heart wound: the fear of making someone feel like they are wrong or don't belong. I ended up going back into the bathroom and talking with her more, and apologizing.

Elissa later pulled me aside and said, "Aj, You have to stay for the aftermath." This lesson was hard to learn because I pride myself on how I have these conversations, but we miss half the learning when we aren't present for others in the conflict. If we decide to talk to someone about a Heart Wound, we can't let it be one-sided conversations. We have to chat it out, hear what they have to say, not just what we want them to say, and be open to feedback.

After looking at your initial response, it may help to have that one degree of separation to look at what happened from their side. Maybe the intention is different from what happened in reality. Even by planning on doing a good thing, we can cause harm. *Intention does not always equal impact.* Be willing to look at the part you played and own that. The other person's feelings are their own, and you don't know how they are operating. Every story has two sides. Yes, it might be challenging, and explaining your perspective may be necessary on occasion.

During the time they are sharing, keep your arms uncrossed and listen. *Stay open.* You might be able to speak to the things they have in their mind, but if you keep talking over and around each other, you won't get anywhere. Stepping back to see what happened initially can save pain and heartbreak in the long run. Here are two questions to keep in mind when listening.

1. Are they speaking out of their hurt?

Did you say something harmful to them? The point isn't to find fault but to bring awareness to the situation. Without being conscious of our feelings, we can slide in comments without realizing their manipulative aim. Being aware helps relieve the tension that might build up otherwise. When this happens to us, we know how we feel. We want to wound or retreat.

We cannot expect to react one way and refuse to acknowledge when others do the same.

Keep an eye out for why people might be responding the way they are. Folks who wrestle with a similar issue to you may react when seeing you struggle and might be projecting. When we don't have tools to show us a healthier way, we can weaponize shame and words. You can ask, "How can I help?" or, "What's coming up for you?" They may say, "Oh nothing," but later take a moment to think about what you said. Even if they are speaking out of their heart wounds, you may need to set new boundaries in place to have a better relationship with them.

Hurt people hurt people; healthy people also hurt people. No one has the corner on that.

2. Are they purposefully hitting yours?

You often see this with siblings, spouses, or toxic friends. In a moment of confidence, you share that you are still afraid of the dark and sleep with rope lights or how you wet the bed until you were in second grade. You never imagine they would betray you. Back-handed compliments are rife with this. We've had couples come over for dinner and lob tiny grenades of resentment at each other and laugh while they do it.[9] Be gentle with those you love. Don't use their weak spots for target practice around others. People might laugh, but they are uncomfortable.

With these types of comments: speak up, shut it down, or move it on out.[10]

SHARING YOUR STORY

Another tool I love is 'The Story I'm making up in my head right now. This tool comes from Brené Brown. See, our brains want to make sense of everything. If the facts don't make sense, our brain will modge-podge ideas together until it does. The modge-podge art piece your brain creates is the Story.

The problem with this is *it is distorted truth.* It's not the entire truth. When we have a one-sided tape playing, we aren't considering the genuine motive or thoughts of the other party, just twisting our own beliefs on what their reasons are.

Our Stories leak and spill out of us, whether through vulnerable sharing or lashed-out anger. Our awareness and willingness to be honest and vulnerable about the Story in our mind can be the difference between the two. Communicating with care and understanding can prevent creating a breeding ground for anger, resentment, and bitterness.

Vulnerably sharing the Story opens the door to have a conversation laced in grace instead of defensiveness.

When I was in Germany, I didn't know how the story I was making up impacted me and thought it was the truth. I was preparing the last Red Tent retreat I would be a part of before moving back to the states. One of our Tent Keepers was a chef, so I gave her free rein for food. When she got back to me, I messaged my co-leader, Elissa, about what we were doing for food, and she replied, "I feel like we're on different pages. Why didn't you talk to me about this? Let's meet in person." In my head, I started making up a story that she was upset, didn't want to do the retreat anymore, was going to say "screw this," leave Tent, and never talk to me again, which would result in Tent and retreat falling apart. Reasonable?

No.

Is it what I led with to immediately defend myself and my actions while laying out why I did everything I did to prove I didn't need to apologize?

Oh, you betcha.

She responded with, "Aj, you just went from 'we need to get on the same page' to the absolute destruction of our friendship, retreat, and Tent in two minutes. What. Is. Up?"

As she said those words, I remembered we were on the same team. She wasn't a prosecuting lawyer I had to defend myself against, she was my friend, and I needed to treat her like it. We were able to sort out the issue, but if I would have led, with "Hey, here's the Story I'm making up in my head right now about why we needed to meet in person, I don't feel like I have all the information I need. What's going on?" We would have had less tension and stress in our meeting.

It turns out she wanted more inclusion in planning this retreat, as, after my move, she was going to lead them and be the primary Tent Keeper, so she needed to know how things worked. I was clinging to leading the retreat because it would be my last one. In my attempt to not feel out of control, I wasn't leaving room for others to have the freedom to lead. Looking back, she laughs and recalls, "Oh yeah, that happened," and sees it as a bump in the road of Tent and our friendship - but not this big to do that I had spun it up to be beforehand. Sometimes we blow situations and our mistakes out of proportion when others haven't thought about it in years.

We use our Stories to prove how the other person is bad or wrong and how we are 100% right. We get so tied up in it that we barely have room to breathe. We spin ourselves into such a cocoon of frustration, fear, and angst that we can't sleep, think, or see anything right. Imagine trying to read a book with drunk goggles on. It's the same idea. Take a few steps back and ask yourself, "what is the Story I'm telling myself about this?" It'll lead to more grace for you and the people around you.

Not only does our Story take over the truth, but if we let it drive, it can lead to manipulation, gaslighting, and bypassing the original problem to make it about ourselves. Instead of lashing out, ask the person if they have time to listen to and speak truth into the story you are creating about them.

Asking in this way allows them to know what is on your mind, so you aren't ambushing them in attack mode. By not being in attack mode and vulnerable about your story, it also lets them off of defense because they are looking for where the story went off track. They understand you are looking to them for assistance instead of blaming them for the story in the first place. Sharing the Story puts you both against the problem instead of the problem coming between you and making each other the enemy.

Being vulnerable allows other people to see us. Remember, your softness and honesty about yourself, feelings, and relationships will create healing spaces. Staying closed keeps the hurt inside—though being open can hurt too. But lovely? That's full-hearted living. As Brené says, remember to have "Strong Backs, Soft Fronts, and Wild Hearts." Because this *is* the point, this is what life is all about, feeling it all and being present for it.

Assumptions go for the flip side as well. When we assume what the other person is saying, we can get ourselves into trouble. I have done this many times by opening my mouth and speaking my assumptions. One time I said, "I know you hate this person, which is why we aren't going." Confused, they respond with something completely different, like, "No, I have a big test in two days, and I am nervous about how I'll do. I'd rather study so I can feel secure about it than go to a party where people will constantly be asking me how I'm doing, and I won't be able to think about anything else."

Ask people for their Story. They may or may not be comfortable sharing with you, but you will still have given them an option to share in a non-judgemental way.

As tempting as it may be, don't stop them in the middle and say, "No, that's not true!" Let them finish. Give empathy, and shed light if you can. Sometimes when we speak out loud the Stories in our heads, we can hear how ridiculous they sound in the light of day.

Kelsey, my best friend, has a phrase I love: it's 'to sing someone's song back to them.' Sometimes our friends and loved ones lose perspective on who they are. If we can hold up a mirror and say, I know this is how you feel, but this isn't who you are, we may help them see themselves in a fresh light. Sometimes it's just hugs and tissues and telling them you hear them. Other times, it may look like an intervention.

Many times being seen and heard is what we are craving most from those around us. As others speak and share, emotions may flare up for you as well, and it's all a part of the process. Be generous with those you love, and let's please finally stop pretending any of us are mind readers.

QUESTIONS FOR FURTHER DISCOVERY

Where do you feel your heart wounds react the most?

When a Heart Wound is hit, what is your initial reaction most often?

Is there someone you need to mend a relationship with due to a misunderstanding?

Where do you need to heal your Heart Wound memories?

BOOK RECOMMENDATIONS

Rising Strong by Brené Brown
Emotionally Healthy Woman by Geri Scazzero
Rebloom by Rachel Maddox

Vulnerability Red Tent

Five minutes before the Tent Begins:
Leader: Lovelies, please put your phones on silent or off, grab your water, snacks, journal, and token and join me in the circle.

Opening:
Leader: Before we begin, I would like to state that this is a safe space. In order to make it so, there needs to be agreement around keeping what is said in circle, in the circle. I'm asking you all to agree to only speak of your own experiences, and only give advice when asked. We will be talking about deeply personal things in the Red Tent. A gentle reminder that we can disagree and still accept each other. Can I have a show of hands for everyone willing to keep this space confidential, for themselves and everyone here tonight?

Shakeout and Grounded Breathing:
Leader: Let us take a minute to stand up, shake out any worries, or frustration from your day. Twist your body, shake your booty, kick your legs, jump up and down. Audibly make sounds while relaxing your jaw. Stretch, or move in a way that feels supportive.

Please have a seat in this circle, and let's do some ground breathing. You can close your eyes, start to relax your shoulders. You can roll your neck from side to side, rest your hands on your stomach, knees, or the ground, whatever is most comfortable for you. Start breathing in from your belly. Take a deep breath. As you exhale, release anything that came before tonight that is on your mind.

Breathe in again, releasing anything to come in the

future. Keep breathing, focusing on the sounds around you, the breath of other women, and your heartbeat. As you release your breath, feel your body settling into this space. In this moment, here with us. You are safe. You are loved. We are glad you are here with us.

Call in:

Leader: We are gathered in our Red Tent, as women, as daughters, as mothers, as workers and dreamers. We come here to speak our heart's desires, our mind's thoughts, and share the song of our souls. We see with our eyes, hear with our ears, and will hum along in our hearts. May this space be open, sacred, and grounded for us here tonight. Let us hold hands as we travel deeper together, learning to better love ourselves, each other, and the world.

Gender Neutral Option:

We are gathered in our Red Tent Tent as humans, as explorers, as workers and dreamers. We come here to speak our heart's desires, our mind's thoughts, and share the song of our souls. We see with our eyes, hear with our ears, and will hum along in our hearts. May this space be open, sacred, and grounded for us here tonight. Let us hold hands as we travel deeper together, learning to better love ourselves, each other, and the world.

Song:

Leader: Close your eyes and think of what you want from this night and this week. It might be friendship, laughter, wisdom. We'll pass the bowl around one person at a time, and you'll say your blessing request, we'll sing the song with your word inside of it, and then after we sing over you, pass the bowl to the next woman. She'll share her blessing word, and we'll sing a blessing over her until we reach the end of the circle.

Call down a blessing x3, Call down, ____before you, ____behind you, ____Within you, and around you

Repeat for each person in the group, end with three call downs.

15: 1st Circle:

Leader: When speaking, please use the talking light, and when you finish, please say "I have spoken," so we know you have completed your thought. You can react with hand snaps, hand on your heart, and facial expressions. Please speak only of your own story, and don't give any advice unless asked.

For our first circle, what is your name, pronouns, your intention for tonight, and what is your first instinct when the word vulnerability comes up.

30: Quote and Response:

Leader: I'll read this quote, and then you can share your response to what comes up for you around it. "Vulnerability is the birthplace of love, belonging, joy, courage, empathy, and creativity" -Brené Brown.

45: Activity 1: Where do you feel vulnerable

Leader: Many times, we hide our vulnerability in fear of what others will say, but sometimes we're all holding similar vulnerabilities, or triggers. When we can hold space for everyone to be human and be nervous, it can create belonging, and help others know where we are vulnerable so they can help protect us too. Write down two to eight things you feel vulnerable about. A few examples are "I don't like being in public without makeup

on", "I'm nervous I'm a bad friend.", "I'm afraid I'm not enough."
Give three minutes for writing

There is no pressure to share if you don't like, but if you would like to share one thing you wrote down you may, and you don't have to explain why. You can say it, and pass the light to the next woman. If you don't want to share, you can pass to the next person.

1:00: Womanhood story:
    Leader: Womanhood stories are a core part of Red Tent, sharing our stories is a brave act. Sometimes they are joy filled, sad, frustrating, or a mix of all of it. The story may include periods, sex, birth, or any part of the woman and human experience. ___ has offered to share her story tonight. ____ the floor is yours.
    See the appendix of the book for reaching out to your women to see who would like to share before the tent day.

After her story:
    Leader: Thank you ___ for sharing your story. Is there anything you need from us? Hug, encouragement, a listening ear during break?
    If they say yes, do what you can to fulfill that need if possible.

1:10: Soul Care Time:
    Leader: Now is our soul care time. This is 20 minutes to stretch, nap, chat, get food, go to the restroom. We do ask that you don't use this time to be on your phone. I'll give us a five-minute heads up to tent, and a one minute come to circle heads up.

· · ·

1:30: Activity Two: I See You[11]

Leader: Let's stand in a circle together. One person will start and turn to the lady on her right, touch her in some way, maybe holding hands, hand on her face, or shoulder, (get permission first), and make eye contact and hold it for a moment.

While still holding eye contact person A says to person B, (B Name), I see you. Take another moment, and really feel the "I see you." Yes, this will be awkward and weird, it's okay, it's not often we let ourselves be seen. B then turns to C, and says to C, (C Name), I see you, and it'll carry on through the circle, till we get back to the beginning.

1:45: Circle

What did that feel like for you? Being seen? Seeing someone else?

2: Closer *Grab your red thread (yarn) and make sure scissors are within reach.*

Leader: Red thread represents our connection to the women around us and those who have come before us. You will take your red yarn and wrap it around your wrist. You can wrap as many times as you want, as you recite your matriarchal spiritual lineage. Your lineage are the women and people who have influenced and loved you.

They don't have to be biologically related, you can claim or not claim anyone you would like. You can say your name, mother of (any children), daughter of x, daughter of y, daughter of daughters, daughter of whatever resonates (Eve, Spirit, the moon, etc). You can also say descendent instead, or daughter of those who _____ instead of names.

When you have finished wrapping, pass the thread to the next person until it has gone all the way around the circle.

You can start the process and do your lineage and wrap and then pass it to the person on your right.

After the Red Thread has come back to you.

Leader: As we are connected, let us sing our song, we'll sing it three times, it goes flow, ebb, weavers, thread, weavers, thread, spiders, web. Sing it with me:

Song: We are the flow we are the ebb,
We are the weavers we are the thread,
We are the weavers we are the thread,
we are the spiders we are the web.
x3

Leader, pick up the scissors, and cut your thread, and as you explain the below, you can have the person to the left tie your thread.

Leader: When cutting the thread to tie bracelets, share your favorite moment and a takeaway. Have the lady to your left tie your yarn, twice in a square knot, and one slip knot, and this way, your thread will not come undone. After you have spoken, pass the scissors to the right, and the next person can go.

After the scissors make their way back to you and everyone has tied their thread, you can share the invitation below. Feel free to hold hands if you'd like.

Invitation to curiosity
   Leader: When you find yourself closing down this

month when you want to be vulnerable, check in to see what needs nourishing or nurturing and how you can give that to yourself. Thank you for being a part of tonight's Red Tent. You are all a treasure, and I'm glad you are here. Our Red Tent is now closed.

HOW WE GROW

When I was younger, I went by Amber instead of Aj. I was happy most of the time, partially because I'm a seven on the enneagram (we're called the *Enthusiasts* for a reason), and partly because I think God sneezed while pouring the joy in when making me, so I have a double portion by default. I especially loved making other people smile and achieving whatever goals I decided to chase. It was a rare day I'd step a toe out of line. [1]

My happy demeanor served me well in school, although I was always curious what it would be like to be the new girl. I never got that chance: I was in the same school system, Kindergarten through 12th grade. I wouldn't trade it for anything because I made fantastic friends and great memories with the show choir, theatre, and dance team. However, the allure of starting fresh and deciding who I would be if I wanted a change always felt like an opportunity that would be amazing. Would I be the mysterious new girl? The glittery one? The sporty one? [2]

I had my first opportunity to be the new girl in college. (Granted, everyone was new because we were all freshmen.)

Our professor took the role in my first college theatre class and asked, "What would you like to be called?"

Her question surprised the hell out of me because I was one of the people being asked. Everybody already knew everyone's names in my old school: whatever you went by in Kindergarten is what people called you senior year. But here? In this new classroom, full of new people, I didn't know anyone's name….and they didn't know mine! As she went down the list, people shortened William to Billy or Alexandra to Alex. The typical name shifts.

I wanted a fresh start, not just for the people who didn't know me but also for myself. I wanted to give myself permission to try new things and explore, so I'm not sure if I truly realized then how much this would be a before/after moment for me. All I knew is that I wanted to answer differently for the first time in my life.

So when she asked me what I would like to go by, I took a deep breath and said, "Aj." I think I stood an inch taller and smiled a bit wider, but for everyone else in the room, it was as if I had gone by Aj my whole life.

I had a friend and a few people who would occasionally call me A.J. growing up, so it wasn't the first time I had used this name. But this time, it was different. Now, going by, Aj[3] felt like a breath of fresh air. It felt like I had given myself wings to fly and explore all my possibilities. And fly, I would as I started letting my curiosity guide me.

We grow in various ways. Sometimes it's moments where we choose ourselves and chart a new path, as I did on my first day of college. Other times it's a community we change in, classes that show us a new perspective, or habits that, over time, wear a new groove into our lives. Sometimes, we grow into someone we weren't acquainted with before. Growth can look like gradual shifts or a sudden growth spurt. Moving to a new place can also help us evaluate who we want to be instead of doing the same routine we've always done. In this new place, we can ask, is this still true? Who do I want to be here?

Whether we like it or not, we're constantly shifting and changing. If we can be aware of *how* we grow, we can use that knowledge to be at the helm of our lives.

GROWING AS A JOURNEY

Being in college opened my eyes to the bigger world around me. There were so many things to do and ways to get involved. I was soaking in new experiences and sharing them with people from every walk of life. I loved every minute of it.[4]

Nearing the end of our college career, Jer brought up the idea of enlisting in the Air Force. Of course, I cried.[5] It was 2012, and jobs were not as widely available for fresh-out-of-college married couples. Jer's older brother was in the Air Guard, so we knew some of what to expect. As we talked, we realized it would be a good fit, and he enlisted.

We move every three years with the Air Force, and I always think of each move as a new adventure. I ask myself, "What's happening here? Where are we going to grow? How can I get involved?" By asking these questions in each place, Jer and I create an oyster of possibilities for us to dive into and then take what we learn to our next home. Some areas are easier than others—I'm still dreaming about going back to Germany but don't feel the need to return to Mississippi.

When things don't go as planned, it can be easy to discount the months or year—*hello, 2020*—that defied the New Year vision. But what I have found is, even during these murky times, we can still have perspective. We can focus on what we gained or learned instead of only on what was lost. We can look back with grateful reflection instead of frustrated regrets over what we 'failed at.'

Even when we have a great year and go after our goals,

334 | RED THREAD

sometimes our focus can be skewed on things we wish had turned out better. This doesn't mean you don't still grieve for the bad or missed moments. But it does mean we don't hate ourselves or dismiss any hope from the season within the same breath.

Make a map of the different periods in your life, whether jobs, houses, relationships, or age ranges. With this map you can see how you've grown or changed over the years. You can be present where you are and uncover your next steps with awareness of where you've been.

Here is my map, with my reflections on how I have grown and what I have learned in my journey so far by using places I've lived:

- In college, I learned I had possibilities I hadn't tapped into and became Aj. I joined a burlesque troupe and discovered I was artistic at the YMCA Summer Camp. I found out who I could be and explored it all.
- In Hawaii, I figured out what I wanted and moved toward it, like mermaiding. Jer and I also bonded in a new way by being far from home, and during his first deployment, I learned how to hold my own and be okay with being alone.
- In Germany, I settled into my bones by finding my style, learned how to apply henna, and dyed my hair purple. I started walking with purpose by letting God and myself define who I was instead of other people. I joined online forums and launched my first Red Tent, which subsequently changed my life.
- In Mississippi, I started walking in who I was. I continued Red Tents and started writing and publishing my work, sharing what I was learning with others. I also learned diligence by setting new business goals, launching In Joy

Productions, and writing the first draft for this book.

- In Texas, I grew deeper roots, and I started thriving. We bought a house, became Texas residents, and planted our first garden. I found a business coach when I brought my business online during COVID, deepened my faith, and started going to weekly SE therapy. I leaped and changed my title from Mermaid Harmony to The Joy Weaver. This book will also be published while I'm in Texas.

What. A. Journey.

Each place has been a layering of the lessons before and applying them to continue growing. Learning helps me alter course for the next base or year, set new boundaries, and make sure I tend my body well.

Knowing there is something new at each base to discover about the world, myself, and those around me thrills me to my toes. There's also a sense of safe adventure; I know that even if this particular place is not my favorite, we'll only be there for a few years. I can look back and see, "Okay, what worked, what didn't? What would I do differently next time?" So wherever I go next, I feel like I have more wisdom to be kinder to myself and others. So in a way, I am the new girl at school, *well, new mermaid on base* every few years. I'm always excited to see what will happen next—to show up fully, offer what I have, and serve well.

So who have you been? Can you appreciate your past selves while celebrating who you are now?

I adored 18-year old me, but she couldn't do some of the things I do now. I need this version of me now. Maybe you chart your path through jobs, or kids, or through moments that have impacted you, but I encourage you to write it down to see what you discover about yourself.

Sometimes military spouses don't like overseas stations for a variety of reasons. I wonder if sometimes, it's because they are tropical flowers that need a lot of sun and rain, and they don't have the resources they need to get grounded. Or, if they are replanted full-grown oak trees, they might feel cut off from their roots.

No matter the type of plant you are, you require specific resources to blossom and grow, and it is okay to seek them out.

If you struggle in different environments, take a moment to understand what is going on and why there is tension. I think people are like plants. Some of us are like oak trees and grow deep roots in one place. Others are like fruit trees who can bear fruit as long as they grow into a compatible atmosphere. Others still, like me, are quick rooting weeds; they'll find a way to live almost anywhere.

Where can you collect the sunshine you need?
Can you dig a bit more to secure your roots?
How resourceful can you get to nourish yourself?

GROWING WITH OUR INTUITION

When did we learn it's okay for other people to follow their gut or Inner Voice, but not for us? I know for me, when someone goes after their dreams full speed, I think, "Get it, babe!" while yearning to have the same courage in my own life.[6] We all have a sliding scale of what we believe is possible. Maybe my path seems outrageous to you, but your journey may look wild to someone else. We can be harsh with ourselves because of the comparison game we learn to play. We gather evidence to believe it's safer to keep ourselves to ourselves. There are also other reasons it might not feel safe to follow your Inner Voice.

Maybe you've been hushed up when you get excited about a new path in your life. Or, when sharing a recent discovery, someone calls you a hypocrite or tells you it's stupid. It may feel safer to keep your ideas to yourself.

There is goodness in you, waiting to bloom. It's already been flowering your whole life, but how often do you cut it back because you think you need to do what others are doing? You might not know what kind of plant you are. Maybe you are a cypress tree amongst strong fearsome oaks or a flower amid sturdy bushes. You are not meant to be what others are. You are undeniably the best *you*.

If you don't have exact coordinates for where you are going with your life, that's okay too. I'm sure you have a few stars that can help you navigate your way; maybe they are kindness, a love of working with computers, teaching, peacemaking, a commitment to prioritize your family, or building community in this season. You might not know ten steps down the line, but the odds are you do know the next right step.

We overestimate what we can do in a year and underestimate what we can do in a decade. Dreams shift and change, and following the flow is half of the adventure. Who we are becoming is also us choosing the direction. Sometimes we don't know, and we're thrown off course. We might think, "Oh, this is different than where I thought I'd be." Sure, it probably will be different than you expected, but if we shoot for nothing and are just meandering, we might stumble into something we'll love. So why not try a little too, and see if you'll get to a place you love even sooner.

338 | RED THREAD

GROWING THROUGH INTENTIONS

The National Fund of Science Research[7] studied people's
conception of how they will or won't change over time. They
asked over 19,000 people, aged 20 to 80, how they thought
they would change in the next ten years versus how much
they had changed over the past ten years. Nearly all the
respondents thought they wouldn't change much in the next
decade but believed they were vastly different from
themselves when they looked back on the previous decade.

We get settled into the idea of having learned everything
we need. "I'll be this way till I die." But if the truth is that
we continue changing and morph into new people as we
grow, and we must acknowledge this fact.[8]

If we constantly change, can we cultivate the grace to
explore old and new dreams with confidence and patience?
We can also remember those around us also learn and
become new people, adding new layers—just like trees grow
a new ring each year. Look back on who you've been and
how being those people have served you in the past.

Who are you now?
What do you love about the person you've become?
What does the person you are now need?

If you stay stuck and think, "Oh, I'm finished learning
after high school or college, I don't need to learn any more
things," you miss out on good stuff. Learning isn't just
school. There is so much to glean and learn from this world.
It's wasteful to assume you won't grow or learn anymore. I
hear "This is just who I am" often from people who say they
don't have anything else to discover. It feels dismissive and
disappointing to who they can be.

We can stay the same instead of transforming and
adapting if we cling to our limiting beliefs. Luckily, we have
neuroplasticity, the ability of our brain to learn new habits

and behaviors. Part of growth and learning new things is figuring out what doesn't work. We take a step, and if it doesn't turn out for the best, we can mistake it for an omen that we are on the wrong path. If you trust your Inner Voice and your curiosity by moving in the direction you need to go in, failing is a part of the story.

Let me repeat: Failing is expected, unavoidable, and standard.

If failure is a guaranteed, unavoidable part of the equation, try to lean into it.

What has made you curious?
What do you want to know more about or learn?
What new possibilities does growth have when you know you don't have to do it perfectly?

Don't limit yourself. Lovely, you have so many growth moments ahead of you. Keep going. Even if it's rough right now, the dawn will come. Find your stars and keep steering. There is hope.

In school, we were all assigned a daily planner. You know these books: a calendar, broken into days with lines to fill in assignments, due dates, tasks, and more. I used to think schedule planners were dumb. Then I started a business and needed one out of necessity. Later, I saw goal planners and thought those were dumb because "Who needs more than one planner?" *Me actually....and many other people.*

Now I have my Elegant Excellence Goals Journal, my morning pages journal I free write in, and my actual planner. Using these tools, I've become a more organized, calmer version of myself, and I'm not near as late as I used to be to everything.[9] Sometimes our growth needs bumpers like in a bowling lane. Your bumpers might be a planner, or an accountability partner, or a bullet journal.

What bumpers can you utilize to stay in the alignment of your growth and goals?

Creating new rhythms, habits, and goals helps us flourish. When I bring up habits to friends, I either get eye rolls or enthusiastic nods. Habits are hard because we think we have to be perfect whenever learning a new one, but they bring us closer to our goals and dreams. Goals don't have to be strict; they can be joyful. There seems to be a general sense that if you fall off the wagon, you might as well blow up the wagon. But the wagon is still there, stopped, waiting for you to hop back on. It's not running off into the distance without you.

Sometimes goals need to be S.M.A.R.T. (Specific, Measurable, Attainable, Relevant, and Time Based). Goals can also be aspirational and indicative of the type of person you want to be. One of my goals right now is "I am a grounded embodied woman." I write my goals in the present tense to help my brain remember how I want to show up, not just ten years from now, but today. As I write out my goals every day (or a few times a week), it's reminding my brain of who I'm becoming. By taking small steps every day and seeing who I am working to become, it's easier to live into my goals now, in the present moment.

Trying to set a new goal or habit doesn't mean things aren't good now. It asks, "What would feel even better?" I have a friend who asked on Facebook if she's allowed to set a new goal to be okay and be financially independent. She's not the only one. It's a trend I see happening, where we see other people struggling and wonder if it's okay for us to be financially secure or healthy while others are worse off. Here's where the rubber meets the road. When we seek wholeness for the sake of community and growing ourselves, we bring others up with us. It doesn't have to be one or the other. Capitalism may say, "I've got mine, screw you!" But we can create better paths for ourselves and those around us simultaneously.

GROWING THROUGH HONESTY

Author and activist Glennon Doyle has a beautiful way of sharing this idea, of living into our possibilities in her book *Untamed*.[10] She asks, "What is the truest, most beautiful story about your life you can imagine?"

When we ask this question, we can get out of the rut of what we should be doing or what others want us to do. What calls to your soul? What dream pulses beneath the surface that you are nervous about speaking aloud? What fills you with a soul-filled yearning?

Sometimes this means we have to be willing to give up something.

To live our most beautiful stories, we have to get centered before moving into them. Maybe you want to travel the world, but you have a medically compromised child and have to stay home. Sometimes there are things you can't give up for your dreams, but what's a way to shift so you can live it now? You can live your vision on a smaller level. Taking a broad brush and saying, "This dream is too big or too complicated to live into," doesn't mean you can't have part of it now.

You may have to get creative. You can do Duolingo with your child as a fun exercise or challenge yourself to cook one authentic recipe from abroad a week. Invite guests and request each bring one travel fact. You can bring your dream into the present, even if it's not the way you originally planned.

If you feel you have regret pooling around your ankles, know there are opportunities to make this next chapter one that feeds your soul and creates a better world all around you.

We can become walking anthropologists in our life, looking for how we are shifting, and uncovering how we want to grow. It's not too late to change.

If you don't like the person you are in this moment,

figure out what you'd like to lean into more, and create a journey of growth:

Would you like more compassion? Kindness? Playfulness? Integrity? Rest?

Who knows who or what will come along to help you grow. Keep your eyes open.

You never know what surprises and gifts lie ahead.

And what a gift this curious exploration is to give yourself.

To grow into and embody the *fullest expression of your soul.*

QUESTIONS FOR FURTHER DISCOVERY

Make your learning timeline. What have you learned in the past from different places, people, or moments?

Have you had a moment of growth? If so, what was that like for you?

Where do you find yourself in your growth journey right now? Are you peeling back layers, learning, resting, or applying new lessons?

BOOK RECOMMENDATIONS

Fierce, Free, and Full of Fire by Jen Hatmaker
Braving the Wilderness by Brené Brown
You are a Badass by Jen Sincero

How we Grow Red Tent

Five minutes before the Tent Begins:
Leader: Lovelies, please put your phones on silent or off, grab your water, snacks, journal, and token and join me in the circle.

Opening:

Leader: Before we begin, I would like to state that this is a safe space. In order to make it so, there needs to be agreement around keeping what is said in circle, in the circle. I'm asking you all to agree to only speak of your own experiences, and only give advice when asked. We will be talking about deeply personal things in the Red Tent. A gentle reminder that we can disagree and still accept each other. Can I have a show of hands for everyone willing to keep this space confidential, for themselves and everyone here tonight?

Shakeout and Grounded Breathing:

Leader: Let us take a minute to stand up, shake out any worries, or frustration from your day. Twist your body, shake your booty, kick your legs, jump up and down. Audibly make sounds while relaxing your jaw. Stretch, or move in a way that feels supportive.

Please have a seat in this circle, and let's do some ground breathing. You can close your eyes, start to relax your shoulders. You can roll your neck from side to side, rest your hands on your stomach, knees, or the ground, whatever is most comfortable for you. Start breathing in from your belly. Take a deep breath. As you exhale, release anything that came before tonight that is on your mind.

Breathe in again, releasing anything to come in the future. Keep breathing, focusing on the sounds around you,

the breath of other women, and your heartbeat. As you release your breath, feel your body settling into this space. In this moment, here with us. You are safe. You are loved. We are glad you are here with us.

Call in:

Leader: We are gathered in our Red Tent, as women, as daughters, as mothers, as workers and dreamers. We come here to speak our heart's desires, our mind's thoughts, and share the song of our souls. We see with our eyes, hear with our ears, and will hum along in our hearts. May this space be open, sacred, and grounded for us here tonight. Let us hold hands as we travel deeper together, learning to better love ourselves, each other, and the world.

Gender Neutral Option:

We are gathered in our Red Tent Tent as humans, as explorers, as workers and dreamers. We come here to speak our heart's desires, our mind's thoughts, and share the song of our souls. We see with our eyes, hear with our ears, and will hum along in our hearts. May this space be open, sacred, and grounded for us here tonight. Let us hold hands as we travel deeper together, learning to better love ourselves, each other, and the world.

Song: Call Down a Blessing

Leader: Close your eyes and think of what you want from this night and this week. It might be friendship, laughter, wisdom. We'll pass the bowl around one person at a time, and you'll say your blessing request, we'll sing the song with your word inside of it, and then after we sing over you, pass the bowl to the next woman. She'll share her

blessing word, and we'll sing a blessing over her until we reach the end of the circle.

Call down a blessing x3, Call down, _____before you, _____behind you, _____Within you, and around you*

Repeat for each person in the group, end with three call downs.

15: 1st Circle:

Leader: When speaking, please use the talking light, and when you finish, please say "I have spoken," so we know you have completed your thought. You can react with hand snaps, hand on your heart, and facial expressions. Please speak only of your own story, and don't give any advice unless asked.

For our first circle, what is your name, pronouns, and your intention for tonight. What does growth mean to you?

30: Quote and Response:

If you have a bigger group, you can have them write down their first instincts (1-3 words) from the poem. If you have a few people, you can ask if anyone would like to share their responses.

"And the day came when the risk to remain tight in a bud was more painful than the risk it took to blossom."—Anaïs Nin[11]

45: Activity 1: Meeting your Future Self Meditation

Meditation script is located at the end of this Red Tent script.

1:00: Journal

Who were you in 7-10 years? What did she have to say to you? What surprised you about meeting her? Where did the two of you meet? What was she like? How do you feel?

Is there anything you need to do? What steps may you need to take as you become her?

1:10: 2nd Circle:

Share anything you learned from your meditation.

1:25: Soul Care Time:

Leader: Now is our soul care time. This is 20 minutes to stretch, nap, chat, get food, go to the restroom. We do ask that you don't use this time to be on your phone. I'll give us a five-minute heads up to tent, and a one minute come to circle heads up.

1:45: Activity Two: Your Guiding Council

Grab your pen and paper. We are going to create a council for you to talk to or look to when you need advice. It doesn't have to be a woman. It can be anyone you look up to, divine, dead, alive, any age, real or imagined. Make a list of 3-10 people. Once you have your list, pick three, and imagine you were them giving you advice for where you are in your life right now. What would they say? How would they encourage you?

After they have written their advice down.

We'll go around the circle and you can share one guide's advice for your life right now if you would like.

2:00: Womanhood story:

Leader: Womanhood stories are a core part of Red Tent, sharing our stories is a brave act. Sometimes they are joy filled, sad, frustrating, or a mix of all of it. The story may include periods, sex, birth, or any part of the woman and human experience. ___ has offered to share her story tonight. ____ the floor is yours.

See the appendix of the book for reaching out to your women to see who would like to share before the tent day.

After her story:

Leader: Thank you ___ for sharing your story. Is there anything you need from us? Hug, encouragement, a listening ear during break?

If they say yes, do what you can to fulfill that need if possible.

2:10: Closer *Grab your red thread (yarn) and make sure scissors are within reach.*

Leader: Red thread represents our connection to the women around us and those who have come before us. You will take your red yarn and wrap it around your wrist. You can wrap as many times as you want, as you recite your matriarchal spiritual lineage. Your lineage are the women and people who have influenced and loved you.

They don't have to be biologically related, you can claim or not claim anyone you would like. You can say your name, mother of (any children), daughter of x, daughter of y, daughter of daughters, daughter of whatever resonates (Eve, Spirit, the moon, etc).You can also say descendent instead, or daughter of those who ____ instead of names.

When you have finished wrapping, pass the thread to the next person until it has gone all the way around the circle.

You can start the process and do your lineage and wrap and then pass it to the person on your right.

After the Red Thread has come back to you.

Leader: As we are connected, let us sing our song, we'll sing it three times, it goes flow, ebb, weavers, thread, weavers, thread, spiders, web. Sing it with me:

Song: We are the flow we are the ebb,
We are the weavers we are the thread,
We are the weavers we are the thread,
we are the spiders we are the web.
x3

Leader, pick up the scissors, and cut your thread, and as you explain the below, you can have the person to the left tie your thread.

Leader: When cutting the thread to tie bracelets, share your favorite moment and a takeaway. Have the lady to your left tie your yarn, twice in a square knot, and one slip knot, and this way, your thread will not come undone. After you have spoken, pass the scissors to the right, and the next person can go.

After the scissors make their way back to you and everyone has tied their thread, you can share the invitation below. Feel free to hold hands if you'd like.

Invitation to curiosity
Leader: This month, evaluate what changes you need to make to feel like you are on a soul aligned path.

Thank you for being a part of tonight's Red Tent. You are all a treasure, and I'm glad you are here. Our Red Tent is now closed.

Future You Meditation

Our meditation today is to meet a possible future you. Nothing is set in stone, it is simply exploring a possibility thread of who you could be, and to explore your dreams and who you are.

Find a place to rest and be comfortable, checking in with your body on how she would like to sit, or lay.

You can rest your hands on the ground, your heart, or sprawl them out around you.

(Pause)

Let your body sink into the ground, or the chair...like you're melting into yourself.

Any thoughts that come in, acknowledge them and let them pass.

Breathe in from your belly, and audibly exhale, letting go of any fears, or notions of what's to come.

With each breath, let yourself sink deeper into your seat, into the ground. You are safe, and you are held.

(Pause)

Envision a path before you.

Begin to walk down it.

What does this path look like? You might be by a beach, a sidewalk, or walking into a forest.

Take a moment to explore the area around you. What time of day is it? Do you hear any sounds of birds or wind, or smell anything?

(Pause)

Find a place to sit and rest. Maybe there is a tree swing, or a bench, or a place under a willow tree.

(Pause)

Soon you see a person coming from the tree line. As they come closer, they feel familiar, and yet different.

This person is a possible you in the future.

It may be five, ten, or even twenty years in the future.

What do they look like?

How does future you move?

How do you feel seeing them?

They may offer for you to walk with them, or they may sit down with you, either is fine.

You relax together for a while, maybe talking, or not saying anything. Future you gently takes your hand, and shows you what your possible life looks like in the future.

Maybe it's in pictures, or in words, or a feeling in your soul. They may also not show you anything, or show you something else. There is no right or wrong way.

(One to two minute pause)

Ask what you are holding onto that you need to let go of.

(Pause)

You notice a basket nearby that you know is for you.

(Pause)

In this basket are the items you need to garden: a trowel, gloves, seeds of possibility, a rake.

You start to dig together.

There may be things weighing on your heart or mind. You can lay down your anger, frustration, or fear—let it be fertilizer for your hopes and dreams.

(Pause)

Put your anxiety and the emotions that are not serving you into the earth.

Dig with your hands, or a trowel, everything you need is nearby.

As you cultivate the earth with your hands, realize you feel lighter as you let go of your fears. You are keeping them safe, they are not forgotten, but they are being put to work here in this space.

There are seeds of possibility in the basket. These are your dreams, ideas, thoughts, hopes.

(Pause)

They may not look like seeds, and maybe there is nothing you plant together, but digging the garden was the work for today.

If there are things to plant, then you can plant them together.

Take note if there are any seeds you thought would be there, that are not.

Or any seeds that are there, that you did not expect.

How do you feel planting these?

(Pause)

They may or may not grow.

Or they may grow slowly, as the dreams of our souls do not sprout overnight, but take tending and time.

(Pause)

You can ask future you how you need to tend these seeds to help them grow to the best of their ability.

(Pause)

Is there anything you need to move out of the way?

Are there any weeds you need to pull? What are these weeds?

(Pause)

Take a few minutes to garden with your future self. You may ask questions or just be.

(Pause for one to three minutes)

When you are ready, look at your garden.

Not everything will grow, and things you never expected to grow just might.

Say your goodbyes and remember you can come back to tend your garden any time.

(Pause)

As you start to walk back on your path how do you feel?

What did you learn?

Do you have new clarity?

(Pause)

Continue walking back to yourself. Walk back to the

sound of my voice, and the feeling of your breath filling your lungs.

Gently bring awareness back into your body, wiggle your toes, your fingers, and on your own time come back to the room by opening your eyes.

CREATING A SUSTAINABLE
RED TENT

*I*f you start a Red Tent, I encourage you to use this book as a jumping-off point, not a rule book. While I wish it could, *Red Thread* won't save you from some of the slip-ups you are bound to make with your specific group of women or help you craft the perfect Tent—Spoiler: it just doesn't exist. Mistakes are a part of life. Things will go wrong, and people will come and go. Women will slip up or be offended. You will mess up and make the wrong decision. It's just a part of being human, but the more gentle we can be with ourselves and others, the better.

Below I've assembled some things that have helped other Tent Keepers and me through the years build sustainable Red Tents. If you have any questions, you are always welcome to email me at TheJoyWeaver@gmail.com. The Red Tent Directory also has a variety of resources, and their *Red Tents* book is a must have on any shelf. They also have a list of Red Tents around the world, if you are interested in seeing if there are any near you.

The idea of making a Tent may feel overwhelming, but Mary-Grace, a radiant coach and Tent woman, shares, "I would say with anything space holding, it's not about you. It's not about you and what you can say or do. Take the pressure off and honor the space and set the tone, invite people to show up fully by making it a safe place to be so. Allow their processing even if it's different than yours. If Tent aims to be transformative and honest, I need to make it safe to be honest. Bring the tools for that to take place and encourage sharing. I need to hold those things in every moment, and sometimes that looks like leading the shape and the time, asking for people to step up or monitoring the more tactical space of it. Whenever people are holding space, there is an ego moment: 'Oh, am I doing this right?' The ego asking, and your nerves are also 100% welcome in Tent.

Allowing people and all their emotions to be held in that space is the most transformative thing you can do as a Tent Keeper. It's not the easiest thing, but set your intentions and then show up the best you can. Sacred space holding goes against so many regular life ideas, which is why it is sacred. Little courtesies add up and go into the feeling you are creating in the Red Tent."

When leading your own Red Tent, you may see parts of the scripts that echo what is in this book. Keep in mind that although you have read the chapter, others have not. The story sections give you a basis of knowledge and provide engaging stories to help you lead your own Red Tent with confidence. Take time before Tent to prepare and center yourself beforehand. Otherwise, you may feel rushed and feel off-center. Know that you set the stage for what Tent will be. It doesn't have to be perfect; you just have to be present.

I've also learned not to hold the reins too tightly. Even if you use an offered script, the conversation or evening may turn out differently than you expected; trust your women got exactly what they needed.

Allow space for your Red Tent to become whatever it becomes. It's okay for your Tent to shift and grow to fit you and your community.

 Michaela, a Tent Keeper, asks herself a few questions before creating her monthly Tent, "What are we going to do this month? What will be engaging and interesting? If we want to find something useful and engaging, what does that look like for our theme this month? What will that be?"

Stay open and curious as you imagine what your Tent will look like. Your living room, a backyard, a community center, a church, a yoga center, or even a local park are all possibilities!

One of my favorite things about Red Tent is how it's a blank canvas to try new things without having them judged right away if they are 'good enough. You can write a poem or share a thought or a new idea. You can draw out what came up in your meditation, and no one is going to say your drawing isn't good. Red Tents are an incubator for your curiosity and creativity to feel it has permission to grow.

Make a list of what is most essential to you when gathering together in a vulnerable space. Is Tent always the 3rd Saturday, falls on the New Moon, or is flexibility the highest priority? Are kids welcome, or is this space for only nursing babies so moms can have some space? Do you want a place to relax and do nothing at all except eat and talk, or do you want activities and a structure? How long will it be? Some Tents are open all day for people to rest in, and in the evening, they have a gathering. If you don't like singing, you can create a different opener. Imagine a buffet in front of you with ideas on what you can do for your Tent. Dream up your ideal Red Tent, talk to your women about what they would love, and then sketch your guidelines from there. You can use the scripts as a starting point and edit them as desired.

 Taylor encourages giving yourself grace when launching a Red Tent or trying anything else. "Try your best to be comfortable at sucking when starting something new. When you have your Inner Critic, they will tell you all of the ways you suck on repeat. I had to tell my brain I'm not doing Red Tent to make money. I'm doing this to have fun and relax. I'm not doing this for you. I'm doing it for me. Go sit down."

Sometimes we just have to show up and trust. If you feel the tug of the Red Thread to start a Tent, I propose you commit for six months. Even if it's just you in your closet, even the small choices we make have immeasurable ripples, and you tending yourself or inviting others into your Tent can change lives for the better.

HERE ARE HELPFUL THINGS TO REMEMBER.

You might be wondering what your Red Tent will look like, and if you'll keep it just you, invite a few friends, or put out a general invite.

As Red Tent spreads, women can have various opinions on whether or not it is for them. Some feel the tug right away, others mull it over, and others are horrified at the wording of 'circle' because they think of witches, assume we are meddling in the occult, and automatically discount what Tent could be for them. Feeling misunderstood about Tents can feel hurtful; (I've been accused of it all) and yet, I know in my bones, helping create Red Tents is part of why I'm here.

Part of the disconnect I found in those questioning what a Red Tent was, is that it's outside of our realm of every day doing. Our society bases the value of gathering around activities, whether this is a game, party, or celebration. The Tent is sober, and no advice given unless asked for. Those are significant shifts from our everyday world, and the idea of not having alcohol and new ways of interacting can make one feel exposed or nervous about what they'll share if they are honest. It's learning how to *be* together. This idea may sound wild to those who have not been a part of Tent. But for others, Tent feels like a whisper of possibility for the women who crave more.

If someone isn't ready, you can say, "I understand; let me know if you ever change your mind." Then the ball is in their court. We have a saying, "Whoever is supposed to be in Tent will be there." Forcing someone to come who isn't ready, can make for an awkward evening. Let them know beforehand what the night will be like, and your vision for the evening so they can prepare.

I've heard people leaving after their first Tent say, "Oh, that was different than I expected!" and are surprised we weren't all in matching robes and chanting all night. On Obbie's first night, as we wrapped our red thread, she said through tears, "This is some Ya-Ya Sisterhood kind of shit." People don't realize places like this exist, so comprehending what's possible when people realize they do exist can be overwhelming.

Know that not everyone is a good fit for Red Tent. Not everyone is emotionally or mentally ready for holding confidentiality or stories. People you think will love it won't be interested, and those you wouldn't expect end up as Tent's biggest fans.

Red Tent is fantastic, unique, and occasionally awkward as we process emotions together. People are not always ready to speak or share. There is never any pressure to do so, but know someone not sharing is not a mark on you. They are setting their boundary for how they feel safe at that moment, and the beauty of Tent is that we can honor their request.

 Obbie shares her perspective on allowing the ebb and flow of attendance within a Red Tent: "As I've gotten older, I've become a firm believer in giving everything at least one chance. If you don't like Tent, you don't have to go back. And if someone doesn't come back, you say she's not ready. We had someone show up once and then a year later and be like, 'Okay, I needed this.' It happens all of the time. When you need it the most, it's there. If you want to open yourself up to it, it's there."

You can create online or physical invitations to invite others to your Tent. People are busy, so reminders are crucial. I usually send out a reminder two to three days before. Because I do my Tent spots through my website, it sends an automatic email when they reserve their spot, and then on the day of, I send an email reminder. I usually invite others based on our conversations or a nudge to share about it after they mention their experiences. If you create a communal event, you can put up posters and flyers and trust those who need to come will be there.

You can bring up books they may have borrowed from the Red Library in the reminders you send out and have a basket at Tent for 'book return.' You may encourage them to bring a donation, wear comfy clothes, bring a journal, and can remind them of the guidelines you've created. Depending on the number of people, I usually ask three women to bring snack food to share. Some tents make soup, and other tents have a few people designated as dinner makers. It varies from Tent to Tent, do what works best for you.

GUIDELINES AND ACTIVITIES

One of our guidelines is no advice unless asked for, and this creates a safe space to ask questions and share what someone is thinking without feeling like she's going to be deluged with opinions on what she should do next.

> DeAnna L'am talks about witnessing this grace of vulnerability in her first Red Moon Circle. "In 1993, I started the first menstrual night; I invited women to tell the story of their first blood. It was amazing how each story resonated with each woman. The details were different, and the backgrounds differed, but each shared's feelings and emotions were identical. There was no pushback. There was an understanding that we were opening a lid to something that had been buried for years."

By creating guidelines, it helps everyone know what to expect and how to listen. I love the "I have spoken" guideline as I pause in thinking to find the right words. Knowing I can take that time without someone else judging me is helpful. It also allows us to listen without having to be 'on' to help and respond with the correct answer.

> Taylor, a Tent Keeper shares: "I got my autism diagnosis the year before I came to the Tent. My social skills did not mature at the rate of my

peers. Red Tent helps women forge meaningful friendships with other women because they didn't know how to before, which has helped me dismantle the wall I built to be in touch with myself more. You hope when you are sharing something that people are giving you their full attention, and when we are going around the circle for Tent, we are told not to advise unless asked, so I can just listen. I don't have to give a wise reply. I can devote 90% part of my brain to actually hearing what people are sharing about themselves.

When I'm in Tent, my mask can come off, and I can say, "I don't have anything to share today." And no one looks at you differently. In and out of Tent, this has changed how I respond to people. That was the fattest permission slip of my life, of hearing "No advice unless asked."

Stories are the glue of Red Tent; when a woman graces you with her story, receive it with as much grace, kindness, and acknowledgment of her bravery as you can.

Even though exercises in these Red Tent scripts may seem ridiculous, these activities help the women see ideas in a new way. Grace can take on a unique tone and feel different when you hold someone's hands, look them in the eye and say, "Kayla, I SEE you." Moving our lessons and tents from our heads to our bodies for embodied learning is an intrinsic part of the way I love to lead Tents.

I love the structure and activities in these Tent scripts because it leans into how we learn. The NTL Institute for Applied Behavioral Science, in 1954, created a learning pyramid that explains learners retain 90% of information by using an interactive, hands-on activity vs. 50% of what they simply hear and see.[1] The Tent creates a broader access point to think about a theme from multiple perspectives and approach it from a few different avenues, whether meditation, journaling, sharing, or art.

When you get into embodied learning, your body starts to process trauma, memories, and ideas, so tears are common. Having tissues nearby and being okay with whatever comes up is helpful as women let down their guard and feel all of the feelings. Michaela shares her learnings around tears, "I realize now it's okay that I cry. Crying isn't a crisis. Having the freedom to safely cry and not feel any embarrassment or hidden remorse afterward is liberating."

TIME BOUNDARIES

Time is essential in a Tent. Time boundaries allow guests to know what to expect and when to expect it. It also gives gravity to your gathering. In our Tent, we are pretty strict about this. Our doors open at 6:30, and you have till 7 pm to arrive. We then close our doors until 9:30, when we finish. We ask women to stay the whole time since we are creating sacred space. This may seem harsh, but imagine this: Someone sobbing their way through a womanhood story, and a new girl opens the door and waltzes into the circle an hour late.

Did you just cringe? Me too.

You can see how awkward everyone would feel. The late woman creates an unsafe space. Even though you know they might be okay; if there is anyone new in your group, they have to adjust to a new person they previously were not expecting. The interruption of someone they don't know may feel like a betrayal of trust in the space. If you want your time boundaries to be trustworthy, you will have to say no sometimes.

Someone may say, "Hey, I'll be there at 7:15", and you'll have to reply with, "I'm sorry, our time boundary is 7. We'll miss you, but hopefully, we will see you next month!" Do not attach any shame or guilt to this. That serves neither you nor them in creating a healthy and productive Tent. It can be a bummer when you want people to come, and then they don't, and you have a smaller group that night. Smaller groups lend themselves to more time for people sharing in the circle and going more in-depth than you could with a larger group. There are pros and cons to each. Trust Tent to become the space it needs to be during the evening. Your job is to prepare and show up.

The one caveat to this is if you decide to structure your Tent differently. If you want your Tent to be a 'come and go as you please' evening, you can share what time you are opening your doors, and the time the Tent closes for the evening. Maybe you have a place people can eat, and a place to rest, or a place to stretch. If you are creating a circle, though, at any point, make it clear for that time when they need to arrive.

GOING AWAYS

If you are a military spouse like me, you may often move or have others move away from your Tent. Leaving is a part of life, and as such, it's also a part of Tent. One of my favorite activities for a going away is writing a thank you blessing. This blessing can either be done on a piece of fabric, journal, or even canvas if you'd like. We had one lady for a while design ones with red, pink, and gold designs glued with a variety of fabric, looking like a mini quilt, and we wrote on that.

If you are not crafty, have them bring their journal that evening. Have each person write a blessing or a thank you in their book. Allow people to write out memories, things they loved about them, how they've impacted their lives, and their hopes for the person leaving in the future. The journal becomes a treasure. I have led this activity at least thirty times, and every time it gives me chills. It is easy to think you've had no impact, or people don't remember you, but when you have your gathering of women all writing down their love for this person, it's harder to forget who you are. They'll carry those words with them, a reminder of Tent, of women singing their song back to them. I have mine from every time I've done it and pull them out a few times a year to be reminded of who others have seen me be.

Other times we speak the blessings. If you decide to do this, set aside at least 30 minutes, and watch the clock. On nights when we have done this, we have often gone over. So you can set aside half the Tent or give each person a minute or two. It might sound harsh, but you also want to respect the time boundaries you have set for the sacred portion of the Tent. People can stay after as well to talk to the person leaving. Another good idea is to have a blessing song, or a poem you read to each person who leaves.

One Tent I know gives the leaving lady a small red bracelet as a reminder of the Tent. Whatever you do, know that Red Tent is a particular sacred space that can be hard to find. Recognizing transitions can be complex. Appreciating the person being a part of your Tent can help anchor their time and inspire them to create a community in their new home.

CREATING A TENT KEEPER CORE GROUP

A Tent is not merely one person, but a single person can start it. The idea of the Tent is to be a communal gathering space for all women. In creating Tents, it's helpful to have a core group of Tent Keepers. Everyone has different skills. Think of this as a guide of responsibilities that help facilitate a Tent. You don't have to have all of them, and maybe you want to start a Tent but aren't sure you want to do it alone. In my experience, some women are excited about getting more involved. Ask around, and see who might be interested in creating a Red Tent with you!

Anyone can be a leader who wants to start a Red Tent

and see it be a thriving space for the women who come. Depending on the size of your group, three to five tent keepers is a good range. Our average is usually four, including the Main Tent Keeper. All the Tents I've led have been near military bases *because I'm a military spouse,* so there's a bit of turnover. We typically add a new tent keeper every six months, so when one moves away, the new lady is up and running and ready to take over. You can rotate the leading role as well as other responsibilities.

Being the leader can become overwhelming if you have a large group, so having a few women to work with to build the space can be helpful so you don't burn out. I've also found therapy and having a mentor has helped me navigate situations as they arise both in Tent and in my own life.

A tent is a place where women share their pain, joy, and struggles. There are times when you may have to ethically decide if and when to act on situations brought to your attention.

Because we are human and make mistakes, if someone struggles with the guidelines, gently bring their attention to them. If there is a big mistake (sharing a story that wasn't theirs in trying to connect) or misunderstanding (they saved the time wrong in their phone and walked in the door mid-Tent), you can have a conversation with them after Tent.

There is a line between mistakes or downright not a good fit for Tent (someone who arrives drunk or maliciously slanders other women). These latter types of conversations need to be had outside of Tent. In one case of a line being crossed, we had a sit down with three of us Tent Keepers and one woman and explained that she couldn't come back to Tent until she sought help and apologized for her actions. Cases like this are rare and challenging for everyone involved. 99% of the time, sharing the guidelines and being a space of grace will be enough.

> Michaela remembers, "We found out there was a situation with kids in a vulnerable situation. By the time we were made aware, police were involved, and the kids were safe. But what if things hadn't resolved and they hadn't been in the custody of a caretaker? We had to ask ourselves this question. So when you create that space, you have it in the back of your mind. Discuss it with your fellow Tent Keepers. How will we handle something unsafe happening?"

Balancing confidentiality and safety is one of the most complex parts of leading. As a Tent Keeper, it's crucial to have support around you and know the resources in your community you can utilize, whether this is food banks, counseling services, or social services.

There needs to be someone who has the central vision in their head, steering the ship. Just like a captain on a boat, you need one for a Tent. We call ours the Main Tent Keeper or Leader. This person has the final say and is ultimately in charge of making sure that Tent happens. You can ask Tent Keepers for help with different tasks, lead Tents with you in other parts of the Tent script, switch off Tents, or have a rotating few months for leading. Here are a few tasks you can share between the Tent Keepers.

Getting the word out: This role can include creating the events on Facebook or invitations and sending them out. They can send out reminders the day or week of the Tent, reach out to past attendees to let them know, or ask for word of mouth referrals.

Money: Red Tents do cost money to run, whether it's just buying food, fabric, or space rental. If you accept donations, keeping track of donations is necessary. Some tents have a box in the corner, and others ask for a donation from each person. Each Tent is different, but Tent should always be accessible for those who come, whether sliding scale or scholarships. If you accept money, is it just cash, or will you use Venmo or Paypal? We have split up donations for menstrual products to a local organization, fabric, plates, bowls, napkins, incense, and adding books to our Red Library, and even workshops to make for a better Tent. I use a google spreadsheet for this.

Depending on your Tent, you may or may not have to register with the state as you are taking money. You may also want to start up a new bank account where you can put the money. We store the cash in a bag, and when we need to buy something, we use that money. Sometimes we roll the money over to the next month to buy a more expensive book or item we need. By keeping track, whoever takes up after you knows what you purchased and how much money is in the waiting pile. Making a spreadsheet is also helpful to keep track of who borrowed what book, who came, and who shared their womanhood story, so you have all your information in one central location. Always if possible, have two people with a link to the donation page, allowing you to make decisions together.

Greeter: Women come to the Red Tent to be seen and heard. Not in a fancy way like at the Kentucky Derby, but in a soul way. *Although, I am always here for fabulous hats.* Holding space for women and seeing them as they are is a core tenant of Tent. Having someone greet people at the door helps set the tone. If it's someone's first time, they might already have jitters as they have imagined the gathering as an emotional tell-all night.

I can't tell you how many times women have come in and gushed over truth-telling, "I don't usually do this, I'm not friends with girls, I'm just one of the guys, girls are untrustworthy, liars, backstabbers, manipulators, and gossipy mean girls." They are stepping out in faith, believing that your Tent will be different. You are essentially asking them to put all that bias aside and try something new. To be in Tent is to be vulnerable and say I'm willing to try again. The least we can do is generously welcome them in.

Check-ins: Check in with the Tent ladies. Let's say there are twelve ladies in your Tent. Pick three a week and message them and ask them how they are doing. You can eat, have a playdate, or catch up via a phone call. They might be going through things that they didn't bring up during Tent. Having someone reach out to them and ask them how they are doing is helpful. For some ladies, Tent is the only community they trust. Be intentional and appreciative; we only have Tent because of these women. This outreach doesn't mean you solve their problems, but sometimes there are things in your ability to work on or give them assistance, which comes through just in the nick of time. We had Village Night on the full moon in Germany, so all the Red Tent women and their families came, and we pot lucked and just enjoyed the evening. Having time outside of Tent is a fun way to get to know people in their day-to-day lives.

Watching women learn how to use their words, stand up for themselves, pick up skills, and remember and claim old dreams is always an honor. Encourage your women. Build them up and speak life into them. As you tend others, don't forget to also tend to yourself. If you are feeling vulnerable, remember Red Tent is for you as well. You help provide the tools, nourishment, affirmations, and space. You give but also receive the beauty that is Tent. Take the time to rest and enjoy and also be held. This space is for ALL the people who show up, including you.

Personally, as a Tent Leader, I love investing in my

fellow Tent Keepers. Many of them want to lead a Tent someday and want space to practice or learn different Red Tent parts. It's easy — *by easy, I mean I've done it* — to let your ego get in the way when you become a leader and hold on tightly to what you think Tent should be. The women around you are brimming with good ideas and new perspectives. Ask them what they want to learn or where they are growing. Challenge them, give them chances to take risks, and learn and try new things in Tent. Maybe it works, perhaps it doesn't.

Every Tent and every Tent Leader starts somewhere. There are activities I've led that work well in my head and fall flat in Tent — it's okay. It's part of the process. Red Tent is a perfect place to experiment and have the women around you try and succeed, and try and mess up. The Tent is theirs as well as yours.

All boats rise in high tide. As a leader, a big part of Tent is saying, "Here I am, here you are," diving in together and encouraging everyone to bloom.

If you want more resources check out the resource list in the back of the book and go to www.TheJoyWeaver.-com/RedThreadResources for the songs, examples of activities, and meditations from this book.

When in doubt, use kind and clear communication to create a Red Tent and life you love.

CONCLUSION AND MOMENTUM

*W*elcome to the end of this book journey and the beginning of new possibility threads in your life around Red Tent, and living an embodied life of joy. You were welcomed into the Red Tent and navigated your relationship to your body and the cycles of life. Along the way, you met some of your archetypes and found places to meditate. You've uncovered and reaffirmed your values, while using your voice to express ALL your emotions and set boundaries to ask for what you needed.

You've realized you're not JUST any one role or facet, and cultivated your wild soul. You were vulnerable and tender with yourself and created sanctuary areas in your life to breathe and be restored in. Hopefully you have inspiration on what your next steps look like on your growth journey.

I am so proud of you for exploring the questions, sitting in the messy middle, and trying something new. That takes bravery my friend, and your growth is no small thing.

I have found this journey of learning and becoming embodied kind of like flowers—we all have layers we're constantly peeling back, and we're continually blooming and evolving. It's the journey of inwards and outwards, of growing up and showing up.

Somedays, I wonder, "When will I arrive?" but I think the truth is we never entirely do. I hope you continue walking forward knowing you are loved, you are seen, you are not a mistake, and that you are worthy of goodness.

I hope your Red Tents become a place of refuge for yourself and those around you to grow and flourish into who you are meant to be and can feel safe being honest and your whole self. If you aren't ready to start your own, you are always welcome in mine.

I can't promise you the embodied journey of togetherness will be easy, but I can guarantee that I have done my best to give you a map with which to forge ahead; to create an embodied life of joy that will have ripple effects for years to come. Let's create new traditions to pass down to the next generation of women and the whole of humanity.

I'd like to end with a blessing for you, the same one I give at the end of Creative Soul Conversations and Joy Guild Tents:

Weaver of the Universe, thank you for this lovely one.
Thank you for her heart,
enthusiasm, bravery, kindness, and love.
Protect her, and grant her peace.
May you bless what she knows, bless what she says,
bless where she goes, and bless what she does.
Above all, bless who she is.
She is a gift to me and many others.
Amen and Amen, so may it be.

RESOURCES

For the downloadable resources such as the meditations, and Red Tent Demo head to
www.TheJoyWeaver.com/RedThreadResources

RED TENT AND RED THREAD SPECIFIC RESOURCES

Red Tents by Mary Ann Clements and Aisha Hannibal
To find the nearest Red Tent to you head to
www.RedTentDirectory.com
Red Tent Temple Movement: redtenttemple-movement.com
Red Tent Doulas- Redtentdoulas.co.uk
DeAnna L'am and the Red Tent Academy:
www.DeannaLam.com
Red Tent class www.Brigidsgrove.com
www.shilohsophiastudios.com
www.WomanUnleashed.com

CHAPTER RECOMMENDATIONS BOOK LIST:

Body is a Temple

As Is by Erin Brown
Mothers, Daughters, and Body Image by Dr. Hillary L. McBride
The Body Keeps the Score by Bessel van der Kolk

Cycles

Moon Time by Lucy Pearce
The Pill: Is it for you by Alexandra Pope and Jane Bennett
Wild Power: By Alexandra Pope and Sjanie Hugo Wurlitzer
I want to punch you in the face, but I love Jesus by Sherri Lynn

Curiosity

The Fire Starter Sessions by Danielle Laporte
The Sin of Certainty by Pete Enns
Walking on Water by Madeleine L'Engle

Creativity

The Artist's Way by Julia Cameron
Creatrix by Lucy Pearce
Big Magic by Liz Gilbert

Voice

A Year of Yes by Shonda Rhimes
Raise Your Voice: Why We Stay Silent and How to Speak Up by Kathy Khang

Daring Greatly by Brene Brown

Value/Values

Falling Upward by Father Richard Rohr
Better than Before by Gretchen Rubin
Essentialism by Greg Mckoewen

Good Girl, Bad Girl, Fully Embodied Woman

Here All Dwell Free: Stories to Heal the Wounded Feminine, by Gertrud Mueller Nelson
The Road Back to You: An Enneagram Journey to Self-Discovery by Ian Morgan Cron
Cultivate: A Grace-Filled Guide to Growing an Intentional Life by Lara Casey

Wild

Untamed by Glennon Doyle-Melton
Burning Woman by Lucy Pearce
Women Who Run with the Wolves Clarissa Pinkola Estés

Anger

How to do the Work by Dr. Nicole LePara
The Dance of Anger by Dr. Harriet Lerner
The Work of Byron Katie by Byron Katie

Boundaries

Boundaries by Dr. John Mcloud & Dr. Townsend
The Subtle Art of Not Giving a F*ck by Mark Manson
Set Boundaries, Find Peace by Nedra Glover Tawwab

Sanctuary

Braiding Sweetgrass by Robin Wall Kimmerer
Searching for Sunday by Rachel Held Evans
Love Does by Bob Goff
An Altar in the World by Barbara Brown Taylor

Vulnerability

Rising Strong by Brené Brown
Emotionally Healthy Woman by Geri Scazzero
Rebloom by Rachel Maddox

How we Grow

Fierce, Free, and Full of Fire by Jen Hatmaker
Braving the Wilderness by Brené Brown
You are a Badass by Jen Sincero

OTHER BOOK RECOMMENDATIONS

I love reading, and the ones throughout the book are my absolute favorites, those are also listed here as well as some others to spark your continual learning shared by the Thirteen Red Tent women in this book.

A Diva's Guide to Getting Your Period by DeAnna L'am
A Generous Orthodoxy by Brian D. McLaren
Away, or Refuse to See by Jess Hill
Becoming Peers: Mentoring Girls Into Womanhood by DeAnna L'am
Becoming Supernatural by Joe Espinoza
Be the Bridge by Latasha Morrison
Brave Women, Strong Faith A compilation by Military Women with Brookstone Publishing Group
Come as You Are by Emily Nagoski, Ph.D.
Craft a life you love by Amy Tangerine

Dance of the Dissident Daughter by Sue Monk Kidd
Drink by Ann Dowsett Johnston
Girl, Wash Your Face by Rachel Hollis
Healing Trauma by Peter A. Levine, Ph.D.
Her Ruck by Richelle Futch
High Performance Habits by Brendon Burchard
How to Keep House While Drowning by KC Davis, LPC
I'm Okay, You're a Brat by Susan Jeffers
In the FLO by Alisa Vitti, HHC
Jesus Feminist by Sarah Bessey
See What You Made Me Do by Jess Hill
Shalom Sistas: Living Wholeheartedly in a Brokenhearted World by Osheta Moore
Soundtracks by Jon Acuff
The 5 am Club by Robin Sharma
The Biology of Belief by Bruce Lipton
The body is not an apology by Sonya Renee Taylor
The Gifts of Imperfection by Brene Brown
The Sacred Enneagram by Christopher L. Heuertz
The Switch on your Brain by Dr. Caroline Lief
The Turquoise Table by Kristin Schell
This Bridge Called My Back edited by Cherrie Maraga and Gloria Anzaldúa
To Dance with God Gertrude Mueller Nelson
Womancode by Alisa Vitti, HHC
You Can Talk to God like That by Abby Norman

WOMANHOOD STORY INSPIRATION STARTER

This is to help come up with your Womanhood Story. You can also find a download to send to your Red Tent attendees in the downloadable book resources.

I'd like to preface that the only expectations I have of you is that you speak YOUR truth, not the perceived view society might have of your story. You do not need to make it like a movie with crazy plot twists to entertain or engage an audience. Share whatever is true for you, and your story. This can be along the lines of: being a woman, your period, birth control experiences, miscarriages, births, assaults, and even what it means for you to be a woman.

Your story could be focused on one day, a chain of events, or on a variety of topics. Each story is different, which is the best part. Even if you feel that you have nothing to share, know that you were asked to share for a reason; someone needs to hear what you have to say. You never know what the ripple effect can be when you speak your story. What I'm asking of you, is for you to show up, and tell your truth. However it looks. I'm here to help, guide, give advice, for whatever you require. Feel free to ask me anything—there are no stupid questions.

You will have about 10 minutes to share your story during tent; you do not have to fill this whole time, either. Let this time be whatever you need. I'm opening the space for you to be vulnerable; it's a place I've been and others have been as well, and we are grateful you said yes.

Free Writing Prompts

Get a sheet of paper or a journal and set a timer for 3 minutes, use these sentence starters below (3 minutes each starter) to write whatever comes to mind—let it flow. If you're stuck, write whatever you think. It might not make sense, but write regardless; you'll be surprised at the words that come out when you let your brain empty out the white noise by writing.

- My experience with my cycle is/has been....
- Growing up as a lady I felt....
- For me, what it means to be a woman is...
- When I think of the word 'vagina' I think....
- What I was told to be as a woman was....

Thought Flow

You can use the below ideas to write down thoughts, make a map, or a bubble chart of ideas. Let them strike up thoughts. If new thoughts arise for you, write them down and don't judge what you write. You aren't sharing any of these thought flows; this is inspiration time to put things on paper. Use pencil if it makes you feel any better, or colored markers, or crayons! Get messy and dig in!

- If my vagina could wear clothing, it would wear:
- My mom represents femininity to me by....
- The way I view myself as a woman is...
- I struggle with being a woman because...
- My first period was... (do you remember, what happened, how old were you? Where were you? What did you think..etc)
- Birth control has been...

Word association

Write down 5 words that you associate with each of the below, it could be more than 5, get creative, see what's attached, follow the rabbit hole. You might just surprise yourself.

Vagina Cycle PeriodWoman Lady Sex Sexual Being Wife Mother Maiden Virginity Orgasms Birth Control

Witch Crone Wild WomanHuman FemmeEmbodiment
Wild Femininity

All of these are just ideas. You don't have to do them all,
although it would be fun. Use them as inspiration; are there
any connections between the words for you? Does a certain
idea keep bobbing up to the surface in your writing? What
do you feel compelled to talk about? Take time to get quiet
with yourself as well. This can indeed be hard—we don't
often share our womb stories so it may feel strange—but you
do have a story. Trust yourself and listen.

NOTES

1. WELCOME IN, LOVELY

1. Composed by Margaret J Nelson found on https://ourchants.org/songs/call-down-blessing
2. Found from https://soundcloud.com/brigidsgrove/sets/red-tent-circle Song is also attributed to Shekhinah Mountainwater
3. We were stationed at Spangdahlem Air Force Base (AFB) in Germany at the time.
4. Don't worry. I only talk about glitter, my publisher said it was impossible to include ACTUAL glitter in the book. I know, I know, I was bummed too.
5. *The Artist's Way* by Julia Cameron
6. www.redtentmovie.com/post/menstrual-hut-and-moon-lodge-history
7. For more information, I recommend watching *Period*, a short film documentary.
8. Aisha, H., & Clements, M. A. (2021). Red tents: Unravelling our past and weaving a shared future. Womancraft Publishing.
9. In our Tent we have Christians, Pagans, Atheists, Witches, and people who are searching. It's all welcome here in Tent. We come together as woman, that's our only guideline. You'd be surprised how similar we all are when we let down our guard enough to share our hearts.
10. This is not true for all Red Tents. The Red Tent Directory has resources on how to identify if a Tent is only for those who menstruate.
11. Within the cycle chapter, there will be content for you, whether you stopped bleeding long ago, bleed like clockwork every 24 days, don't bleed because you are on birth control, or have never bled at all.
12. A token is a small piece each woman brings to represent her which could be a memento, a ring, or even the keys from her purse. Yes, it's 100% inspired by the *Pirates of the Carribean*'s take on the Nine Pieces of 8.
13. www.TheJoyWeaver.com/RedThreadResources Also included is a video example of a Tent you can watch.
14. Wikipedia. I know, I know. But it says it all so well. https://en.wikipedia.org/wiki/Meditation
15. *Return to Love* by Marianne Williamson, Harper Collins, 1992.

2. BODY IS A TEMPLE

1. Ancestry sites: Cutting down family tales and exposing secrets since people willingly started handing over their DNA.

2. You better believe there were a few situations of drama, especially one time when a girl stepped on another's dress by accident and the girl freaked out—but on the whole those who competed had hearts of gold, and gorgeous dresses I swooned over.
3. What started in the basement of our college theatre, now lives on the community stage in Cedar Falls with multiple night shows, fundraising thousands of dollars for charities each year.
4. Sometimes photos of others looking embodied in the way they love gives us permission to do the same.
5. Orders are what we call assignments to move to a new location in the military.
6. Mother Daughters and Body Image by Dr. Hilary McBride
7. *Shameless* by Nadia Bolz-Weber page 152
8. Pockets are always a plus as well.
9. Jen Hatmaker, *Fierce, Free and Full of Fire* pg. 45
10. Not actual Hogwarts because copyright infringement is expensive.
11. I'd rather run off for a whole year to magic college, but I'll take a weekend.
12. Mcbride 99 Mothers, Daughters and Body Image

3. CYCLES

1. I regret to inform you, dear reader; it was not.
2. Your energy will drop as your progesterone rises. So you can save yourself some heartache by acknowledging this in advance.
3. Vitti, A. (2014). From Vicious cycle to delicious cycle. In *Womancode: perfect your cycle, amplify your fertility, supercharge your sex drive, and become a power source* (p. 147). New York: HarperOne.
4. I see you smiling, recovering-people pleaser. I see you.
5. Pope, A., & Hugo, S. (2017). The Inner Seasons. In *Wild power: discover the magic of your menstrual cycle and awaken the feminine path to power* (p. 186). England: Hay House.
6. We all know there was room on that door, Rose!
7. Pope, A., & Hugo, S. (2017). The Inner Seasons. In *Wild power: discover the magic of your menstrual cycle and awaken the feminine path to power* (p. 95). England: Hay House.
8. *She Power* by Lisa Lister
9. https://www.drnorthrup.com/what-is-optimal-hydration/
10. Raging against the machine is one thing, raging against your own body is a whole other story.
11. A personal favorite is The Agenda.Period app www.theagendaperiod.com
12. Lister, L. (2015). Pills 'n' Thrills and 'Bellyaches. In *Code Red* (p. 22). SHE Press.
13. Grace space means planned downtime to breathe and rest.
14. This handy piece of information is even more critical when you are only using the rhythm method of protection.

15. I'd rather lay in a hammock than wear one, but you work with what you've got.
16. Hot water seals protein stains, which means if you wash your blood-stained white pants with hot water, the blood isn't going to budge. Your white pants just became your newest item on your tie-dye to-do list, but it's okay. Tie-Dye is back in style.
17. https://www.healthlinkbc.ca/healthlinkbc-files/toxic-shock-syndrome
18. As horrible as this sounds, if you wouldn't want to put it on the inside of your mouth, don't put it in your vagina.
19. Maybe don't use your family's passed down spaghetti pot, though.
20. Find an example of this activity in the downloadable resources in the back of the book.

4. CURIOSITY

1. Okay, maybe not those last two questions. *Queen* already asked them for us in the *Bohemian Rhapsody*.
2. I'm not saying it's easy, but we can reroute, and rewire our mindset and thoughts.
3. Except in the case of the mysterious stranger that is Aragorn—I'd follow him anywhere.

5. CREATIVITY

1. Pg. 257 Creatrix
2. Marion Woodman quote found in Handbook for the Soul by Benjamin Shield, and Richard Carlson
3. If you've ever been a camp counselor, you know it is a blast—but it is anything but relaxing!
4. Ironically, two years later, that same 16-year-old counselor ended up being the Art Program Head and was fantastic.
5. Pro Tip #2: Always bring more carving supplies than what you think you need.
6. Make sure you have a licensed professional for that.
7. *Playing Big* by Tara Mohr
8. Playing Big Tara Mohr page Published by the penguin group in 2014
9. Odds are the system is broken as well. While in a broken system, what can you do to either change it, or survive and thrive within it in the meantime? What do you need? What would feel supportive?
10. TLC stands for Tender Loving Care, although listening to TLC is also a great choice.
11. Not all criticism is bad. We need instruction and feedback to grow. Feedback doesn't need to be belittling and shaming to be accurate and helpful. Give your concise, clear, constructive feedback. As someone who repeated 'Red is Love' to herself when getting edits back to this book, I can tell you feedback is essential, and good for growth, even the good kind hurts a little bit sometimes.

12. Magic Lessons Podcast with Brene and Liz Gilbert
13. PS. Now that this book is in your hands, I just hand her a copy and ask if she wants to talk about anything she read.
14. Y'all, I'm 100% here for the cape revolution—but we must throw off the shame capes and guilt cloaks.
15. Mary Daly Quote from Beyond God the Father (1973)

6. VOICE

1. Sometimes there are rounds of bad luck as well, or situations outside of your control. Controlling how we show up and navigate tricky situations with good boundaries and awareness can change more than you might expect.
2. www.yourhormones.info/hormones/adrenaline/
3. Proverbs 18:21
4. Introverts, I see you gearing yourself up to walk into a room. Introversion is how you store energy, so for you, I encourage you to look at how you enter into conversations with those you love for an accurate assessment of your energy.
5. I'm 100% done with this theology.

7. VALUES

1. I joke that by being together we ended the Romeo and Juliet story the right way, without any murder and bloodshed.
2. I had told him Settlers of Catan was my favorite board game, but I didn't own a copy of it.
3. In riding in the car together he belted all the lyrics to *Beauty and the Beast*'s *"Be Our Guest"*, which is also when I knew he was a keeper.
4. The Lovenox, even when given correctly over the next two weeks was excruciatingly painful for me, and after the initial course, I never wanted to have to endure that drug again.
5. My friend, only you can choose the risks that are worth it to you. Don't let anyone ever judge you for your family choices. Families come in all shapes and sizes, some are blood, and some are not. All are equally valid.
6. The healthcare system is hard enough as a married woman without children, but for single childless women it's nearly impossible.
7. Toko-pa Turner, Excerpt From "Belonging" (belongingbook.com)
8. I'm not sure where I originally came to this conclusion, but I think it's a combination of predestination theology, the three fates and their threads, quantum theory, and free will.
9. I regret to inform you that even when you are content, others may not be. That's okay. Remember your reasons and trust your Intuition and your path.

10. Love your Lady Landscape Lisa Lister 62-63
11. https://www.goodreads.com/quotes/1246213-there-is-a-voice-inside-of-you-that-whispers-all

8. GOOD GIRL, BAD GIRL, FULLY EMBODIED WOMAN

1. https://aras.org/about/what-are-archetypes
2. https://scholar.harvard.edu/files/shleifer/files/stereotypes.q-je_.october2016.pdf
3. Mothers, Daughters, and Body Image by Hillary L. McBride
4. The shoving down of our truth is also why I think so many women go through a 'screw it' phase when they turn around 40 and start speaking up more for themselves. They got sick of staying quiet.
5. www.DeanStreetSociety.com
6. *Burning Woman* by Lucy Pearce pg. 63
7. Burning Woman Lucy Pearce
8. https://www.goodreads.com/author/quotes/15042371.Roy_T_Bennett
9. Find an example of this activity at www.TheJoyWeaver.com/RedThreadResources

9. WILD

1. Our group chat was filled with everything from fishnets, capes, flowing dresses, to pinterest boards brimming with magical body painted ladies as inspiration.
2. To learn important things to keep in mind for fire dancing, check out Lucy Pearce's book, *Burning Woman.*
3. Hillary L. McBride, *Mothers, Daughters, and Body Image* (New York: Post Hill Press, 2017),98-99
4. I understand why shoes are important, I would still rather be barefoot or in whimsical tall rainbow boots. I just don't like shoes that feel like angry corsets on my feet.
5. I'm now that fancy garden person though, and am loving it. Although I do have rogue squash growing in the grass because the seeds fell out of the packet when I didn't notice.

10. ANGER

1. There is a difference between wrestling and feeling our deep emotions, and clinical depression and anxiety. If you are struggling and can't see any hope, please call a helpline, or seek a therapist.
2. Worst summary of LOTR ever: A magical being named Sauron tells everyone he's making fancy magic rings for the different rulers. He secretly makes his the most powerful and then tries to destroy and take

over the world. The One Ring gets lost and found, the ensuing chaos is the story LOTR follows with tiny hobbits having to trek through half the known world to chuck it into a volcano.

3. Sadly, my Grandma Julie died before I was born, but I've learned from her nonetheless through stories my mom and Aunt have shared with me.
4. We've come to accept that tears are a part of life, and crying is how our bodies prefer to process emotions the most.
5. If alcoholism runs in your line and you are nervous, I encourage you to try a 21 or 90 day alcohol break. Sometimes a break can show us how we use alcohol in healthy or unhealthy ways. If you'd like more support, attending Alcoholics Anonymous can also be life changing.

11. BOUNDARIES

1. Pg. 50 *Set Boundaries, Find Peace* by Nedra Glover Tawwab
2. Erin Brown *As Is* pg. 153
3. My other favorite question is "What is bringing you joy lately?"
4. *Anything you Want* by Derek Silvers
5. *Big Magic* by Liz Gilbert
6. Page 61 *Set Boundaries, Find Peace,* by Nedra Glover Tawwab

12. SANCTUARY

1. https://languages.oup.com/google-dictionary-en/
2. https://adaa.org/understanding-anxiety/facts-statistics
3. PS: This is called Comparative Suffering, and it helps no one.
4. For reference this was said as I was writing this book, running Red Tents online amidst a pandemic, and launching new programs all while my husband was away with the military. We often don't have great perspective when we are neck deep in our lives.
5. Ari also burned out during the same year I did. It's a good reminder to remember that the people we often idolize for 'doing it all' often have or need help, and are human too. No one is perfect, and putting people on pedestals often hurts those elevated, and alienates those doing the elevating.
6. https://pubmed.ncbi.nlm.nih.gov/15834840/
7. Check out the book *Burnout* for a more in-depth explanation of how stress interacts with our body and how you can process it.
8. https://www.nih.gov/news-events/nih-research-matters/gene-identified-people-who-need-little-sleep
9. Sleep deprived Aj is not my favorite version of me.
10. *Essentialism* by Greg Mckeown is where I learned this sentiment. It's a great resource for paring down.
11. Not that there were many dangers in Iowa, but better safe than sorry.
12. Great sale at the bookstore is also a valid option here.

13. Hello, reasoning behind half the wars of our human history.

13. VULNERABILITY

1. If you struggle with shame from the purity culture movement I HIGHLY suggest grabbing Linda Kay Klein's book *Pure*.
2. We all have Heart Wounds and fear. We're all just in various stages of healing.
3. Madeleine L'Engle https://www.goodreads.com/quotes/64058-when-we-were-children-we-used-to-think-that-when
4. From the book *Rising Strong* by Brené Brown
5. Lovely, if you need time to gather a wise response ask for it. Worst they say is no. A little time and space can be exactly what you need to collect your thoughts.
6. Don't worry, my retreats now have plenty of grace space and rejuvenation time built in.
7. If you are charting your cycle, your waxing and full moon stage are great times to have a hard conversation. New moon? Not so much.
8. *Healing Trauma* by Peter Levine
9. Most of these marriages aren't together anymore
10. Laughing and poking fun can be done in a good way. Have open discussions with friends on what is able to be made fun of. My clothing choices, and glitter are fair game, my cleaning routine is not. If you lift up the people around you in your vicinity, you'll be more fun to be around I promise. Mocking doesn't need to be the bedrock of friendship.
11. If doing this activity virtually have Person A look into the camera, and Person B look at Person A's eyes on the screen to feel like there is eye contact.

14. HOW WE GROW

1. The one time I stayed out past curfew, I got pulled over by the cops because I forgot to turn on my lights.
2. I kept pulling my hamstring while on the track team, so the Sporty One was not going to be my role.
3. I use Aj because I thought A.J. felt too masculine for me, and the periods felt like they got in the way. I should add here; I also met five Ambers on my first day of college, which may have played a small part in wanting to differentiate myself.
4. Except finals week. I don't think anyone loves finals week.
5. I had been watching Army wives, which does not help matters when your husband talks of enlisting.
6. The funny thing is, people look at me the same way. I think it's time we start giving ourselves some credit for the steps we have taken so far. Let's not be our own harshest critics.

7. https://science.sciencemag.org/content/339/6115/96
8. Although we can get stuck in our thinking and behaviors.
9. My friends especially appreciate this shift.
10. *Untamed* by Glennon Doyle
11. https://www.goodreads.com/author/quotes/7190.Ana_s_Nin

15. CREATING A SUSTAINABLE RED TENT

1. "NTL Institute for Applied Behavioral Science, 300 N. Lee Street, Suite 300, Alexandria, VA 22314. 1-800-777-5227."

ACKNOWLEDGMENTS

I always read the acknowledgments because I believe it takes a village to write a book. I feel like it's a sneak peek into inside jokes, memories, and abundant love. I didn't realize how true that was until I wrote one. I already know I'm going to miss someone. If that someone is you, know that I'm grateful to my bones for the lessons, gifts, and encouragement you have lent to me and this book. Thank you, thank you, ten house points to you.

God: You are the Weaver of the Universe and I'm grateful for how you've pulled things together. Thank you for holding me, and loving me always, even when I forget.

Jer: Thank you for being my best friend and reminding me to take a bath or go to the forest when I was frazzled. Thank you for being my adventure partner and love of my life.

Callie: Thank you for saying yes to my proposal of this book and putting your faith in what this book could be (and is I think). Thank you for going along with my wild hair ideas and answering my gazillion questions. Best publisher a mermaid could ask for.

Kelsey: My twin flame. Thank you for believing in me

and the countless calls, and introducing me to the Artist Way. You know all the words. Love you.

Elissa: Your red lipstick is great, but your heart is even better. Thank you for leading Tent beautifully and for loving me well. Your words have been a grace and a balm, and this book and I are better for it.

Lucy Pearce: I am on this path because you followed yours.

St. Pauls: Thank you for becoming home and a place I can bring my whole wild-hearted soul, no shrink-wrapping required.

Dangerous Women and especially Idelette, Kathleen, and Shaley: You taught me paradox was possible and opened the door to what if. Thank you for teaching me I could ask questions. We love a dangerous God, so let's be dangerous women. Amen and Amen, so may it be.

My parents: Thank you for the check-ins, and all the love, and for always having blankets for everyone and anyone at the house..

To the OG Four who walked the forest path in Germany and said yes to starting a Tent with me: Your ripples of trust are innumerable.

Ayesha, and Brooke: Thank you for the forest soul talks, and for your friendships during this book.

Olivia: SE therapy is life-saving. Your friendship is soul food. Thank you for both.

Anna: Thank you for helping me discover my numbers, and for your help sorting out thoughts and your coaching in discovering what's possible.

Mary-Grace: Thank you for reminding me it's okay to listen to God and to tune out the noise, and remember I can listen to my nudge and be in full joy. Thank you for walking alongside me with grace and maracas.

Bjornsborg: You are what we didn't know we needed in our life. Specifically Bjornlings and Moon Clan. Thank you for the dancing, singing, and open-armed landing place for me these past two years. More specifically: Kit, Vera, Petra, & Emma.

Red Ladies: From all the Tents I've been in, thank you for being in Tent with me, and for sharing your heart. You have changed me forever. I love you all. May you always have blessings called down upon you.

Cat: Thank you for your developmental edits, and wisdom in formatting this book. It's beautiful, and your insight is a treasure.

Star Tribe: Elissa, Steph, Michaela, Chanera, Ya'll. Thank you for listening to my videos and the planning sessions. You know what Tent means, and you made sure its magic is woven into this book so that others can have it too —what a gift.

TFL: Laura, Kelsey, Riley, and Mandy: For the check-ins, laughs, and reminding all of us who we are to each other.

Megan: Thank you for fighting for me, but thank you for fighting for me and reaching out that day with a scholarship to Speak Up, and teaching me Red is Love. I'm grateful God brought us together.

N+H: I never expected either of you, but your warmth and magic have been a deep comfort to me.

To my 13 women who trusted me with your stories and heart for this book, your ripples will be seen for years to come. You are a gift to me and many others. Thank you for your words.

Beta Readers/Editors and Red Tent Betas: This book is what it is because you sent back chapters dripping in red ink. Thank you for your clear feedback and enthusiasm. Red is Love, and you made this book better for everyone who will touch it.

Betas: Brooke, Crystal, Lindsay, Jenness, Jillian, Lisa S.S., Angela, Alicia, Gretchen, Cat, Danielle, Sunny, Meghan, Melissa, Aeleen, Chrissie, Kathleen, Michaela, Lilith, Heather, Stephany, Dee, Jake, Sean R, Elisa Marie,

Becky, Michaela, Jenna, Hope, Chandler, Mary-Grace, Lisa S, Tori, Jamie, Laura, Eve.

This book was also brought to you by: The forest clearing by my house, cookies, mug-a-ritas, dancing, fire nights, prayers, hot baths, naps, Viking and Disney Music in equal measure, and Sanctuary Days.

ABOUT THE AUTHOR

Aj Smit is a writer, speaker, glitter enthusiast, and professional weaver of Joy. She loves God, dancing in the forest, and being in sacred space with others. She is an Enneagram 7, enthusiastic Hufflepuff, and makes delicious chocolate chip banana bread. She is a military spouse to her husband Jer, and they have two puppies, house plants galore, and a rogue garden. Aj has led various Red Tents, retreats, and workshops internationally for organizations, retreats, and schools over the last ten years.

She offers in person and virtual Red Tents, one on one Creative Soul Conversations, henna adornment services, and more to help others discover how to weave creativity and curiosity into their lives and work. Join her free group

Embodied in Joy on Facebook. You can work with her at TheJoyWeaver.com

Email Aj with any questions, requests, or to share stories from your experience with this book at TheJoyWeaver@gmail.com

Photo by: Rosey Tones Photography

[f] facebook.com/thejoyweaver

[o] instagram.com/thejoyweaver

[p] pinterest.com/thejoyweaver

ABOUT THE AUTHOR

Aj Smit is a writer, speaker, glitter enthusiast, and professional weaver of Joy. She loves God, dancing in the forest, and being in sacred space with others. She is an Enneagram 7, enthusiastic Hufflepuff, and makes delicious chocolate chip banana bread. She is a military spouse to her husband Jer, and they have two puppies, house plants galore, and a rogue garden. Aj has led various Red Tents, retreats, and workshops internationally for organizations, retreats, and schools over the last ten years.

She offers in person and virtual Red Tents, one on one Creative Soul Conversations, henna adornment services, and more to help others discover how to weave creativity and curiosity into their lives and work. Join her free group

Embodied in Joy on Facebook. You can work with her at TheJoyWeaver.com

Email Aj with any questions, requests, or to share stories from your experience with this book at TheJoyWeaver@gmail.com

Photo by: Rosey Tones Photography

facebook.com/thejoyweaver

instagram.com/thejoyweaver

pinterest.com/thejoyweaver

CPSIA information can be obtained
at www.ICGtesting.com
Printed in the USA
LVHW041645211121
704019LV00006B/27